Contents

edexcel
advancing learning, changing lives

Edexcel GCE History

British Political History 1945–90: Consensus and Conflict

Geoff Stewart

Series editors: Martin Collier   Rosemary Rees

Unit 2 Student Book

A PEARSON COMPANY

Published by Pearson Education Limited, a company incorporated in
England and Wales, having its registered office at Edinburgh Gate,
Harlow, Essex, CM20 2JE. Registered company number: 872828
www.pearsonschoolsandfecolleges.co.uk

Edexcel is a registered trade mark of Edexcel Limited

Text © Pearson Education Limited 2010

First published 2010

12 11 10

10 9 8 7 6 5 4 3 2 1

British Library Cataloguing in Publication Data
A catalogue record for this book is available from the British Library

ISBN 978 1 846905 05 6

Copyright notice

Edited by Karen Hemingway
Designed by Florence Production Ltd, Stoodleigh, Devon
Typeset by Florence Production Ltd, Stoodleigh, Devon
Cover photo © PA Archive /Press Association Imagery
Printed in Italy by Rotolito Lombarda

Acknowledgements

The author and publisher would like to thank the following individuals and organisations for
permission to reproduce:

Photographs:

p.163 Alamy / Trinity Mirror / Mirrorpix; p.7 Corbis / Bettmann; p.2 Corbis / Bettmann;
p.113 Getty Images / Hulton Archive; p.161 Getty Images / Hulton Archive / John Downing;
p.178 Getty Images / Hulton Archive / Steve Eason; p.75 (t) Getty Images / Time & Life
Picvtures / Joseph Scherschel; p.145 Getty Images / Time & Life Picvtures / Ken Goff;
p.3 Imperial War Museum; pp.21, 23, 47, 10, 65, 82, 92, 175, 177 Political Cartoon Society;
pp. 135, 169 Political Cartoon Society / the Observer / Wally Fawkes; pp.85, 89, 116, 119
Reproduced by kind permission of PRIVATE EYE magazine; p.75 Topfoto; pp. 106, 133,
162 University of Kent Cartoon & Caricature Collection /Express Newspapers; p.137
University of Kent Cartoon & Caricature Collection / News International Syndicate;
pp.2 (t), 26, 38, 78, 138, 174, 177 University of Kent Cartoon & Caricature Collection /
Solo Syndication

Written Sources:

p.4, p.26, p.55, p.66 Sir John Colville, *The Fringes of Power: Downing Street Diaries 1939–1955*,
reproduced by permission of Hodder and Stoughton Ltd.; p.5, p.184 Sir John Betjeman,
In Westminster Abbey, 1940; p.6 Alex Danchev, *War Diaries 1939–1945*, Field Marshall Lord
Alanbrooke, Orion; p.9, p.41, p.45 Excerpts by Kenneth Harris from *Lord Attlee* (© Kenneth
Harris, 1968) are reproduced by permission of PFD (www.pfd.co.uk) on behalf of Kenneth
Harris; p.10 Tribune, February 1945; p.12, p.22 Peter Hennessy, *Never Again: Britain 1945–51*,
Jonathan Cape; p.13, p.39, p.100, p.120, p.144, p.146 Excerpt by Denis Healey from *Time of
My Life* (© Denis Healey, 1989) is reproduced·by permission of PFD (www.pfd.co.uk) on
behalf of Denis Healey; p.14 Crown copyright material is reproduced with the permission of
the Controller of HMSO; p.15 *English History 1914–45* by Taylor, A J P (1965) By permission
of Oxford University Press; p.16 Correlli Barnett, *The Audit of War: The Illusion and Reality of
Britain as a Great Nation*, Macmillan, 1986; p.16 Juliet Gardiner, *Wartime Britain 1939–45*,
Headline, 2004; p.22, p.98, p.132, p.169 Peter Clarke, *Hope and Glory: Britain 1900–2000*,
reproduced by permission of Penguin Books Ltd; p.26, p.80, p.181, p.185 *Britain Since 1945:
The People's Peace* by Morgan, Kenneth O (2001) By permission of Oxford University Press;
p.27 Alan Sked and Chris Cook, *Post-War Britain: A Political History*, Penguin, 1979; p.29, p.38,
p.106, p.167, p.184 Andrew Marr, *A History of Modern Britain*, Pan Macmillan, London.
Copyright © Andrew Marr, 2007; p.32, p.40 Ben Pimlott, *Hugh Dalton*, Pan Macmillan, 1985;
p.39, p.50, p.60 Peter Hennessy, *Having it so Good; Britain in the Fifties*, 2006, David Godwin
Associates; p.42, p.55, p.62 *"Chips": The Diaries of Sir Henry Channon* edited by Robert Rhodes

James, Weidenfeld & Nicolson, London; p.43, p.61, p.84 R. A. Butler *The Art of the Possible*, Hamish Hamilton, 1971; p.43 Anthony Howard, *RAB: The Life of R A Butler*, Macmillan Publishers, 1987; p.44, p.57, p.94, p.181 John Charmley, *A History of Conservative Politics 1900–1996*, Macmillan Publishing, 1996; p.45 Robert Blake, *The Conservative Party From Peel to Churchill*, Eyre & Spottiswoode, 1970; p.48, p.64, p.105, p.120, p.164 Roy Jenkins, *A Life at the Centre*, Pan Macmillan, London. Copyright © Roy Jenkins 1991; p.54 Charles, Lord Moran, *Churchill: The Struggle for Survival*, Constable, 1966; p.57, p.87 Samuel Brittan, *The Treasury under the Tories 1951–64*, Penguin, 1966; p.58 Nigel Fisher, *Iain Macleod*, Andre Deutsch, 1973; p.58, p.59 Alistair Horne, *Macmillan Volume I 1894–1956*, Macmillan 1988; p.60 Norman Macrae in *The Economist* 13 February 1954; p.62 *The Economist* 23 April 1955; p.64 © 2007 Kenneth O Morgan, by permission of HarperCollins Publishers Ltd; p.66, p.67 Robert Rhodes James, *Anthony Eden*, Orion, 1986, by permission of CurtisBrown Group Ltd; p. 67 David Butler et al, *The Nuffield Studies of British General Elections from 1950 to 1987*, Faber & Faber, 1951–88; p.71 Dominic Sandbrook, *Never Had it So Good*, Little, Brown Book Group, 2005; p.71 David Maxwell-Fyfe, *Political Adventure: The Memoirs of the Earl of Kilmuir* (1964) Weidenfeld & Nicolson; p.76 *Seeking a role, The United Kingdom 1951–1970* by Harrison, Brian (2009) By permission of Oxford University Press; p.79 Malcolm Pierce and Geoffrey Stewart, *British Political History 1867–1995*, 2nd edition, Routledge, 1996; p.82, p.126 Michael Cockerell, *Live from Number 10: The Inside Story of Prime Ministers and Television*, 1988, courtesy of Michael Cockerell; p.93, p.103, p.110 Philip Ziegler, *Wilson*, Weidenfeld & Nicolson, London; p.98, p.125, p.150, p.157, p.177, p.187 John Cole, *As It Seemed to Me: Political Memoirs*, Weidenfeld & Nicolson, London; p.99, p.134, p.141 *THE PRIME MINISTER: The Office and its Holders since 1945* by Peter Hennessy (Allen Lane The Penguin Press, 2000) Copyright © Peter Hennessy, 2000. Reproduced by permission of Penguin Books Ltd; p.100, p.114, p.168, p.169, p.173, p.174, p.175 Tony Benn, *The Benn Diaries*, Selected, Abridged and introduced by Ruth Winstone, Hutchinson, 1995; p.102, p.103, p.139 James Callaghan, *Time and Chance*, Politico's Publishing, an imprint of Methuen; p.103 *The Crossman Diaries 1964–70: Selections from the Diaries of a Cabinet Minister* by Richard Crossman. Introduction and Editing by Anthony Howard, Hamish Hamilton 1979 Copyright © Richard Crossman, 1979. Reproduced by permission of Penguin Books Ltd; p.107 Paul Johnson, Editorial, *New Statesman*, June 1970; p.107 Susan Crosland, *Tony Crosland*, Jonathan Cape, 1982; p.108, p.145, p.179 A N Wilson, *Our Times*, Hutchinson, 2008, by permission of Random House and Aitken Alexander Associates; p.109, p.115, p.139, p.140 *Michael Foot: A Life* © (2007) Kenneth Morgan, reproduced with permission of HarperCollins Publishers Ltd; p.114 Anne Perkins, *Red Queen: The Authorised Biography of Barbara Castle*, Pan Macmillan, 2003; p.115 Harold Wilson, *The Labour Government 1964–70, A Personal Record*, Weidenfeld & Nicolson 1971; p.117, p.132, p.172 Douglas Hurd, *Memoirs*, Little, Brown Book Group, 2003; p.118 Michael Foot, *Loyalists and Loners*, Collins, 1986; p.124 Reproduced by kind permission of PRIVATE EYE magazine; p.128 (x2), p.155, p.180 Geoffrey Howe, *Conflict of Loyalty*, Politico's Publishing, an imprint of Methuen; Reginald Maudling, *Memoirs*, Sidgwick & Jackson 1978; p.134, p.153, p.161 John Campbell *Margaret Thatcher*, Vintage, revised edition 2009; p.135 Edmund Dell, *A Hard Pounding*, OUP,1991; p.135 Peter Hennessy, *Whitehall*, Pimlico. By kind permission of Peter Hennessy; p.138 *Wall Street Journal* 29 April 1975; p.142(x2) *Diaries of Barbara Castle* 3 April 1977; p.151 Percy Cradock, *In Pursuit of British Interests*, John Murray, 1997; p.152, p.160 Hugo Young, *One of Us*, Pan Macmillan, London. Copyright © Hugo Young 1989; p.154 'Why the Tories must halt the charge of Margaret's Light Brigade, by a Tory', *Observer*, 17 February 1980; p.155 Francis Pym, *The Politics of Consent*, Hamish Hamilton, 1985; p.157, p.170 Kenneth Harris, *Thatcher*, Weidenfeld & Nicolson, London; p.159, p.160, p.179, p.187 Alan Clark, *Alan Clark Diaries-Into Politics 1972–82*, Weidenfeld & Nicolson, London; p.176 Paddy Ashdown, *The Ashdown Diaries*, Allen Lane, 2000; p.180 Eric Evans, *Thatcher and Thatcherism*, 2nd edition, Routledge, 2004; p.186 Malcolm Pearce and Geoffrey Stewart, *British Political History 1867–2001*, Third Edition 2002

Disclaimer

This material has been published on behalf of Edexcel and offers high-quality support for the delivery of Edexcel qualifications.

This does not mean that the material is essential to achieve any Edexcel qualification, nor does it mean that it is the only suitable material available to support any Edexcel qualification. Edexcel material will not be used verbatim in setting any Edexcel examination or assessment. Any resource lists produced by Edexcel shall include this and other appropriate resources.

Copies of official specifications for all Edexcel qualifications may be found on the Edexcel website: www.edexcel.com

Introduction

This book offers a study of 45 years of British political history, between the ending of the Second World War and the fall of Margaret Thatcher, the first woman to hold the office of prime minister. It is primarily concerned with domestic developments, rather than the decline of a great power on the global stage and the unscrambling of the greatest empire the world had ever seen. Britain's international position, however, cannot be totally ignored. The burden of trying to maintain great power status had an undoubted impact on domestic developments and from time to time, as in 1956 and 1982, international crises directly affected political events in Britain.

Political parties

There is a focus throughout on the personalities of politics. Policies often cannot be really separated from personalities but many of the bitterest and often most amusing rivalries were within the same party rather than across the party divide. However, rivalry between the Labour Party and the Conservative Party for power inevitably figures with extensive coverage of the thirteen general elections fought in these years. Six were won by Labour and seven by the Conservatives. But for all the sound and fury generated at elections there was a wide degree of agreement between the two parties about the way Britain should be governed, hence the inclusion of the word 'consensus' in the title of this book. Politicians from different parties were often personal friends as well as agreeing on the fundamental issues of the day. The two rivals for the post of Chancellor of the Exchequer in the early 1950s, Hugh Gaitskell of the Labour Party and Richard Butler of the Conservatives were so similar in approach, that their policies were given the name of 'Butskellism.' Conflict was much more evident within the Labour Party, where allies of Gaitskell and supporters of Gaitskell's rival, Aneurin Bevan were barely on speaking terms. Where there was personal hostility between party politicians of different parties, as between Harold Wilson and Edward Heath in the 1960 and 1970s, this had little to do with fundamental differences in policies but was the result of personal dislike.

Work and the economy

Certain themes run through the whole 45 years. Possibly the most crucial was the attempt to manage the economy in such a way as to prevent a return to the unemployment of the inter-war years. At the same time both parties were anxious to cooperate with the trade unions, whose power and influence had been much increased by the Second World War. The attempt to pursue both these policies had a detrimental effect on the efficiency of the British economy which proved slow to adapt to new technologies and new working practices. Trade unions were often resistant to change, which they felt threatened the jobs of their workers, and without the discipline imposed by the threat of unemployment, organised labour often saw no reason to accept the need for change. The result was that from the 1950s Britain fell slowly behind most of Western Europe in living standards, gradually becoming the 'sick man of Europe'. Both parties came to see the necessity of reforming the trade unions and both failed in the 1960s and 70s. Eventually reform was achieved in the 1980s but at the price of social and political conflict.

The welfare state

These years were also marked by far reaching reforms in welfare services, carried out initially by the post-war Labour government but accepted and continued by successive Conservative governments. The result was a degree of social security for the British people hitherto unknown. Educational opportunities were also massively extended by both parties, with a huge increase being made in the percentage enjoying further education. The period also saw the growing popularity of comprehensive schools. Initially pushed and developed by both parties, it was becoming controversial by 1990, with questions being asked as to whether it really had served the interests of bright working-class children. Had not selection by ability been replaced by selection based on where one lived, or, in view of the increase in fee-paying schools, on the ability to pay for education?

British society

There had also been sweeping changes in the laws affecting social behaviour. Abortion and homosexuality had been legalised. Divorce became easier to obtain and freedom of expression on sexual matters in print, on the stage and in film increased considerably. In all these ways the Britain that Margaret Thatcher governed in the 1980s was very different from the one that Clement Attlee and Winston Churchill had governed in the 1940s.

Continuity

For all this, there was considerable continuity in British life over these 45 years. Much that was traditional continued, the monarchy, the House of Lords, the method of electing the House of Commons all remained essentially unaltered. The dominance of the two main parties was not really challenged until the 1980s and even then the challenge was not effective. The British people showed an interest in the game of politics from time to time but for the most part remained uninterested in political ideas. Sport elicited much more interest and passion. Perhaps these characteristics were the secret of the nation's political stability.

1 Britain in 1945

What is this unit about?

This unit shows how Britain in 1945 was different to Britain in the 21st century and introduces some of the key features of the country's political system. Without understanding these features, it will be very difficult to tackle this option. The unit also introduces some of the various types of sources historians work from and draws attention to some of their strengths and weaknesses.

Key questions

- What was Britain like socially and economically in 1945?
- What were the key features of the British political system?

Timeline

1939	September	Outbreak of war
1940	May	Churchill becomes prime minister at the head of a coalition
	May/June	Dunkirk evacuation of the British Army
1941		Lend-Lease introduces massive US aid to Britain
1942		Publication of the Beveridge Report urging a system of national insurance and comprehensive welfare
1944	June	D-Day – successful invasion of France by Britain and the USA
	August	Butler Education Act
1945	May	Germany surrenders
	July	General election – Attlee forms the first majority Labour government
	September	Japan surrenders

Introduction

The Britain of 1945 might appear to be a strange, grey and deprived world to those alive in the 21st century. Its rubble-covered bomb sites, its queues for limited supplies of goods and its relative absence of cars mark a society very different from the one it evolved into 60 years later. It is a doubly alien place.

1 The Britain of 60–70 years ago was very different in social customs and its economy, even without the impact of the most destructive war in our national history.

2 The immediate impact of the Second World War is another great chasm separating then from now. Even when peace came in May 1945, the signs of war were everywhere and millions of young men were still in uniform, their wives and girlfriends abandoned. The prospect of peace brought wild rejoicing as Sources A, B and C indicate.

Source A

'Be funny if the siren went now, wouldn't it?' (19 August 1945)

1.1 Cartoon by Carl Giles, *Sunday Express*, 19 August 1945

Source B

1.2 VE celebrations in Piccadilly Circus on 8 May 1945

Source C

1.3 *VE Day street party, 1945* by Edwin La Dell

SKILLS BUILDER

1 In what ways do Sources A, B and C differ in value as historical evidence?

2 Which, in your opinion, is the most and which the least useful?

3 How might Sources A, B and C be used together by a historian?

A lost world

Working class men really did wear flat caps and there were many more engaged in heavy manual labour than there are today. Over half a million were members of the National Union of Mineworkers and coal mining was a major industry, producing over 200 million tons in most years. The coal literally coloured Britain with soot-engrained buildings and dank smog-covered cities. Coal heated most houses and was used to power most industries. It was a key component in the British steel industry, which was still massively important to the British economy and was the fourth largest in the world. Shipbuilding in Britain was still operating on a large scale, with production second only to that in the USA. Coal mining, steel production and shipbuilding may all have been depressed in the inter-war years, but all seemed to have recovered by 1945. There were still plenty of large textile factories in the North West working five and a half days a week, the hooter at midday on a Saturday signalling the start of 'the weekend'. New industries, like motor car and electrical goods manufacturing, had grown up in the Midlands and around London in bright, light factories, but manufacturing was still largely associated with the grimy North, South Wales and Scotland. The transport system still relied heavily on the railways. There were as yet no motorways. Steam engines puffed and chugged from one end of the country to the other. The railway closures of the 1960s were still two decades away and, although there was much talk of modernisation and electrification, new steam locomotives like the Britannia class were still being built in the late 1940s and early 1950s.

By the standards of the 21st century, living standards were low, but they had been rising throughout the 20th century as had life expectancy. In 1945, £5 per week was a good wage and a man earning it was a well-paid worker. Few married women worked, especially if they had children and it was still widely accepted, even by women, that 'a woman's place was in the home'. Before the war foreign holidays had been extremely rare and impossible during the war, but the annual weekly holiday to the seaside had become established and was quickly resumed in the late 1940s. Entertainment throughout most of the year centred around the radio, which most families possessed, and the cinemas, which drew millions of viewers every week. The *Daily Mirror* or the *Daily Express* were likely to be the newspapers of choice. In many households, newspapers were eventually torn up and used in the lavatory. The public house still attracted many men, but alcohol consumption had fallen sharply since Edwardian times as taxes on beer and spirits had been increased. Sport was a national obsession. Football matches drew vast crowds of well-behaved supporters and the Wembley FA Cup final was a major national occasion, blessed by the presence of the royal family. In summer, cricket transcended all classes. Large numbers played in village and club teams and the likes of Yorkshire's Len Hutton were national heroes.

The better-off working class shaded into the middle class, but the badges of class were much more distinctive then. White shirts not blue marked the middle class, as did the bowler hat or trilby rather than the flat cap. The possession of a car (just over two million were owned in 1940), a telephone (there were just over three million) and a bank account were middle-class traits. That Victorian badge of middle-class respectability, the possession of servants, was disappearing, but it was the middle classes who enjoyed new labour-saving devices such as the vacuum cleaner. Houses clearly pointed to the occupants' class. Detached or even semi-detached houses conferred respectability. Newspapers like the *Daily Telegraph* or, in the North, the *Manchester Guardian* signalled middle-class status; perhaps at a pinch, so did the *Daily Mail*.

The middle classes shaded into the upper or ruling class. Here, a private education at one of the more ancient public schools followed by three years at Oxford or Cambridge were features, as well as ownership of not just an imposing house but also an estate. Wartime had imposed all manner of hardships, but key aspects of the old lifestyle survived. Membership of a London club, participation in shoots and hunts, and the possession of servants were still the norm. Churchill's young private secretary John Colville, later Sir John, records his return home, in his diary entry for 2 May 1945:

Source D

Went home to find the married couple whom mother has engaged had arrived and also that she had discovered that the man had just completed a three year sentence for fraud and embezzlement. This was something of a shock, but we decided after dining at the 'Good Intent', that we ought to give him a chance to make good. Besides his wife seems honest and hardworking. All the same, an 'old lag' for a butler with several previous convictions, is something of an experiment.

From John R. Colville, *The Fringes of Power: Downing Street Diaries 1939–1955*, published in 2005

The awareness of class was a pervasive aspect of British society at the time, commented upon by many writers and journalists. The American reporter Ed Murrow wrote in 1946 about his impressions of England on his arrival in the 1930s: 'I thought your streets narrow and mean; your tailors over-advertised; your climate unbearable; your class-consciousness offensive.' The poet John Betjeman also drew attention to this feature of English life in a poem written during the war.

Source E

Think of what our nation stands for,
Books from Boots and country lanes,
Free speech, free passes, class distinction,
Democracy and proper drains,
Lord, put beneath Thy special care
One-eighty-nine Cadogan Square.

From John Betjeman, 'In Westminster Abbey', published in 1940

The education system both reflected and helped to reinforce class differences. The word 'system' is perhaps misleading, implying some element of planning. It had merely grown up with the state at various times filling in a bit here or there, for example Forster's Education Act 1870 or Balfour's Education Act. In the 1930s, most children attended elementary school, which they left aged 14. Only 14 per cent attended secondary school. Half of these paid fees, even in the state grammar schools. These grammar schools tended, therefore, to draw from the middle and lower middle classes. Only a minority were fully paid for, through scholarships, by the state or local authorities. In this way, a handful of bright working-class boys and girls could get on the ladder of social advancement. At the top were the ancient 'public schools'. (Only the English would think of calling their most exclusive and private institutions 'public'.) Less than 3 per cent of an age group went on to university, hardly any improvement since 1918. Education was clearly ripe for reform.

Education had, in part, been bedevilled by religion. The rivalry in the 19th century of the Church of England (the state church) and the non-conformist chapels prevented the setting up of a wholesale education system such as had been established in the USA and Prussia. Religion still remained a major force in Britain in the 1930s and 1940s despite a decline in church attendance. Churches and chapels still often served as centres for social activities whether amateur dramatics or sport. Ministers of religion exercised considerable influence and there was a widespread belief in God. As Chief of the Imperial General Staff from 1941 to 1945, Churchill's chief military adviser Field Marshall Lord Alanbrooke recorded in his diary on 8 May 1945:

SKILLS BUILDER

Use Sources D and F and your own knowledge to answer the following question. What are the strengths and weaknesses of diaries as sources of evidence?

Source F

I am not a highly religious individual according to many people's outlook. I am however convinced that there is a God all powerful looking after the destiny of this world. I had little doubt of this before the war started, but this war has convinced me more than ever of this truth. Again and again during the last six years I have seen his guiding hand controlling and guiding the destiny of this world toward that final and definite destiny which he has ordained. The suffering and agony of war in my mind must exist to gradually educate us to the fundamental law of 'loving our neighbour as ourselves'. When that lesson has been learned, then war will cease to exist.

From Field Marshall Lord Alanbrooke, *War Diaries 1939–1945*, published in 2002

The whole value system of British society differed from that of the 21st century in many important ways.

- It was a much more communal and collective age. Most people travelled by public transport, not in the privacy of their own car. They watched the screen together in the cinema. They lived much more on top of one another, children sharing bedrooms, or even beds, with their siblings. Even the very wealthy shared their mansions with their servants, from whose eyes they could not escape.

- Moral codes were clear and, by the standards of later times, repressive. Abortion was illegal and the shame of pregnancy outside marriage was devastating. Homosexuality was a criminal offence and prosecutions were common. The theatre was still carefully regulated by the Lord Chamberlain's Office and anything unduly sexual was deleted from plays. Novels like D.H. Lawrence's *Lady Chatterley's Lover*, written in the 1920s, was banned from publication.

- The press censored itself in reporting the lives of the rich and famous and, as long as a man or woman avoided the divorce court, no breath of scandal would be publicised, even where it was common knowledge between politicians and journalists. For example, no hint of the private life of Robert Boothby, Tory MP and friend of Churchill, entered the public domain. His long-standing affair with the wife of Harold Macmillan, another Tory MP and future prime minister, and his homosexual liaisons within the London underworld never surfaced until a much later, more open age.

- If the system was more repressive, society was more law abiding and fundamentally cohesive. It was riddled with petty snobberies. Jews were still often excluded from golf clubs or abused in the East End, but in general there was a horror of the brutalities inflicted on Jews by the Nazis. Only in Northern Ireland and possibly Glasgow did the primitive tribalism of Catholic–Protestant antagonism survive. In Liverpool and Manchester, it subsided into mere football rivalry. The British thought of themselves as 'decent' and, on the whole, behaved decently. There were none of the genocidal lunacies that disfigured Russia and Germany in the 1930s and 1940s nor anything equivalent to the isolated atrocities carried out by the Ku Klux Klan in the USA. Most of the population, regardless of their party political loyalty or class, were attached to their society and its customs. The monarchy had successfully come to express this stability.

The political system

The British had evolved a very effective method of governing themselves. It delivered order with freedom, two desirable goals very difficult to obtain at the same time. England, overwhelmingly the largest and most important of the four components of the United Kingdom, had enjoyed nearly 400 years of economic growth and not had a civil war since 1648 nor a revolution since 1688. Since that revolution, the population had multiplied by a factor of eight to reach over 40 million. Living standards and life expectancy had risen dramatically and this small island off the coast of Europe had conquered a fifth of the globe and settled many areas of it with emigrants. English was bidding to become the world's most important language.

The political system, which appeared to be so successful, was not easy to comprehend. There was no written constitution, as in the USA. Yet there were rules, and respect for rules and the rule of law was perhaps one of the key elements in its success. There was still a monarchy when much of Europe had followed the French example and removed theirs. Yet in Britain the monarchy had virtually lost all political power. It was merely decorative. It seemed nonetheless to function as a focus for loyalty and robbed the wielders of real political power of the adulation they might otherwise have received in a republic. The German dictator Adolf Hitler was always grateful to the German Social Democrats for removing the German monarchy in 1918 and leaving the field open to him. George VI, the British king in 1945, was a shy, stuttering chain-smoker, who even had his own ration book, number CA 570011. Only very rarely did he exercise a direct political influence on events.

- When Churchill proposed to visit the newly invaded France on D-Day, at great personal risk, the king stopped him by insisting that he would accompany his prime minister.
- In July 1945, he influenced Attlee's choice in Cabinet appointments by suggesting that Ernie Bevin be made Foreign Secretary and Hugh Dalton Chancellor of the Exchequer, rather than the other way round as Attlee proposed. It was only a suggestion, but one that Attlee chose to follow.

Real political power was centred in the position of prime minister. In theory the holder was appointed by the king and had to go to the royal palace to be formally confirmed as such. He then exercised most of the powers that a monarch in the 16th or 17th century would have exercised. The king could not appoint whom he wished. The prime minister had to have the support of a majority of MPs in the House of

1.4 King George VI

Commons in order to get laws made and taxes approved. This meant that the prime minister was usually the leader of the largest party in the House of Commons. In 1940, in rather special circumstances, the king had appointed **Winston Churchill**, merely a leading member of the largest party, when the existing prime minister and leader of the **Conservative Party** Neville Chamberlain lost the confidence of many MPs. Churchill thus become prime minister in May and formed a coalition government, uniting all the parties in the House of Commons. When Chamberlain died in November that year, Churchill was promptly elected Conservative leader, restoring normality.

Definition

Conservative Party

The name 'conservative' dated back to the 1830s and was devised by Sir Robert Peel as a way of repackaging the old 'Tory' Party and making it more acceptable to the increasingly influential middle classes. It was traditionally the party of the landed gentry and the Church of England. It gradually became more and more middle class itself, with business men replacing landed gentlemen and aristocrats as its leading members. All the leaders from 1911 to 1940 had business backgrounds, including Neville Chamberlain whom Churchill replaced.

Biography

Winston Churchill (1874–1965)

Churchill was the grandson of a duke, so he marked a break from his three predecessors and almost a return to tradition. However, he was a maverick and not personally rich. He made his living in the 1930s by writing. He had been elected as a Conservative in 1900, but changed parties to become a Liberal and served as a leading Liberal Cabinet minister before and during the First World War. He then rejoined the Conservatives in 1924, but was regarded with deep suspicion by many in the party and it was with deep reluctance that many accepted him as leader in November 1940.

A British prime minister was no dictator. He had great powers in making appointments in government, but he could be removed by a vote in the House of Commons. In reality, he had to govern with the consent and cooperation of the senior members of his party whom he appointed to his **Cabinet**. The relationship of the prime minister to his Cabinet colleagues

Definition

The Labour Party

This was the new party of the 20th century, being originally established in 1900 as 'The Labour Representation Committee', an alliance between three small political groups and the trade unions. It won 29 seats in 1906 and changed its name to the Labour Party. After the First World War it expanded rapidly at the expense of the Liberals and formed a government for the first time in 1924. In 1918 the Party adopted a new constitution which committed it to 'socialism'. The Labour Party drew its support from the big cities and the mining areas. The parliamentary party tended to be a mixture of trade unionists and middle-class intellectuals.

Definition

The Liberal Party

The Liberals had been the dominant party in Britain between 1832 and 1886. It was essentially the party of reform and drew its support from the middle classes and non-conformist churches. It enjoyed one last spectacular burst of power between 1905 and 1915 when Liberal governments introduced a spate of reforms which laid the basis for the welfare state. The party split in 1916 which gave the new Labour Party a chance to take its place as the main challenger to the Conservative Party.

Definition

Cabinet

The Cabinet was at the heart of government in Britain. It was a committee of the senior members of the government, meeting regularly under the chairmanship of the prime minister to discuss and approve the general line of government policy. Senior ministers like the Foreign and Home Secretaries and the Chancellor of the Exchequer would always be members. Sub-committees of the Cabinet were often established for more detailed work and these reported back. Government ministers not in the Cabinet are normally referred to as junior ministers.

Biography

Clement Richard Attlee (1883–1967)

Attlee was very much a product of upper middle class late Victorian/Edwardian England, After education at private school and Oxford, he was called to the bar and then served in the First World War, rising to rank of major. He worked for charitable causes in the East End and this attracted him to Labour politics.He became a Labour MP for Limehouse in 1922 and served in the Labour governments of 1924 and 1929.

varied with the personality of the occupant of number 10 Downing Street, the official home of the prime minister. Churchill was a larger-than-life figure capable of brilliant speeches and flashes of wit and genius but also interminable monologues and time-wasting. It was a brave man, however, who could tell him of his short-comings. **Clement Richard Attlee**, the Labour Party leader and deputy prime minister in the coalition, was such a man as Source G makes clear.

Source G

I have for some time had it in mind to write to you on the method or rather lack of method of dealing with matters requiring Cabinet decisions . . . You have set up a number of committees, over some of which I have the honour to preside to deal with various aspects of our affairs. . . . I doubt if you realise the length of time and the amount of work entailed on busy ministers not only by attendance at these committees, but by reading the relevant papers and by seeking advice from persons of knowledge . . . The conclusions of the Committees are brought to the cabinet in memoranda which we try to keep as short as possible in an attempt to save members the trouble of reading long disquisitions.

What happens then?

Frequently a long delay before they can be considered. When they do come before the Cabinet it is very exceptional for you to have read them. More and more often you have not read even the note prepared for your guidance. Often half an hour and more is wasted in explaining what could have been grasped in two or three minutes reading of the document. Not infrequently a phrase catches your eye which gives rise to a disquisition on an interesting point only slightly connected with the subject matter. The result is long delays and unnecessarily long Cabinets imposed on Ministers who have already done a full day's work and who will have more to deal with before they get to bed.

From a letter from C.R. Attlee to Winston Churchill, 19 January 1945 Quoted in *Attlee* by Kenneth Harris, 1982

SKILLS BUILDER

Use Source G to answer the following questions.

1 What are Attlee's criticisms of how the Cabinet's committees system is functioning?

2 What are the problems for the historian in using letters as sources of evidence?

Source H

Mr. Attlee has consistently underplayed his position and his opportunities. He seems determined to make a trumpet sound like a tin whistle. He brings to the fierce struggle of politics the tepid enthusiasm of a lazy afternoon at a cricket match.

From an article in *Tribune*, February 1945

Attlee was the antithesis of Churchill in almost every way. Small and lacking in charisma, he was a poor orator and was at his most effective when chairing committees. He had become leader of the Labour Party in 1935 following a devastating election in that year in which all the senior Labour figures had lost their seats in parliament. Attlee was elected leader for want of anyone better and regarded as a stop-gap. Churchill referred to him as 'A modest little man with much to be modest about'. His great loves were his wife Vi, who acted as his driver, cricket and *The Times* crossword. He was often brief to the point of silence, never using one word where no word would do, as one colleague pointed out. Aneurin Bevan, a colourful left-wing Labour MP and editor of the left-wing Labour magazine *Tribune* in 1945, wrote an article about the leader of his party (see Source H).

Perhaps not surprisingly Attlee's leading party colleagues almost overshadowed him, as Source I makes clear.

Source I

1.5 Cartoon by David Low published in the *Evening Standard*, 9 October 1947

Attlee's senior colleagues shown in the cartoon were all much more charismatic and colourful than their leader and many felt that they should replace 'little Clem'. There was the bald, booming old Etonian, Dr Hugh Dalton, who was to become Chancellor of the Exchequer in July 1945. There was Ernie Bevin, the squat formidable trade union boss, who had left school at 14 and only entered parliament or government in 1940, when he was 59. He then became the second most powerful man in the country, first as wartime minister of Labour under Churchill and then as Foreign Secretary in 1945 under Attlee. His personality was as large as Churchill's and his backing for Attlee was vital. The bespectacled Herbert Morrison was a powerful figure in the Labour Party machine and the boss of the London party. He constantly sought to replace Attlee, but as Bevin reassured his leader, 'You leave that little bugger Morrison to me.' The last of the four was the eccentric but imposing figure of Sir Stafford Cripps, a product of Winchester and a leading QC. He was a devout Christian and left-wing socialist, whom many on the left of the Labour Party preferred to Attlee.

Civil servants

Beneath the senior politicians who took the big strategic decisions were the professionals, civil service mandarins and military advisers. By the mid 20th century, Britain had acquired a very sophisticated and skilled corps of such professionals to advise and assist the elected politicians. Two of Churchill's closest collaborators in the conduct of the war have already been encountered through extracts from their diaries, which are major sources on the wartime government of the country. Field Marshall Alanbrooke was Churchill's principal military adviser and vital in heading off many of the more crackpot ideas that Churchill embraced from time to time. In a more junior role, as his private secretary, John Colville wrote letters sent out under Churchill's name and, as he describes in one diary entry, he became very skilled at imitating Churchill's style. Colville played a significant part in defusing tension between Churchill and Attlee over Attlee's letter of complaint (see Source G). He failed to send off Churchill's initial aggressive response and when Churchill had calmed down suggested an alternative, milder response, which Churchill agreed to.

Senior civil servants could have an enormous impact on policy. One of the most influential was **Sir William Beveridge**. He had been a civil servant before and during the First World War and then served as the Director of the London School of Economics. He returned to **Whitehall** during the Second World War. He played a leading role in devising the rationing system, which fairly and efficiently allocated scarce resources, in the process raising the diet of the poorest. He was then asked to undertake a survey on the working and reform of the existing welfare system. It was intended as a mere tidying operation. Beveridge published his report in

Biography

Sir William Beveridge

He was an economist who at the early age of 30 became director of the new labour exchanges set up in 1909. He moved between government jobs, academic life and politics and was briefly a Liberal MP before ending up as a member of the House of Lords. He was one of the 'great and the good' in British national life and was one of those who, largely behind the scenes, pulled the strings and shaped modern Britain.

Definition Box

Whitehall
Originally the site of Cardinal Wolsey's London palace it was seized by Henry VIII and became a great royal palace but was largely burnt down in 1698. The site became occupied over the next two centuries by government departments such as the Admiralty, the Treasury and the Foreign Office. The word became a synonym for government and the civil servants who worked there.

November 1942. It had an enormous impact, selling 100,000 copies within a month and eventually 635,000 copies. A modern History text on the period describes the essence of its 200,000 words.

Source J

Stripped to its core the Beveridge Report was targeted on 'Five Giants on the Road to Recovery' which he identified in bold, capital letters – **WANT, DISEASE, IGNORANCE, SQUALOR and IDLENESS.** To defeat them Beveridge devised a comprehensive welfare system (though oddly, he never cared for the phrase 'the welfare state' preferring to call it 'the social service state') based on 'three assumptions' – a free national health service, child allowances, full employment (which he defined as less than 8.5% unemployment).

From Peter Hennessy, *Never Again: Britain 1945–51*, published in 1992

The report became the basis of much of the post-war Labour government's reforms and it shaped the whole nature of post-war Britain.

By 1938, there were 376,491 civil servants and during the war their numbers expanded even more. Without such a large body, with a very able body of men and women at the top, the efficient government of Britain would have been impossible and ministers would have been mere voices crying helplessly in a political wilderness.

Parliament

Civil servants might propose schemes to ministers or carry out the schemes ministers had managed to pass into law. The lawmakers were the ordinary members of parliament (MPs) and members of the House of Lords. MPs who were not holders of a government position were known as 'back benchers' because, in contrast to ministers who sat on the front benches of the House of Commons and House of Lords, they sat behind the front bench. There were 615 MPs, the majority Conservative (432 elected in 1935). Most MPs were middle or upper class in origin and had attended privately paid for public schools. The largest single group by profession were lawyers and these figured in all parties. Most MPs followed their leaders, hoping for promotion to government office or other rewards such as titles and honours. MPs were, however, also open to pressure from their constituents who had put them there. It was perceived public opinion that gave such a boost to the Beveridge Report and prevented economy-minded ministers kicking it into touch.

Members of parliament represented constituencies where local Labour and Conservative parties operated and selected their candidates to stand as MPs. Sometimes the choice was determined by tradition. For example, a member of the Cavendish family traditionally represented West Derbyshire. The family, based in the grand house of Chatsworth, owned much of the county. It was something of a shock when they lost the seat in a by-election in February 1944. In places like County Durham and Barnsley in South Yorkshire, the National Union of Miners had a similar hold to the Cavendish family in West Derbyshire. In other areas without a dominating interest, local activists competed. Throughout the country only a minority were involved in such political activity. The majority only became involved during a general election or when some great issue surfaced and determined the public mood. The Beveridge Report is one such issue, when interest went beyond the usual activists and forced politicians to respond to a mood change in the electorate.

By 1945, all men and women over 21 could vote and usually did. Turn-out tended to be over 70 per cent and sometimes reached over 80 per cent. Elections were supposed to take place every five years under the Parliament Act of 1911. The last general election had been in 1935, when the Conservatives had won with a large majority. Because of the war, the election due in 1940 was postponed. There was every sign that the Labour Party was gaining in popularity and the Conservatives were losing it. Since 1935, the Conservatives had lost in 27 by-elections. The next general election when the war ended was likely to be exciting.

The impact of war

It is difficult to exaggerate the impact of the Second World War in shaping the mentalities of all those who fought and struggled in it. Denis Healey went from being a student at Oxford into the army. He later became a Labour MP and Cabinet minister.

Source K

Working in an office as part of a large headquarters was something for which my wartime experience prepared me well. I found my army staff training invaluable – as did other ex-officers at Conservative Party headquarters, such as Enoch Powell and Reggie Maudling. Indeed post-war politics in both parties was largely shaped by men who had learned a new way of looking at problems as a result of their practical experiences in the services during the war. That is why 'Rab' Butler was able to covert the Conservative Party to economic planning and the welfare state. Thatcherism became possible only when the wartime generation was passing from the stage.

From Denis Healey, *The Time of My Life*, published in 1989

SKILLS BUILDER

Refer to Source K. What are the problems for the historian in using memoirs as sources of evidence?

By 1945, Britain had been at war for six years and in many ways the war had been, in Churchill's famous phrase, the country's 'finest hour'. Britain had declared war on Germany in 1939 to prevent Germany dominating the Continent. When Germany unexpectedly defeated France in six weeks in 1940, Britain might have been expected to make peace. Hitler was prepared to offer generous terms, yet Churchill persuaded the nation to fight on and was backed by the coalition he led. The country was mobilised into undertaking a heroic crusade for liberty with the vision of a better world emerging. On 18 June, as France prepared to surrender, Churchill delivered one of the greatest speeches in the English language.

Source L

Upon this battle depends the survival of Christian civilisation. Upon it depends our own British life, and the long continuity of our Empire. Hitler knows that he will have to break us on this island or lose the war. If we can stand up to him all Europe may be free and the life of the world may move forward into broad, sunlit uplands. But if we fail, then the whole world, including the United States, including all we have known and cared for, will sink into the abyss of a new Dark Age, made more sinister by the lights of perverted science. Let us therefore brace ourselves to our duties and so bear ourselves that if the British Empire and its Commonwealth last for a thousand years, Men will say: 'This was their finest hour.'

From a speech by Winston Churchill, broadcast over the radio, 18 June 1940

SKILLS BUILDER

To what extent do Sources J, K and L suggest that the war years helped to create an expectation of reform in Britain?

Churchill and his colleagues were gambling that the USA would ultimately come to Britain's rescue. In the meantime everything was turned to the war effort and war production soared. By 1941, Britain was out-producing Germany in planes and much war material, but at the heavy cost of mortgaging the future.

In frustration with Britain's refusal to make peace, Hitler turned against the USSR in June 1941. The result was a war on two fronts for Germany of the sort that Hitler had always warned against. The assault on the USSR brought relief to Britain as the German air force moved east. The USSR now became Britain's ally and the Soviet dictator Stalin became beneficent 'Uncle Joe'. As Churchill pointed out at the time, 'If Hitler invaded hell I would at least make a favourable reference to the Devil.' With the USSR as an ally, there was some hope of victory and a great boost was given to the credibility of left-wing politics and principles in Britain.

However, if Russia gave hope, it was the USA that provided the crucial aid to keep Britain fighting and make ultimate victory possible. By 1941, Britain was almost bankrupt, unable to pay for essential imports. Through the Lend-Lease Agreement of that year, the USA made money and credit available. Five billion pounds of goods were borrowed from the USA. This was a colossal sum in the 1940s. When Hitler foolishly declared war on the USA in December 1941, Churchill claimed that he could sleep easily in his bed for the first time as victory was assured in the long run. Troops and goods trickled from the USA in 1942, but they became a flood in 1943 and 1944. Trucks and radios modernised the Red Army, and food and even railway engines enabled the Soviet economy to continue to work miracles of production. United States products helped to modernise Britain. Ferguson tractors appeared in ever greater numbers, enabling British food production to grow. American troops and military equipment made the reinvasion of France possible in 1944.

The war was sold as a crusade for liberty and a better world. Deprivation and suffering were accepted, but it was hoped that the power of the state, much enlarged in the quest to defeat Hitler, would be turned to social engineering inside Britain. After the defeat of Nazi Germany, Beveridge's '5 giants' (see Source J) would be slain by the same powerful state. It was not only Liberals like Beveridge or socialists like Morrison and Dalton who embraced state power to produce a better life for ordinary people. R.A. Butler, a talented young Tory, appointed by Churchill as Minister of Education, was determined to solve some of the deficiencies in British education and produced a far-reaching *Education Act* in 1944. The Act ended fees in secondary schools and massively extended opportunities for bright working-class girls and boys. It appeared that conflict had created consensus for reform.

Victory, however, did not come without a horrendous price. The Second World War had cost Britain much more than the war of 1914–18. Fewer lives were lost, but that was because much of the fighting on land was left to the Russians. Nevertheless, a huge air force had been created and a navy of 929 major warships. Britain was a great power in terms of armaments, but the economy had been weakened. Exports were considerably lower and twice the amount of overseas assets had been sold off as had been sold in 1914–18. To fight the war, the country had been on a huge spending binge and was likely to wake with a massive economic hangover.

For 20 years or so after the end of the war, the prevalent view among historians was one that viewed the war as a positive experience for Britain. This was probably most famously expressed by the left-wing A.J.P. Taylor in the conclusion of his volume of the *Oxford History of England*.

Source M

In the second World war (sic) the British people came of age. This was a people's war. Not only were their needs considered. They themselves wanted to win . . . The British were the only people who went through both world wars from beginning to end. Yet they remained a peaceful and civilised people, tolerant, patient and generous. Traditional values lost much of their force. Other values took their place. Imperial greatness was on the way out; the welfare state was on the way in. The British Empire declined; the condition of the people improved. Few now sang 'Land of Hope and Glory'. Few even sang 'England Arise'. England had risen all the same.

From A.J.P. Taylor, *English History 1914–1945*, published in 1965

SKILLS BUILDER

Refer to Source M. What is A.J.P. Taylor suggesting were the main consequences of the Second World War?

However, the consensus engendered by the war broke down in the 1970s as Britain's economic failings became more obvious. Some historians began to take a more cynical view of the war as a disaster for Britain, leaving it with an exaggerated view of its own importance and strengthening damaging traits within British society and the economy. Such traits were identified as: more powerful trade unions that were hostile to innovation, an expectation of welfare benefits without the economic performance to pay for them and an overblown state inefficiently interfering in the economy. The conservative historian Correlli Barnett reflected these attitudes in a famous attack, *The Audit of War.*

Definitions

GNP

A measure of the total value of the goods and services produced in a country and its overseas earnings from trade and investments. Divided by the number of people, GNP will give an approximate indication of standard of living. It is a useful way of comparing the relative economic importance of countries.

New Jerusalem

This is a phrase often used in this period and comes from the language of religious visionaries like William Blake, whose famous poem talks of Jerusalem being built in 'England's green and pleasant land'. It refers to the creation of a near perfect environment for human beings.

Source N

And so it was that, by the time they took the bunting down from the streets after VE Day and turned from the war to the future, the British in their dreams and illusions and in their flinching from reality had already written the broad scenario for Britain's post-war descent to the place of fifth in the free world as an industrial power, with manufacturing output only two fifths of West Germany's, and the place of fourteenth in the whole non-communist world in terms of annual **GNP** per head.

As the descent took its course the illusions and dreams of 1945 would fade one by one – the imperial and commonwealth role, the world power role, the British industrial genius, and, at last **New Jerusalem** itself, a dream turned into dank reality of a segregated, subliterate, unskilled, unhealthy and institutionalised proletariat hanging on the nipple of state maternalism.

From Corelli Barnett, *The Audit of War: The Illusion and Reality of Britain as a Great Nation*, published in 1986

More recently, in her detailed study of wartime life, Juliet Gardiner finishes on a different note.

Source O

But even with a husband taking his seat in the reform-minded new Labour House of Commons, and with her own hopes for a revitalised post-war Scotland, Naomi Mitchison still recognised sadly that 'we are going to have hell trying to get people to work the peace, trying to give people a worth-while-ness in their peace time lives comparable with the worth-while-ness of working together during the war. We shall probably fail.'

From Juliet Gardiner, *Wartime: Britain 1939–1945*, published in 2004

SKILLS BUILDER

Why might the authors of Sources M, N and O see the legacy of the Second World War in starkly different ways?

Unit summary

What have you learned in this unit?

This unit has covered a considerable amount of information. You have learned about some of the ways in which Britain in the mid 1940s was different both physically and in its attitudes to Britain in the 21st century. You have also encountered the most important features of how Britain was governed. Finally you have been asked to think about and understand the impact of the Second World War on Britain and its political system.

What skills have you used in this unit?

You have been introduced to various different types of sources and asked to consider their strengths and weaknesses as sources of evidence for historians. You have begun to examine small groups of sources, comparing and contrasting their evidence to enable you to answer a specific question.

Exam style question

This is the sort of question that you will find on the examination paper as an (a) question. Use only the sources provided, but none of your own knowledge.

Study Sources G, H and I.

How far do the sources support the view that Attlee was 'a modest little man with much to be modest about'?

Explain your answer using the evidence of Sources G, H and I.

Exam tips

- Don't bring in a lot of your own knowledge. All (a) questions focus on the analysis, cross-referencing and evaluation of source material. Your own knowledge won't be credited and you will therefore have wasted time.
- Don't write out the sources.
- Do use the attribution to put the source into context and use it where appropriate to evaluate the source as evidence.
- Do draw inferences from the sources where appropriate.
- Do remember to cross-reference the sources for similarities and differences.

RESEARCH TOPIC

Local history

Look carefully at your local built up area (nearest town or city to you) and research the answers to the following questions.

- Which buildings standing today existed in 1945?
- Find out what notable buildings that existed in 1945 have been destroyed or abandoned?
- What buildings have been converted to new uses? What does this tell you about changing lifestyles?

UNIT 2 Victory and reform: Labour in power, 1945–48

What is this unit about?

This unit shows why the Labour Party won such a convincing victory in July 1945, and why and how the new government carried out a series of major reforms affecting both welfare and the economy in the period from 1945 to 1948, despite massive economic problems. It also shows how important a major loan from the USA was in under-pinning the much-weakened British economy.

Key questions

- Why did the Labour Party win the general election of July 1945 with a large majority?
- What were the key features of the reforms carried through?
- How important was the USA in providing financial help?

Timeline

1945	**7/8 May**	End of the war in Europe
	23 May	Churchill ends wartime coalition
	4 June	Churchill's 'Gestapo' radio broadcast
	5 July	General election
	26 July	Attlee forms the first majority Labour government
	21 August	Truman ends the Lend-Lease Agreement
	September	Japan surrenders
	December	US loan agreement
1946	**March**	Bank of England nationalised
		Bevan unveils plans for the National Health Service
	May	Trades Disputes Act repealed
		Bread rationing announced
		National Insurance Act
		National Health Services Act
	December	Coal shortages shut down some industries
1947	**January**	Coal mines and Cable and Wireless nationalised
	January–February	Severe cold – energy crisis worsens
	March	Gales and flooding
	April	School leaving age raised to 15

	April	Dalton's third Budget – tax rises
	July	Sterling becomes convertible – sterling crisis
	July	Government draws up 'famine food programme'
	August	Food rations cut and petrol ration abolished – no pleasure motoring
	September	Cabinet plot to remove Attlee – the PM survives
	October	Foreign travel allowance abolished
	November	Dalton resigns over Budget leak – replaced by Cripps Potato rationing introduced
1948	**January**	Railways nationalised
	March	Last £25 million of USA loan drawn
	April	European Recovery Programme – Marshall Aid Electricity nationalised First Cripps Budget
	May	First public announcement about British nuclear bomb programme
	5 July	National Health Service inaugurated

The end of the coalition

The German army surrendered at Rheims on 7 May and two weeks later the British coalition government came to an end and Britain returned to traditional competitive party politics. Churchill, Attlee and Bevin favoured continuing the coalition until Japan was defeated, which was expected to take until 1946. However, a Labour Party conference at Blackpool pushed Attlee into a decision to end the coalition by October. On 21 May, he telephoned Churchill to this effect and Churchill decided that in this case the sooner the coalition ended the better and the earlier the election, the better it would be for the Conservatives. It was felt by most politicians and knowledgeable commentators that Churchill, as the great war leader, would carry the Tory party to victory. Attlee was not optimistic and the best he hoped for was a reduced Conservative majority.

On 23 May, the coalition came to an end and Churchill formed a 'caretaker' Tory Cabinet until an election could be held. It was decided that parliament would be dissolved on 5 June and voting would take place on 5 July. The votes would not be counted until 25 July to allow the many millions in uniform a chance to vote and to collect their ballot boxes. There were many soldiers still fighting the Japanese on the frontiers of India and there was a sizable British fleet in the Pacific. In addition, there was a very large British garrison occupying defeated Germany. It would be a very unusual election.

Although the country was about to return to party politics, with the usual trading of insults and competitive jibes, in a very real sense the war had established a comradely consensus. Young MPs of both parties had served in the forces. Captain Roy Jenkins and Major Denis Healey of the Labour Party now faced Lieutenant Colonel Heath and Brigadier Enoch Powell of the Tories. All had been civilians before the war and Powell, for example, had risen impressively from private to brigadier entirely on his own merit and abilities. Leading Labour politicians had served for five years with leading Conservatives. Attlee and Eden, Churchill's deputy, addressed one another in letters as 'My dear Clem' and 'my dear Anthony'. Churchill had a very real respect for his former Labour Party colleagues, particularly Attlee and Bevin. At a farewell meeting in the Cabinet room, tears poured down his face as he declared that, 'The light of history will shine on every helmet.' This was a far cry from Chamberlain's attitude to the Labour front bench in the 1930s. When urged by Baldwin not to treat them like dirt, he replied, 'Intellectually they are dirt.'

In 1945, not only was there a personal consensus of men who had served together in a common cause, there was also a wide consensus of what had to be done. Both front benches essentially agreed on foreign policy. Bevin, no less than Churchill, could think of Britain as no less than a great power with worldwide responsibilities. Both parties supported a close relationship with the USA; the wartime alliance. Both parties embraced an extension of welfare at home. Churchill's caretaker government introduced child allowances in its short existence and Butler had already established the broad pattern of post-war education policy with his 1944 Act. However, with an election to fight, consensus was about to give way to conflict, even if much of the conflict was simply ritual.

General election, 1945

Churchill was to stand in his North London constituency of Woodford, which he was expected to win comfortably. As the cartoonist Vicky pointed out, the Conservatives tried to give the impression that he was standing everywhere.

SKILLS BUILDER

Look carefully at Source A.

What is the message of this cartoon?

Source A

"...YOU CAN'T VOTE FOR WINSTON CHURCHILL UNLESS YOU HAPPEN TO LIVE IN WOODFORD"
– SIR WILLIAM BEVERIDGE

TORY DREAM

2.1 Cartoon by Vicky, *News Chronicle*, 30 May 1945

The Conservatives were relying heavily on Churchill for victory as Source A makes clear. He toured the country in a grand cavalcade. Attlee energetically campaigned up and down the land, driven by his wife Vi in his little Standard motor car. The two leaders' styles inevitably reflected their different personalities, but Attlee was to be no push-over. On 4 June, the day before parliament was dissolved, Churchill opened the election campaign in a radio broadcast with a typically bombastic outburst aimed at the Labour Party.

Source B

No Socialist Government conducting the entire life and industry of the country could afford to allow free, sharp or violently worded expression of public discontent. They would have to fall back on some form of Gestapo, no doubt very humanely directed in the first instance.

Churchill speaking on the radio, 4 June 1945

The next day, Attlee effectively demolished his opponent (see Source C).

Source C

When I listened to the Prime Minister's speech last night, in which he gave such a travesty of the policy of the Labour Party, I realised at once what was his object. He wanted the electors to understand how great was the difference between Winston Churchill the great leader in war of a united nation and Mr Churchill, the Party Leader of the Conservatives. He feared lest those who had accepted his leadership in war might be tempted out of gratitude to follow him further. I thank him for having disillusioned them so thoroughly.

Attlee speaking on the radio, 5 June 1945

Source D

That elaborate confection of rhetorical exaggeration did Churchill great harm. It made him sound ludicrous rather than eloquent, a crude partisan rather than the wise statesman above the fray. It was a gift to the Labour Party such as few Conservative leaders have presented in 20th century elections and Labour made effective use of it, starting with Attlee himself when he broadcast his reply.

From Peter Hennessy, *Never Again: Britain 1945–51*, published in 1992

Many, including Conservatives like R.A. Butler, felt that Churchill's broadcast damaged the Conservatives and some historians still point up its role (see Source D).

Other historians disagree and downplay its importance.

Source E

Churchill reverted to type as a narrowly partisan campaigner. Afterwards, one of his extravagant claims, that the same Labour colleagues with whom he had worked for five years against Hitler were about to introduce their own Gestapo into Britain, was blamed for losing votes. But according to the opinion polls, the Conservatives actually gained support during the campaign; in the spring of 1945, they were 20% behind Labour and closed the gap to 8 per cent on polling day in July.

From Peter Clarke, *Hope and Glory: Britain 1900–2000*, published in 1996

Why did Labour win?

In fact, Labour had many advantages. They were consistently ahead in the opinion polls as Source E makes clear. The Conservatives were paying the penalty for all the suffering and mistakes of the 1930s. The unemployment was held against them and fears of its return were widespread. The British government's dealings with Hitler before the war at Munich and the policy of appeasement were now looked on with shame and blamed on the Conservative Party, who were in government at the time. The fact that Churchill had opposed it and that the Labour Party had consistently opposed re-armament until 1939 did not seem to count now. The sins of the past were heaped onto the Tory Party, and the Labour Party, as the opposition, was absolved. The long-standing hostile attitude of the bulk of the British press had been partially reversed by the shift of the *Daily Mirror* to support Labour just before the war. Beaverbrook's *Daily Express* was still hostile, as was the *Daily Mail*, but the *Mirror*'s circulation was increasing rapidly to have the biggest circulation in the country by 1950. Labour also appeared better organised than the Conservatives. Dalton told John Colville, 'that while the Tories had left the constituencies unattended, their agents being for the most part away fighting, he, like Herbert Morrison, had spent much time and effort in ensuring that Labour's electoral machinery was in good order'. The Labour campaign was also more professional, with effective targeting of marginal seats.

Perhaps most important of all, there had been a mood change since the last election of 1935. Deference towards those in a higher class had declined and there was clearly an increased faith in the power of the state to produce a fairer society in which old evils should and could be removed. This was not a spirit of revolution but one of faith that the country that had defeated an intolerable moral evil in the shape of Nazi Germany could now slay Beveridge's giants of evil – want, disease, ignorance, squalor and idleness. William Temple, Archbishop of Canterbury since 1942, was a socialist sympathiser and many others of all classes now felt that the time was right 'to build Jerusalem in England's green and pleasant land'.

Attlee, who in many ways was a deeply conservative figure with his attachment to his old public school and cricket, embodied this feeling and expressed it effectively in his radio response to Churchill. He argued that the Labour Party was now the all-embracing national party, representing 'all the main streams which flow into the great river of our national life'. By comparison, the Conservatives were a 'class party' representing 'property and privilege'. This seems to have struck a chord with the electorate. The party that had dominated British elections since 1918 now seemed old-fashioned. It was time for a change and the Labour Party cashed in on this sea change. Churchill's attempts to scare the electorate were unconvincing. After the Gestapo reference there was a concerted attempt to emphasise the power and influence of the left-wing of the Labour Party, embodied in the person of Professor Harold Laski of the London School of Economics, who was elected Party Chairman in May. The Beaverbrook Press ran a campaign stressing his influence and suggesting that the Labour Party was an extremist party.

SKILLS BUILDER

Look closely at Source F. How does the cartoonist show his disapproval of the Conservative campaign regarding the importance of Laski within the Labour Party?

Source F

But what's your PROGRAMME ?

2.2 Cartoon by George Whitelaw, *Daily Herald*, 4 July 1945. A voter is trying to ask Churchill a question whilst Lord Beaverbrook, owner of the *Daily Express* and a keen Tory, tries to whip up fear of the Left.

Source G

Dear Laski,

Thank you for your letter, contents of which have been noted.

C.R. Attlee

Letter from C.R. Attlee to H. Laski, written in response to a long letter sent by Laski to Attlee on 24 May 1945

The electorate remained unconvinced of Laski's influence. He had tried to persuade Attlee to resign in a long memorandum to the Labour leader, written on 24 May. Attlee's response was a typically terse one as seen in Source G.

SKILLS BUILDER

Use Source G to answer the following questions.

1 How far does Attlee's letter indicate that Laski exercised limited influence on Attlee as leader?

Who won the election?

The results of the election were a national landslide. 432 Conservatives had been elected in 1935. Now there were only 213. Only 154 Labour MPs had been elected ten years previously; now there were 393. There were only 12 Liberals returned, compared with 20 in 1935. In almost every region, Labour did well. They had a convincing majority in London and even a slight majority in the rest of southern England, which was traditionally Tory. In the North, Midlands and Wales, Labour was comfortably ahead. Scotland was much closer than might be expected, given the near elimination of the Conservatives in Scotland by the 21st century. Labour was ahead overall but by only 37 to 29. In every region, Labour had won a majority of the seats and now, for the first time in the history of the Labour Party, could form a government with a strong base in parliament. Labour's programme could be carried out, as long as the state of the economy allowed it.

Forming a Labour government

Churchill and Attlee were both somewhat surprised by the result, which became clear on 26 July. Churchill's wife sought to comfort her husband with the suggestion that it might be a blessing in disguise. Churchill grumpily retorted that at present it was very effectively disguised. Attlee immediately faced a plot to replace him, organised by Herbert Morrison, who suggested that there be a leadership election among the new MPs, an election Morrison expected to win. Ernest Bevin, the Labour heavyweight in every sense of the phrase, suggested that Attlee go to the palace immediately and get appointed before Morrison could organise anything. Attlee was driven promptly to Buckingham Palace by his wife and, after expressing his surprise to the king at being there, accepted the king's commission to form a government. As Morrison continued to make trouble, he was forcibly informed by Bevin, 'to stop mucking about or he wouldn't be in the bloody government'.

Biography

Herbert Stanley Morrison (1888–1965)

Morrison, who had left school at 14, was the son of a London policeman. He rose through local politics to become the Leader of the Greater London Council (GLC) from 1934–40. He was a London MP and served in the Labour Cabinet of 1929–31, but lost his seat in that year and so missed his chance of the leadership when Attlee succeeded George Lansbury in 1935. He returned to parliament later that year in the general election and he always felt that he deserved to be leader rather than Attlee. He served in Churchill's wartime government as Home Secretary and as a senior figure in the War Cabinet from 1942. He became very proud of his quiff, which the cartoonist David Low made famous (see the figure on the right of Source I, Chapter 1, page 10).

Attlee rapidly put together a strong team. Bevin went to the Foreign Office; Dalton to the Exchequer. Herbert Morrison became Leader of the House of Commons, responsible for the management of government business, and Lord President of the Council, an ancient title, which supported Morrison's oversight of Labour's domestic programme. Stafford Cripps was the fifth member of Labour's senior team as President of the Board of Trade. The one great surprise choice was that of the difficult and fiery Welshman, Aneurin Bevan as Minister of Health. At 47, he was considerably younger than the others. The average age of Cabinet members was over 60. In many respects, the Cabinet was oddly conservative despite the programme of reform. Attlee demonstrated this in his background and tastes. Colville had been appointed to serve under Attlee to help with the transition between governments and in his diary for August 1945, he recollects a conversation at Chequers (see Source H).

Biography

Sir Richard Stafford Cripps (1889–1952)

Cripps was from a wealthy legal family and became a very successful barrister himself. He was a devout Christian and this brought him into left-wing politics. He was a major opponent of re-armament in the 1930s and a supporter of the 'Popular Front' in opposition to Fascism. However, he never saw any incompatibility between his two positions, which irritated realists like Bevin and Dalton. He became a major figure in Churchill's wartime government. He was personally austere as a vegetarian and teetotaller, and a suitable Chancellor of the Exchequer for the period of maximum austerity from 1947 onwards, when he replaced Dalton.

Biography

Aneurin Bevan (1897–1960)

Also known as Nye, Aneurin Bevan was the son of a Welsh miner and was one himself at the age of 13. He rose rapidly as a union official and became Labour MP for Ebbw Vale in 1929. He was an inspired and inspiring speaker and became a noted left-wing member of the party. During the war, he was one of the few to criticise Churchill, who responded by describing him as a 'squalid nuisance'. He clashed frequently with Bevin and, in response to the advice, 'Never mind Nye, he's his own worst enemy,' famously retorted, 'Not while I'm alive, he isn't.' He often appeared lazy and vain, but he proved himself to be an able administrator at the Ministry of Health.

Source H

Attlee asked me what I thought of Geoffrey De Freitas who was there to be vetted as a candidate for Parliamentary Private Secretary. Charming, I said, and highly intelligent. 'Yes,' replied Attlee, 'and what is more he was at Haileybury, my old school'. Churchill, though he sometimes said nice things about me, never included in his recommendations that we were both Old Harrovians. I concluded that the old school tie counted even more in Labour than in Conservative circles.

From John R. Colville, *The Fringes of Power: Downing Street Diaries 1939–1955*, published in 2005

Source I

The Attlee government, even with such prominent left-wingers as Bevan, Shinwell and Strachey, was anything but a doctrinaire socialist administration. Attlee's personal dedication to Haileybury public school, Dalton's to the rowing fraternity of King's College, Cambridge, alone belied the fact. In the summer of 1947, a new splinter-group of fifteen left-wing MPs formed the 'Keep Left' group in protest at the government's promotion of the **mixed economy** at home and, more especially, its hard line Cold War policies overseas.

From Kenneth O. Morgan, *Britain Since 1945: The People's Peace*, published in 1990

Definition

Mixed economy
This refers to the presence of both state run and privately run economic ventures. Extreme socialists wanted most economic ventures to be state owned and run.

SKILLS BUILDER

How far does Source H support Source I in its views about Attlee's government?

However, for all the personal conservatism of some of the leading Labour ministers, there was a real sense that something monumental had happened in the election. John Freeman, a new young Labour MP, expressed it eloquently in his speech in reply to the king's speech opening parliament on 15 August: 'Today we go into action. Today may rightly be regarded as D-Day in the battle for the New Britain.'

Source J

" MAKE WAY ! "

2.3 Cartoon by David Low, *Evening Standard*, 27 July 1945

SKILLS BUILDER

What image does Low's cartoon present?

Creating the new Britain (1): The welfare state

Possibly the greatest achievement of the post-war labour government was the establishment of what became known as the welfare state, cradle-to-grave support for the entire population against poverty and sickness. This achievement was embodied in the *National Health Service Act* and the *National Insurance Act*, both in 1946 and the *National Assistance Act* in 1948.

It is often believed that Labour created the welfare state from scratch, and/or simply implemented the recommendations of Beveridge. Neither are strictly true. A national welfare system goes back to the reign of Elizabeth I and in its modern form to the major reforms carried through by the Liberal government before the First World War. Old-age pensions, national insurance against sickness and unemployment all existed for some people by 1914. These were gradually extended by 1939. Even before Beveridge produced his famous report late in 1942, the Labour Party was committed to an extensive overhaul and extension of welfare provision.

Beveridge is important in giving a major boost to welfare reform. It was a propaganda triumph, which made it difficult for any post-war government not to extend welfare provision. Point (c) of the Labour programme of 1942 (see Source K) was actually carried out by the Tory caretaker government of 1945.

National Insurance Act 1946 and the National Assistance Act 1948

The key element in Labour's programme of reform was 'universality', i.e. that benefits would apply to all; rich and poor. There would be no means test, such as had been a hated feature of the dole in the 1930s. On the other hand, benefits were paid for by insurance contributions, not given free. The whole social security system of the 1946 Act was established on a sound calculated basis, i.e. it was paid for by contributions from workers and employers, not taxation. A minimum number of contributions had to be made before benefits could be drawn. Only school children, pensioners, married women and the self-employed earning less that £104 a year were not covered. Demands from left-wing Labour MPs for the absolute right of the unemployed to benefits were defeated. Old-age pensions were established at 26 shillings for those over 65 and 42 shillings for a married couple.

The unemployed and those who had failed to make contributions were dealt with in the later *National Assistance Act* 1948. Here, personal means tests were applied by regional offices of the National Assistance Board. This was kept separate from the Minister of Social Security established under the 1946 National Insurance Act. The widespread support for welfare reform was shown by the fact that the Conservatives failed to oppose either the second or third readings of the Bill.

The two acts made considerable difference to all but the wealthiest members of British society. It did not create a welfare system from scratch but building on the existing provisions, it broadened them to give almost universal security from extreme poverty. It was a much appreciated change, yet the even more dramatic changes brought about by the National Health Service have somewhat overshadowed the achievement.

Source K

The Labour Party conference in 1942, having accepted a motion moved by James Griffiths, had called for a) one comprehensive scheme of social security; b) adequate cash payments to provide security whatever the contingency; c) the provision of cash payments from national funds for all children through a scheme of family allowances; and d) the right to all forms of medical attention and treatment through a National Health Service.

From Alan Sked and Chris Cook, *Post-War Britain: A Political History, 1945–92*, published in 1979

National Health Service Act 1946

There was far more controversy over the other great Act of 1946. Here the Conservatives attacked the details, if not the fundamental principles behind the scheme, announced by Aneurin Bevan, the new Minister of Health. The key aims were laid down at the beginning of the Act.

Source L

1 It shall be the duty of the Minister of Health to promote the establishment in England and Wales of a comprehensive health service designed to secure improvement in the physical and mental health of the people and England and Wales and the prevention, diagnosis and treatment of illness and for that purpose to provide or secure the effective provision of services in accordance with the following provisions of this act.
2 The services so provided shall be free of charge except where any provision of this act expressly provides for the making and recovery of charges.

From The National Health Service Act 1946

SKILLS BUILDER

What are the main principles of the new National Health Service as outlined in Source L and why might they create opposition?

Early on, Bevan took the decision to, in effect, nationalise all hospitals in place of the chaotic mix that then existed. There were locally run hospitals, many of which had originally been attached to workhouses. There were also charity hospitals, some of which were teaching hospitals. He was initially opposed in Cabinet by Herbert Morrison, who believed strongly in local control. Bevan carried his point, receiving strong support from Hugh Dalton, the Chancellor of the Exchequer, who agreed to provide 80 per cent of the costs from taxation. Only 20 per cent of the cost of the health service was to come from national insurance contributions. The plan was for 388 hospitals to be run by 14 regional hospital boards centred on the medical faculties of a university. Bevan felt that only the state could pay consultants of the quality necessary to ensure a spread of talent throughout the entire country. The consultants were persuaded to go along with the scheme by the concession that they could continue their private practices while receiving generous salaries from the National Health Service (NHS). They were to become the demi-gods of the new system.

Bevan's biggest fight was to be with the British Medical Association (BMA), the body representing general practitioners (GPs). There was real hostility from most doctors, who feared being turned into mere state employees, a course favoured by the Socialist Medical Association (SMA). Bevan compromised, in their eyes letting down his left-wing supporters. Doctors who agreed to join the NHS were to be paid a small salary topped up by fees on the basis of the number of patients enrolled. This gave freedom to doctors and patients. Private practice could continue. As with the consultants, Bevan had bought off the doctors with generous terms: 'I stuffed their mouths with gold.'

State-run hospitals and state-funded and supervised GPs were supplemented by various local health services administered by local authorities, for example, maternity and child welfare clinics, health visitors, vaccination and ambulance services.

By 5 July 1948, 90 per cent of GPs had agreed to join and the whole scheme could be launched. Bevan had shown great skill and flexibility in piloting his Bill through Cabinet and parliament and in negotiating with powerful bodies such as the BMA. The fire-breathing Welsh socialist had proved himself a pragmatic, political operator. The whole scheme turned into an enormous, popular success. Thousands now received treatment, which they previously had felt that they could not afford. The NHS became not only the biggest employer in the country, but an almost sacrosanct national institution, such as the Royal Navy had been. There was, in fact, an irony that as one new national icon was being created, the other was being destroyed. Between 1945 and 1948, 10 battleships, 20 cruisers, 37 aircraft carriers, 60 destroyers and 80 corvettes (convoy escorts) had been scrapped. The nation's priorities were changing.

The new NHS was not without criticism then or since. A recent popular study of modern Britain by the journalist Andrew Marr makes the following balanced judgement.

Source M

When the NHS opened for business on 5 July 1948, there was a flood of people to surgeries, hospitals and chemists. Fifteen months later Bevan announced that 5.25 million pairs of free spectacles had been supplied, as well as 187 million free prescriptions. By then 8.5 million people had already had free dental treatment. Almost immediately there were complaints about cost and extravagance, the surge of demand for everything from dressings to wigs. There was much anecdotal evidence of waste and misuse. There certainly was waste. The new bureaucracy was cumbersome. And it is possible to overstate the change – most people had had access to some kind of affordable health care before the NHS, though it was patchy and working class women had a particular difficulty in getting treatment. But the most important thing it did was take away fear. Before it millions at the bottom of the pile had suffered untreated hernias, cancers, toothache, ulcers and all kinds of illness, rather than face the humiliation and worry of being unable to afford treatment. There are many moving accounts of the queues of unwell and impoverished people surging forward for treatment in the early days of the NHS, arriving in hospitals and doctors' waiting rooms for the first time not as beggars but as citizens with a sense of right.

From Andrew Marr, *A History of Modern Britain*, published in 2007

Housing and town planning

If the introduction of the NHS was to prove one of Labour's most enduring and popular reforms, the most urgent issue in 1945, and the one that concerned most people in contemporary surveys, was the issue of housing. By 1945, there was a crisis of major proportions. Not only had building and slum clearance been largely halted by the war, German bombers had added to the problem by destroying the homes of many thousands of families. By 1945, there were 700,000 fewer houses than in 1939. As Minister of Health, Nye Bevan was responsible for housing, but made it less of a priority. As one saying of the period had it, 'only keeping half a Nye on it'.

He was responsible for two Housing Acts, extending the powers of local authorities, and with them he hoped to achieve an end to social segregation with people of all classes living in council houses. Possibly the most notable success of the period was the construction of 157,000 prefabricated houses as temporary accommodation. In fact, Bevan disliked these, referring to

SKILLS BUILDER

List the positive and negative comments on the National Health Service referred to in Source M. Overall, in what ways does it tend to be more positive than negative?

them as 'rabbit hutches'. Part of the reason he did not meet the government target of completing 300,000 houses a year was his insistence on high standards, increasing the minimum floor area and insisting on upstairs and downstairs lavatories, at a time when many older properties did not have an inside lavatory at all. Despite a slow start in 1945–46, 750,000 new homes had been provided by September 1948; a considerable achievement.

Closely associated with the drive for more housing was the whole issue of planning, which in the best wartime tradition was taken up enthusiastically by the government. If all land was not going to be nationalised, then it would, at least, be subject to rigorous government control. The Town and Country Planning Act was passed in 1947 and came into effect in 1948. Agricultural land was to be protected and urban development carefully controlled, in contrast to the chaotic development of Victorian Britain. 14 new towns were to be built to help solve the housing shortages of the older cities. These included Stevenage, among many others, to solve the problems of Greater London, Peterlee in County Durham and Corby in Northamptonshire. National Parks were also to emerge from the same planning process, a cause very dear to Dalton, the Chancellor of the Exchequer.

Creating the new Britain (2): Education

Although the key piece of education legislation had been passed before Attlee became prime minister and it was a Conservative, R.A. Butler, who had been the minister responsible in 1944, it was left to the Labour Government to implement the reform and to bring about much needed changes. It was a woman, Ellen Wilkinson, who was appointed Minister of Education and had the difficult task of producing change at a time of financial stringency. Her greatest achievement against pressure from the Treasury was to get the school leaving age raised to 15 in 1947. An emergency building programme got temporary huts built for the extra pupils and a crash-training programme produced 35,000 extra teachers from de-mobilised service personnel. A further massive building programme produced 928 new primary school buildings by 1950.

The tripartite system of secondary education envisaged by Butler's *Education Act* (see Unit 1 page 15) was implemented as far as finance would allow. It was never fully tripartite as many areas failed to produce the technical schools, simply dividing children into a selected 25% who went to grammar schools and 75% who went to the secondary moderns. Despite this failure, the Act had a tremendous impact in providing opportunities for bright working class boys and girls and contributed massively to social mobility over the next thirty years. Many were to enjoy an education up to and beyond university which had been outside the reach of their parents before the war.

Creating the new Britain (3): Seizing the commanding heights of the economy

The Labour Party felt that the other great initiative with which it could transform Britain was by taking control of the economy through what it termed socialisation, more commonly called nationalisation. The party was committed by clause 4 of its 1918 constitution to 'the common ownership of the means of production, distribution and exchange'. This commitment had been publicly restated at a party conference in December 1944. The conference overwhelmingly carried a motion supporting public ownership, which had been moved by a young left-wing activist, Ian Mikardo. After his triumph, a gloomy Herbert Morrison placed a hand on Mikardo's shoulder and said, 'You do realise that you have lost us the general election.'

The **king's speech** of August 1945 referred to a large number of nationalisation proposals, which would bring 20 per cent of the economy under public ownership. Like the welfare reforms, these examples of seemingly radical politics were in reality less radical than they superficially appeared. All the proposed victims of nationalisation were already under some degree of state regulation and control. The approach adopted to running the newly nationalised industries was the public corporation. This device had already been adopted by Conservative governments to run the BBC in 1927 and the British Overseas Airways Corporation (BOAC) in 1939. Nationalisation made little change to workers within the industries and usually left the same managers in place. The complete non-revolution of this process was well illustrated by the nationalisation of the Bank of England in March 1946. There were no howls of protest from stricken capitalists and the existing governor and deputy governor were immediately reappointed and invited for a glass of sherry with the socialist Chancellor of the Exchequer. This was a far cry from the Bolshevik revolution in Russia. Civil aviation was brought fully under state control in August and the coal industry and the communications company Cable and Wireless in January 1947. Transport and electricity were taken over in 1948 and gas in 1949. The only really controversial area was nationalisation of the iron and steel industry, which was bitterly resisted by the Conservatives and left until 1951.

Given that there already existed a tradition of state control of such services as the BBC and temporary control of railways and mines in wartime, the takeovers were hardly great political issues. In general, the government was either taking over monopolistic utilities such as electricity supply, against which the Conservatives had no arguments, or 'basket cases', i.e. industrial enterprises that were no longer viable without state help. The railways were no longer profitable and the shareholders in the four great companies were grateful to receive government stock in compensation for their shares. Mine owners received £164 million, a very generous deal for a run-down, antique industry in need of much modernisation. For the miners, however, it was a symbolic victory over an ancient enemy. The managers tended to be the same, but miners received improvements in working conditions.

The most basic economic activity of the country, the production of food through agriculture, was not neglected, although the 1930s commitment to the common ownership of land was forgotten. An ex-Yorkshire miner, Tom Williams, found himself Minister of Agriculture and actually ended up endearing himself to farmers and landowners although not to rural romantics. The *Agriculture Act* of 1947 gave farmers guaranteed prices and modernisation grants to encourage production and easy access to a government-run scientific advisory service. Output increased to 146 per

Definition

King's/queen's speech
The speech given at the beginning of a parliament or a session of parliament that sets out the government's agenda or programme. It is usually delivered by the monarch but is written by the prime minister and his colleagues. Private Eye had a famous front cover in October 1964 with the Queen delivering the Wilson government's programme with a speech bubble coming from her mouth with the words, 'and I hope you realise I didn't write this crap'.

SKILLS BUILDER

Refer to Source N. What were Dalton's Budget strategies?

Definitions

Direct taxes

These are taxes on income that include the basic income tax and 'surtax', a higher rate charged on higher incomes. Such taxes are said to be 'progressive' because they hit the rich harder.

Indirect taxes

These are taxes on the buying and selling of goods such as excise duty on alcoholic drinks.

cent of 1939 levels and an age of 'industrial' farming blossomed. Williams became known as 'the farmer's friend' and on his retirement, the Duke of Norfolk organised a farewell thank-you dinner at Claridges Hotel in London.

Creating the new Britain (4): Paying for it

As indicated above, far from decreasing with the arrival of peace, the role of the state in peoples' lives continued to grow. Some of the changes could be paid for by shifting expenditure from defence to welfare and in this sense the war made the implementation of the Labour programme easier. Dalton proved a shrewd Chancellor of the Exchequer and genuinely radical in helping to build the new Britain. His biographer, Ben Pimlott, summarised his Budget strategies (see Source N).

Nevertheless, high taxes were not enough to sustain the new Britain. The end of the war produced a major financial and economic crisis as the USA suddenly and without warning cancelled Lend-Lease in August 1945. Without Lend-Lease, Britain would not be able to pay for food imports let alone cover the costs of massive defence commitments overseas, as in occupied Germany, Greece and the Middle East. The only solution, without inflicting even more sacrifices on the British public in terms of rationing and lower living standards, was to take a massive loan from the USA. One of the world's greatest economists and adviser to the Treasury, **John Maynard Keynes**, believed that he could extract an interest-free loan or even a gift of $6 billion and was duly dispatched across

Source N

The redistributive aim was disguised because Dalton reduced the total burden of taxation as compared to wartime levels, added nothing to income tax, and showed a preference for **indirect** over **direct taxation**. However, tax cuts were heavily in favour of the worst off. Dalton's first two budgets took two and a half million people in lower income groups out of tax altogether (by raising personal allowances and earned income relief) and substantially increased surtax. Dalton also revealed his socialism by what he deliberately neglected to do. He did not dismantle the tax structure that had been erected to meet wartime needs. As Anthony Crosland put it later, 'he maintained and even extended the great advance to income equality that was made during the war'. For those paying tax, the effect was 'to steepen the slope of graduation, and to make all tax on income more sharply progressive than before.' At its highest level, taxation on income reached 19s. 6d in the pound (97.5%).

From Ben Pimlott, *Hugh Dalton: A Life*, published in 1985

Biography

John Maynard Keynes (1883–1946)

By 1945, Keynes was one of the most eminent economists in the world. He was born into a Cambridge academic family and became a celebrated figure in Cambridge. He established an international reputation, criticising the economic consequences of the Treaty of Versailles in 1919. His great work was *The General Theory of Employment, Interest and Money* which was published in 1936. He appeared to offer a means of controlling the vagaries of the market by government policy, thereby offering an alternative to the two opposed viewpoints of the period, namely free-market capitalism and state socialism. His ideas dominated British government policy from 1947 to the 1970s.

the Atlantic. The USA did not see things quite as simply as the brilliant Keynes, whose wit and arrogance produced distrust. It was a case of brains versus power and power had the upper hand. Eventually, after four months of gruelling negotiations, which contributed to Keynes' death of a heart attack in 1946, the USA agreed to a 50-year loan of $3.75 billion at 2 per cent interest. Another condition imposed by the US administration was that within 12 months of the loan beginning, the pound should become freely convertible, i.e. it could be freely traded for dollars and other currencies on the world money markets. This was storing up trouble for 1947, but in the short-term it was paying for the new Britain.

Crisis and misery

The rationing and deprivations of wartime continued well after the war ended. There was a serious shortage of dollars with which to pay for imports after the US ended Lend-Lease. British exports had collapsed and it was a priority for the government to boost these so that the goods produced by the new peacetime Britain had to be exported to earn currency to pay for necessary imports. One role of the heavy taxation meted out by Dalton was to restrain spending power in Britain, driving firms to export. The post-war economic situation was made worse by serious shortfalls in coal production, on which Britain was dependant for 90 per cent of her energy. Manny Shinwell, the Minister of Fuel and Power, was absorbed in carrying through the nationalisation programme and was blithely optimistic, believing that the miners would deliver what was necessary once they were freed from the 'oppressive capitalist owners'. Nationalisation could not make good years of under-investment and poor management. By December 1946, there were serious fuel shortages affecting the whole economy and in January/February 1947, the weather intervened to produce a crisis hitherto unseen in 20th-century Britain. Siberian cold swept in. Many writers have described its impact (see Source O).

The Conservatives coined the phrase 'Shiver with Shinwell'. In March, floods replaced the cold as the snow began to melt. Selby in the Vale of York was cut off and the water level in the low-lying areas around the Rivers Ouse and Wharfe reached levels never known before or since. As the horrors produced by nature receded and a fine summer began, new problems were caused by the need to accept the convertibility of the pound, as part of the deal for the US loan. No sooner was it possible to freely buy and sell pounds in July, than a sterling crisis developed. Dollars poured from the country and by August convertibility was stopped. The government began to plan for famine and the prospect of Britain not being able to import sufficient food. Rations were cut further than they had been in wartime and private consumption of petrol stopped. In November, even potatoes were rationed, something that had never happened even during the worst phases of the war.

In these circumstances, there was an inevitable knock-on effect in politics. Plots abounded to get rid of Attlee and replace him with either Cripps or Bevin. Dalton and Morrison were in the forefront, but Bevin remained

Source O

Everyone who remembers 1947 has his own winter story. At Beaumont in Essex, the local postmaster walked 16 miles through head-high drifts to the nearest town to collect rations for his hungry village. On the morning of 29th January, the fireman of the 6.23 a.m. train from Huddersfield to Bradford glanced out of his cab and was knocked unconscious by a large icicle hanging from a bridge. On a national scale, the story was one of unrelieved disaster. By the end of the first week in February two million men were out of work, and there was no electricity at all for industry in the South Midlands and the North West. Several power stations closed for lack of coal; a hundred and twenty-five colliers were storm bound on the Tyne. Parsnips were being dug out of the ground with pneumatic drills.

From Susan Cooper's chapter 'Snoek Piquante' in, *The Age of Austerity 1945–51*, edited by Michael Sissons and Philip French, published in 1963

SKILLS BUILDER

What is the impression of the winter of 1947 given in Source O?

steadfast and Attlee showed himself a smart political operator. First, Cripps was promoted in September to a new ministry in charge of economic planning, sidelining Morrison, who had hitherto had a general oversight. When Dalton made the mistake in November of speaking to a journalist about the contents of his Budget, just before announcing it to the Commons, he had to resign and Attlee replaced him with Cripps. The modest little prime minister had neatly defused the situation and neutralised his critics. The economic situation, nevertheless, remained grim.

Unit summary

What have you learned in this unit?

This unit has covered a considerable amount of information. You have learned why Labour won the general election of 1945 and about the ways the new government tried to transform Britain. In particular, you should appreciate the major changes in welfare provision and the big increase in government management of the economy. Some of the financial problems have been addressed, as well as aspects of the very severe economic crisis that developed in 1947.

What skills have you used in this unit?

You have encountered a large number of secondary sources relating to this period as well as some primary ones and been asked to consider their strengths and weaknesses as sources of evidence for historians. You have begun to use sources in various different ways.

Exam style question

This is the type of question that you will find on the examination paper as a (b) question. You will use the sources provided, with your own knowledge.

Study Sources J, M and N.

How far do you agree with the view that the Labour government transformed Britain in the years 1945–48?

Explain your answer using the evidence of Sources J, M and N, and your own knowledge.

Exam tips

- Do be clear about the question focus – what is being offered for debate? In the question below the key word is 'transformed'.
- Use the sources both for and against the proposition. They won't all point in the same direction. Sometimes a single source can be ambivalent and can be used in both support and contradiction as Sources M and N can be here.
- Develop each point by reference to your own wider knowledge, using it to reinforce and/or challenge the points derived from the sources.
- Evaluate the conflicting arguments.
- Present a judgement in a clear conclusion.

RESEARCH TOPIC

Try to validate or contradict Andrew Marr's judgements in Source M on the impact of the National Health Service by interviewing some of those alive today who can remember its introduction in 1948.

3 Austerity and defeat: Labour in power, 1948–51

What is this unit about?

This unit shows how and why the Labour Party imposed a policy of austerity on the country and what the consequences were. It is necessary to look briefly at some aspects of defence and foreign policy, which had considerable impact on developments within Britain. The reorganisation and reform of the Conservatives was also a major development of these years, which was to bear fruit in the two elections of 1950 and 1951, the latter bringing to an end six years of Labour rule. Finally, there is an assessment of the Attlee Labour government.

Key questions

- How and why did the Labour Party continue with a policy of austerity?
- What were the economic achievements of these years?
- In what ways did the Conservatives reform themselves?
- What happened in the general elections of 1950 and 1951, and why?
- What was the legacy of the Attlee government?

Timeline

1948	April	European Recovery Programme – Marshall Aid
	June	Berlin Blockade confrontation with the USSR
	29 July	Olympic Games open in London
1949	March	Clothes rationing ends NATO set up
	May	Gas nationalised
	December	Parliament Bill passed – reduces powers of the Lords
1950	February	General election: Labour 315, Conservatives 298, Liberals 9, others 3
	April	Strike in London Docks
	June	Outbreak of Korean War
	July	First British troops reach Korea
	August	UK defence estimates trebled
	September	National Service extended to two years
	October	Cripps resigns as Chancellor of the Exchequer – succeeded by Hugh Gaitskell
	November	China intervenes in the Korean War

1951	January	Bevan becomes Minister of Labour
	February	Iron and steel nationalised
	March	Bevin leaves the Foreign Office
	April	Gaitskell's first Budget
		Bevan and Wilson resign from the Cabinet
	25 October	General election

The impact of foreign and defence policy on British politics

Although this study is not primarily concerned with foreign and defence policies, it is impossible to understand the nature of British domestic politics without understanding something of the foreign policy context. Britain was still a 'great power', if a slightly moth-eaten one. British troops were garrisoned across the world: once again back in Hong Kong and Singapore in the Far East and until 1948 in India. The British army had a vast base in Egypt, near the Suez Canal, with smaller garrisons in Aden and elsewhere in the Middle East, where Britain was still the dominant power. In addition to all the old imperial commitments, there were new calls for military power in Europe, occupying conquered Germany and battling Communists in Greece. In the spring of 1948, there were still 940,000 troops in the British Army and conscription was still in force to provide this number. It was only by 1950 that it fell to around 750,000. To put figures into context, the size of the current British Army is around 100,000 strong.

The Cold War

However, it was not only old Imperial obligations that kept defence spending high. No sooner had Nazi Germany been removed as a threat, than a new totalitarian power seemed to be bidding for European if not world domination. Soviet Russia, with her vast Red Army occupying all of Eastern Europe and part of Germany, now seemed to threaten Western democracy. Stalin's brutal dictatorship extended its methods of barbaric terror to Poland, Hungary and the other countries of Eastern Europe.

Definition

Cold War

The expression was coined to describe the confrontation between the USA and Britain on one side and the Soviet Union on the other. It developed almost immediately after the 'hot war' with Nazi Germany. Although it never led to a direct military conflict, there were many close shaves and indirect confrontations such as in Korea. It finally ended in 1990 with the collapse of Communism in Eastern Europe and the disintegration of the Soviet Union. It is an essential part of the background of the time period covered by this book.

Communist puppet governments were installed even in Czechoslovakia, which had a tradition of democracy. The Gestapo had been removed to make way for the **KGB**. In 1948, the year Czechoslovakia had been forcibly taken over, Stalin tried to force the British and Americans out of Berlin by denying land access across Soviet-occupied territory. The result was the **Berlin airlift** and the very real threat of a new world war. Attlee and his foreign secretary Ernie Bevin responded to Soviet aggression with a toughness worthy of Churchill. Both realised that Britain and Western Europe needed the USA as protector and helper, and Bevin played a large and important part in re-engaging the US with Europe. He was instrumental in securing both **Marshall aid** and the setting up of **NATO** (North Atlantic Treaty Organisation) in 1949. This was to elicit criticism from left-wing Labour MPs, who were suspicious of the USA as the world champion of capitalism and still had a sneaking admiration for the Soviet Union. Some such MPs were Communist **fellow travellers** and even Soviet agents. Bevin hated them with a passion, which was returned in equal measure.

Definitions

KGB

These initials stand for the feared post-war secret police of the USSR. Before the war, they had been called the NKVD and between 1936 and 1938 had arrested, tortured and shot hundreds of thousands of Soviet citizens. In 1938, Lavrentiy Beria had taken over management of the organisation and he was still the dreaded chief after the war.

Berlin airlift

On 24 June 1948, the Soviet Union closed all land routes to Berlin in breach of post-war agreements. The Western powers were faced with either using force against the vastly superior Red Army or accepting defeat and the abandonment of their occupation of Berlin. They hit on the idea of using their superior air power to fly food and supplies to the two million West Berliners. In all, 272,000 sorties were flown and, in May 1949, Russia lifted the blockade.

Marshall aid

This was the programme of economic aid to Europe proposed by George Marshall, the US foreign secretary in 1947. The suggestion was enthusiastically encouraged and helped by Bevin. Congress agreed in 1948 and set up the European Recovery Programme. Eventually $13 billion was spent. Britain and France were the two chief beneficiaries. The aim was to reduce the influence and attraction of Communism, very strong in France, and to enable Western Europe to buy US products. It was enlightened self-interest by the USA, but it was generous and did much to help Europe develop as a prosperous, free and essentially capitalist corner of the globe.

NATO

A multi-national organisation established in 1949 which agreed to a system of mutual defence between members. If one of the members of NATO was attacked, all other members would come it its aid. The main threat that it faced off against was the Soviet Union and its communist allies. The first NATO Secretary General famously stated the goal of NATO was 'to keep the Russians out, the Americans in, and the Germans down'.

Fellow travellers

This is a phrase used to describe secret Communist sympathisers, who had chosen to stand as Labour MPs knowing that they stood little chance of being elected if their true colours as Communists were known by the electorate.

Bevin's position is well expressed by the contemporary cartoonist David Low and more recently by the journalist turned historian Andrew Marr.

Source A

3.1 Cartoon by David Low, *Daily Herald*, 12 January 1951

Source B

The key to Bevin, from NATO to directing the British fight against insurgents in Greece was that he believed in liberty as essential to the building of a fair society. He believed in a welfare system to keep the wolf from the door and full employment for unionised workers, which could be delivered by taking some of the economy into public ownership. Because of his huge wartime powers he was a great believer in the State. He once told some American correspondents that he believed it was possible to have public ownership and liberty. 'I don't believe the two things are inconsistent . . . If I believed the development of socialism meant the absolute crushing of liberty, then I should plump for liberty because the advance of human development depends entirely on the right to think, to speak, and to use reason, and to allow what I call the upsurge to come from the bottom to reach the top.'

From Andrew Marr, *A History of Modern Britain*, published in 2007

SKILLS BUILDER

In what ways do Sources A and B explain Ernest Bevin's support for the US alliance?

Bevin and Attlee's determination that Britain should both remain a great power and closely cooperate with the USA to contain Communism had enormous implications for domestic politics. It created a real bond with the Conservative opposition and was a key element in consensus. In sharp contrast to the 1930s, when foreign policy and re-armament had created bitter party political divisions, Tories and Labour essentially agreed on

Britain's role in the world. Bevin persuaded Attlee and the small Cabinet committee considering the matter that Britain should become a nuclear power. In Bevin's words, he wanted an atom bomb 'with a bloody Union Jack on the top of it'. When North Korea attacked South Korea in June 1950 using heavy equipment supplied by the Soviet Union, Attlee and the Labour government aligned themselves completely with the USA and sent a British brigade to fight alongside US troops. The Korean War and the need to confront Soviet threats in Europe through NATO forced a programme of re-armament upon the Labour government that added to the financial strain.

In his study of Britain in the 1950s, Peter Hennessy emphasises the cost, as highlighted in Source C.

The Young Denis Healey, working as International Secretary for the Labour Party (in effect a party researcher who briefed Bevin from time to time), comments in his memoirs on the political costs for Bevin.

Source D

Bevin had enormous difficulty in winning the approval of the Labour Party itself while he was alive, and had to contend with at best grudging acquiescence from many of his cabinet colleagues. Much of the party still took a Utopian view of world politics. Many at every level of the movement still had their pre-war illusions about Stalin's Russia as a workers' paradise. An even larger number distrusted the United States. Above all, there was a general reluctance to accept that the defeat of Hitler and Mussolini had not in itself created the conditions for a lasting peace. With so much to do at home, the idea of continuing to divert resources to defence was universally unwelcome.

From Denis Healey, *The Time of My Life*, published in 1989

Source C

Despite imperial withdrawal from the Indian sub-continent, the handing over of military responsibility for the defence of Greece and Turkey to the USA, two punishing sterling crises in 1947 and 1949, the worsening Cold War and continuing imperial commitments, the unquestioned appetite of Attlee and his senior ministers that Britain should remain a great power resulted in defence spending in 1951 (because of the Korea-related surge) accounting for 20% of total public expenditure or 7.6% of GDP (gross domestic product).

From Peter Hennessy, *Having it So Good; Britain in the Fifties*, published in 2006

Cripps and austerity

Perhaps even more than Clement Attlee, the prime minister and the bulky figure of Ernie Bevin, the Foreign Secretary, it was the new Chancellor of the Exchequer, Sir Stafford Cripps who symbolised the Labour government in the years 1948–50. He carried with him a moral certainty that could repel but also inspire. 'There but for the grace of God, goes God' was Churchill's comment on him. A vegetarian and teetotaller, it was popularly believed that, as he grew older, he lived on a diet of pea shoots grown on his office blotting paper. He was the ideal man to demand discipline and restraint from the country.

Cripps had to encourage production to rise, but the products should primarily be for export to cover the cost of necessary imports. In other words, domestic living standards had to be held down while hard work was encouraged. Cripps hoped to encourage such restraint through budgetary methods rather than the physical controls of rationing, but the end product was the same – self-denial and a drab sufficiency. Petrol rationing and taxation ensured that many of the small cars being produced went for export and the £30 currency limit made any foreign travel difficult. Clothes were 'utility' ware and the national appearance similar in many respects to that associated with Eastern Europe under Communism. The standard rate of income tax remained at 45 per cent, but surtax was payable on top of this by the wealthy. A bachelor lucky enough to have an income of £10,000 per annum kept £3501 of it after tax. Taxes on beer reached record levels in 1948, seven times what it had been in 1939. Cripps needed the high revenue, not only as a way of controlling domestic spending, but also to fund the foreign policy commitments referred to above and the escalating costs of the health service, which far exceeded expectations. Full employment ensured that the great expenditure on welfare could be cut back on its 1930s level, but pressure had to be applied to Bevan's housing budget and the numbers of houses built in 1949 fell compared with 1948.

Despite a good year for exports in 1948 and the help via Marshall Aid, a major **balance of payments** crisis developed in 1949 as a result of a temporary downturn in the USA economy and a subsequent slump of British exports to the USA in consequence. Hugh Dalton, once again back in the Cabinet but in a more junior position, tells the story of an unfolding crisis in his diary for 15 June 1949.

Definition

Balance of payments

This refers to the relationship between payments made by the country for imports and the earnings gained from exports. If the cost of imports exceeds that of earnings from exports then there is a negative balance and the country is effectively spending more money than it is earning. Ultimately if this persists over a long time then an economic crisis can ensue as the country gets into high levels of debt.

Source E

Very Serious dollar situation. Gap widening and reserves running down. Cripps says that the danger is that within twelve months, all our reserves will be gone. This time there is nothing behind them, and there might well be a complete collapse of sterling. Cripps gets authority to stop all purchase of gold and dollars. As we go out Addison says, '1931 over again'. I say 'It reminds me awfully of 1947.' Shall we never get free?

From Hugh Dalton, *The Political Diary, 1918–40, 1945–60*, published in 1987

The next month Cripps, whose health was failing, had to go to Switzerland to recuperate. He was firmly opposed to devaluing the pound as an answer, as was Ernie Bevin. Devaluation was an acknowledgement of the fundamental weakness of Britain compared with the USA. Dalton, Wilson, the President of the Board of Trade, and some other younger government members decided that devaluation was inevitable and persuaded Attlee. On Cripps' return, he was left with no alternative and, together with Bevin, went to Washington in September to negotiate an economic package to go with devaluation. In general they got what they wanted, more Marshall Aid, lower US tariffs to encourage British imports and agreement to a new pound/dollar ratio. The pound was to fall substantially from $4.30 to the pound to $2.80. Bevin wanted to know what it would do to the price of a loaf of bread. The economic experts told him it would rise from four and a half pence to five and a half pence. Bevin decided that the working classes would stand for this especially if the bread could be whiter. The austerity bread with bits of husk in it made him belch and, like many working men, he liked his 'butties' of white bread. This led to a furious argument with

Cripps, who was something of a food fad and regarded brown bread as superior and thought it would be conning the working classes to pretend that this more expensive loaf was better because it was white. Thus class distinction affected even the most important of economic policy decisions.

Attlee's problems throughout all of this were horrendous, indicating that a prime minister's lot is not a happy one, especially a prime minister faced by such assertive colleagues and very difficult economic circumstances.

Source F

The next two weeks were very difficult for Attlee. Alexander, threatened to resign if there were cuts in defence, Bevan was threatening to resign if there were cuts in the social services, and Cripps, his nerves frayed by insomnia, seemed, as Attlee said, 'ready to resign about anything'. Even Ernest Bevin spoke of going if defence suffered damage, though Attlee thought later that this was to provide countervailing strength against Bevan.

From Kenneth Harris, *Attlee*, published in 1982

SKILLS BUILDER

Use Sources E and F, and your own knowledge. What were the problems facing Britain in the summer of 1949?

In the country at large there were signs of discontent. Labour lost control of the London County Council in 1949, which it had held before with a large majority of 90 to 28. A middle-class pressure group, the 'Housewives League', was established and complained about rationing, queuing and all the petty indignities and controls of life under Labour. These could be remarkably stupid as the following extract makes clear.

Source G

The Ministry of Food prosecuted a greengrocer for selling a few extra pounds of potatoes, while admitting that they were frostbitten and would be thrown away if not cooked at once. The Ministry clamped down on a farmer's wife who served the Ministry snooper with Devonshire cream for his tea. A shopkeeper was fined £5 for selling home-made sweets that contained his own ration of sugar. Ludicrous penalties were imposed on farmers who had not kept strictly to the letter of licences to slaughter pigs; in one case, the permitted buildings were used, the authorised butcher employed, but the job had to be done the day before it was permitted; in another case the butcher and the timing coincided but the pig met its end in the wrong building.

From David Hughes' article, 'The Spivs' in *The Age of Austerity*, edited by Michael Sissons and Philip French, published in 1964

The mood of the country became almost rebellious and was expressed in two popular films of 1949, *Passport to Pimlico* and *Whiskey Galore*. Both celebrated the triumph of the individual and their 'illegal appetites' over the all-controlling state. The first imagined a part of London freed from the all-embracing regulations of Labour Britain and the joys this would entail. The title of the other, set on a Scottish island, almost speaks for its theme. Both celebrated freedom and satirised the controlling bureaucracy. By 1949, after nine years of high-minded self-denial in the name of a greater good, there was clearly a growing demand for freedom and choice. Sir Stafford Cripps' time was passing.

Yet, for all the grumbles, there were very real achievements.

- Despite setbacks and sterling crises in 1947 and 1949, exports soared from £266 million in 1944 to £2.2 billion by 1950.

- Devaluation had a real impact and British goods, now cheaper abroad, poured through the ports.

- The fact that it was a Labour government and that there were very real improvements in welfare care enabled them to get the cooperation of the trade union leaders. In April 1948, the Trade Union Congress (TUC) agreed to what amounted to a wage freeze.

- This wage freeze was to last well into 1950 and the whole period of the Labour government was marked by an absence of strikes. Only nine million working days were lost in the years 1945–50 compared to 178 million 1918–23. There were even the first signs of consumer prosperity and rising living standards.

- At the Board of Trade, **Harold Wilson** progressively removed articles from rationing.

- Television began to spread throughout the land supplementing the entertainment provided by radio and the cinema. Alexandra Palace began transmitting in the London area in June 1946, in Sutton Coldfield in the Midlands in 1949 and in Holme Moss in the north in 1951. The number of television licences increased from 15,000 to 344,000. On the whole it was only a middle-class southern minority who enjoyed television, but the numbers were growing.

The Conservatives in opposition

The election defeat of 1945 was a shattering and demoralising blow to the Conservative Party, which had dominated politics since 1918. Sir Henry Channon, the Conservative MP for Southend and one of the great political diarists of the 20th century wrote in his entry for 28 July 1945:

Biography

Harold Wilson (1916–1995)

A young Labour MP, he had just been elected in 1945 at the age of 29. He had had a brilliant academic career at Oxford where he had been a noted Liberal. During the Second World War he worked as a civil servant. He became the youngest Cabinet minister since the 18th century politician William Pitt the Younger, when he became President of the Board of Trade in 1947 and at that time he seemed to have a brilliant political career ahead of him.

Source H

On 10 July I was operated on at the London Clinic for hernia and for ten days was prostrate, too ill and angry to react seriously on the disastrous Election results. I am stunned and shocked by the country's treachery, and extremely surprised by my own survival. I predict the Socialist regime will soon come to grief: I give it three years, and then we shall be returned to power: but do we deserve to be?

From Chips Channon and R.R. James, *'Chips': The Diaries of Sir Henry Channon*, published in 1996

R.A. Butler, another Essex Conservative MP more politically powerful than Channon, explained the Conservative problems in his memoirs.

Source I

But the strength of the Labour government's position was reinforced by the magnitude and difficulty of our Conservative predicament – our need to convince a broad spectrum of the electorate, whose minds were scarred by inter-war memories and myths, that we had an alternative policy to Socialism which was viable, efficient and humane, which would release and reward enterprise and initiative but without abandoning social justice or reverting to mass unemployment. Until the progressive features of our thought had been fully exposed to public view, no one (to adapt Charles II's epigrammatic cynicism) was going to kill Attlee in order to make Churchill king.

From R.A. Butler, *The Art of the Possible: The Memoirs of Lord Butler*, published in 1971

SKILLS BUILDER

With reference to Sources H and I, explain what Channon means by the 'country's treachery'.

How far do the two sources agree on the problems facing the Conservatives?

It was not easy to persuade Churchill of this view. As Source I indicates, the problem of defeat was compounded by Churchill as leader who, although he had no intention of stepping down and handing over to a younger man, was frequently absent from the Commons. He became busily, and profitably, involved in writing his war memoirs, thus giving little thought to conducting the Opposition. The initiative passed to others, but at least Churchill appointed key figures to produce change. Lord Woolton, the wartime Minister of Food, was persuaded first to join the Conservative Party and then to serve as its chairman, with a brief to improve organisation and funding. R.A. Butler, the talented author of the 1944 *Education Act*, was appointed to head the Conservative Research Department and give a new intellectual thrust to the party. Butler and his team produced the Industrial Charter in 1947. The aim was to emphasise that the Conservative Party was one of conciliation and cooperation in industry not the party of hard-faced bosses associated with wage cuts and unemployment. Butler, who was married into the wealthy Courtauld family, was much influenced by the progressive approach of his father-in-law's business, which he saw as a model for the country. Churchill was less than enthusiastic about the Industrial Charter, as the following extract makes clear.

SKILLS BUILDER

How far do Sources I and J indicate that Churchill was a key obstacle to the recovery of the Conservative Party?

Source J

At the Party Conference at Brighton in October 1947, Churchill requested Reginald Maudling, as his speech writer, to put into his speech 'five lines explaining what the Charter says'. When they were produced, the Party Leader read them slowly and then disconcertingly, announced, 'But I don't agree with a word of this.' Fortunately, however, by then the document had been triumphantly passed by the Conference with only three dissentients and Maudling was able to reply 'But, Sir, this is what conference adopted', leaving Churchill to take refuge in a discontented grunt, 'Oh well, leave it in.'

From Anthony Howard, *RAB: Life of R.A. Butler*, published in 1987

I appreciate the pun

Woolton laboured away to improve funding and membership with remarkable success. He wished to make the party more dependent on a large number of small subscriptions rather than a handful of big ones, which kept constituency parties in the control of a few wealthy individuals. Candidates were forbidden to contribute more than £25 to the local fund in an attempt to encourage less-wealthy applicants. Membership leapt from just under a million in 1945 to 2,250,000 by June 1948. Woolton even toyed with the idea of changing the name of the party, but gave up on it. He did, however, stress the need for Conservatives to refer to the Labour Party, which sounded honest and English, as the Socialist Party, which sounded foreign and subversive. This tactic was followed until 1959, when it was discovered that a large number of voters thought that Labour and Socialists were two different parties. Nevertheless, the positive impact of Woolton's work is made clear in Source K.

Source K

A committee headed by a leading KC, David Maxwell-Fyfe, reported in 1948, recommending that the contribution of MPs to local associations should be limited to a token amount and that election expenses should be borne by the party centrally to a much greater extent. This did not clear out the augean stables overnight, indeed it could be argued that it did not clear them out to any great extent, but it did make it possible for more men like Edward Heath, Enoch Powell and Reginald Maudling to find winnable seats; to this extent the reform did its job in providing an entry into politics on the Conservative side for young meritocrats who through the accident of birth, fate had neglected to provide with sufficient funding.

From John Charmley, *A History of Conservative Politics 1900–1996*, published in 1996

Changing ideas

The parties of the left have often claimed the moral high ground but also at times the intellectual high ground as well. The Tories have sometimes been seen not just as the 'selfish' party but also as the 'stupid' party. This might be unfair to notable Conservatives, but at times like 1945, when Marxism or at least faith in the role of the state to solve problems was fashionable, it was easy to believe that the intellectual tide was behind socialism. In the late 1940s there was a reaction. Professor F.A. Hayek published an influential book in 1944, *The Road to Serfdom*. It warned of the dangers of the enhanced powers of the state as a threat to freedom. Writers like George Orwell, hitherto a man of the left, showed his disillusion with the Communist experiment in *Animal Farm*, published in 1945 and then later in the novel *1984*, his chilling vision of a socialist Britain a quarter of a century on. Robert Blake, a leading Conservative historian and peer, drew attention to this important development.

Source L

The Conservative revival was helped by an intellectual movement in their favour. Statism which had been all the rage in the 1930s lost its charm in the highly regimented England of the war and post-war years. A very influential book at this time was Professor F.A. Hayek's *Road to Serfdom*, published in 1944. It was essentially anti-socialist in its implications. The universities saw a notable revival of conservative sympathies among the undergraduates and to some extent among the professors too. The Conservative Research Department, headed by R.A. Butler, contained as members at times during the period Edward Heath, Reginald Maudling and Enoch Powell – people of whom many things have been said, but not that they were stupid. The Labour Party had lost its near monopoly on intellect and ideas.

From Robert Blake, *The Conservative Party From Peel to Churchill*, published in 1970

Thus, by 1950, the Conservative Party was in a far stronger position to fight an election with the prospect of winning.

Decline and fall of the Labour government, 1950–51

If the Conservatives were looking more formidable, Labour was increasingly divided and exhausted. The losses in the London local elections of 1949 have been referred to above (see page 41). The question of how to respond to defeat produced division. Morrison, a London politician and acutely aware of the popular mood, urged the need for caution and consolidation. He wished to avoid raising the tax burden, which he already felt was too high.

Source M

The incentive to effort for workers as well as professional and technical people and employers is seriously affected by this (tax) burden, which in turn reacts on our costs, and our capacity to earn dollars. It seems difficult to believe that revenue can be maintained even at present levels without pressing on the limits of the taxpayer's endurance.

From a paper drawn up for the Cabinet by Herbert Morrison, August 1949

Bevan's position was diametrically opposed.

Source N

Bevan ardently advocated 'advance'. He publically pressed three points: there must be more nationalisation; Tory attacks on the conduct of the nationalised industries by the Labour Party must be countered by denunciations of the iniquities of private industry; the Labour Party must put forward a list of industries to be nationalised for instance, chemicals and shipbuilding. If the party would not put its weight behind this three point programme said Bevan, it would lose the next election.

From Kenneth Harris, *Attlee*, published in 1982

SKILLS BUILDER

Refer to Sources M and N. What were the tensions within the Labour Party in 1949–50?

Attlee decided to go to the country in February 1950 rather than struggle on to the last possible moment in July. The result was a well ordered, almost model general election with an amazingly high turnout of 84 per cent. Labour campaigned on its record and increased its vote by a million and a quarter, securing 46 per cent of the votes cast. The Conservatives focused on the evils of nationalisation and government control. They secured a 3.3 per cent swing in their favour. The Liberals made a major effort in fielding 475 candidates, which it was thought might hurt the Tories. In fact, most of the Liberals lost their deposits and the Liberal Party gained only nine MPs and virtually bankrupted themselves. Despite the increase in the Labour vote, Labour lost many seats as much of the increased turnout was in safe Labour areas and merely increased existing Labour majorities. The big losses were in southern England (excluding London), where Labour seats were reduced from 91 to 54 and the Conservatives increased their seats from 88 to 144. In London, the Conservatives made no gains, but Labour lost 17 as a result of the abolition of seats to take account of declining inner-city populations. It was this redrawing of boundaries, largely carried out under the direction of the Labour Home Secretary, Chuter-Ede, which probably damaged the Labour Party more than anything else. The final tally was Labour 315, Conservative 298, Liberal 9, others 3.

This gave the Labour government a majority of 5 instead of 146. This could pose serious problems in getting measures through, especially as the Conservatives were now on the offensive and were going to fight everything every inch of the way. They were also fighting an aging and increasingly sick Labour team. Bevin was dying, under the strain of ten years in high office. Cripps was also gravely ill and surrendered the Exchequer in November. He was succeeded by one of the rising stars of the party and another product of Winchester College, Hugh Todd Naylor Gaitskell. This appointment irritated the great man of the left, Aneurin Bevan, who was kept as Minister of Health and then offered the Ministry of Labour early in 1951. He felt he deserved more of Attlee, and a greater bitterness arising from personal vanity and spurned ambition was now added to differences over policy.

The events of 1950 were to show how fragile the British economy was. The year had started well with dramatic improvements in exports, following devaluation and the first real sense that prosperity was round the corner. By the autumn, the economy mirrored the season. Spring was gone and a new winter of gloom approaching. The Korean War had broken out in June and British forces joined the United Nations Army, in resisting North Korea. A major British re-armament programme became necessary, partly as a result of events in Korea, but also due to the perceived Soviet threat in Europe. Gaitskell's first Budget was likely to be a tough one. Furthermore, the outbreak of war in Asia pushed up the cost of **commodity prices** worldwide, producing a new balance of payments crisis in Britain. The trade unions were increasingly impatient of wage restraint. There had been a series of unofficial strikes in 1949, which the

Definition

Commodity prices
These are the costs of various raw materials needed for industry to produce finished goods, and are a vital ingredient in the balance of payments. Britain needed to import large amounts of raw materials, notably oil. If the commodity prices fell on the world market then Britain benefited.

government believed were Communist inspired. The TUC conference in the summer of 1950, reflecting grass-roots opinion, rejected further wage restraint and it appeared that the good industrial relations of the post-war years were about to come to an end.

However, it was his Cabinet colleagues who were to pose the greatest problem to Attlee in 1951. Bevin finally reached the stage where he could not continue. He had to be moved from the Foreign Office in March and then died in April, holding the office of Lord Privy Seal. Attlee pondered on his replacement and apparently favoured another working man and trade-unionist, the Durham miners leader, Sam Watson. Unfortunately, he hated going south of Durham, which was something of a disadvantage in a Foreign Secretary. Eventually, Attlee appointed Morrison, who knew little of foreign affairs and was not a success. Attlee himself then fell ill just as Gaitskell was preparing to announce his Budget. With Attlee in hospital, a major Cabinet row broke out. Bevan and Wilson hotly contested Gaitskell's proposals.

- Bevan argued against the imposition of prescription charges as striking a blow against the principles of an NHS, free at the point of delivery.

- Wilson opposed the scale of re-armament.

Together with John Freeman, a junior minister and future television performer, they resigned. This clearly weakened the government and became the increasing subject of press comment, as the following cartoon indicates.

Source O

"SOCIALISTS!"

3.2
Cartoon by Vicky, *News Chronicle*, 25 July 1951

SKILLS BUILDER

What is the message of Source O?

The bitter division, with the constant stress of functioning with a tiny majority, made a general election look likely sooner rather than later. Attlee had been toying with the idea for some time and seemed to have settled on the autumn of 1951 because the king was to go on a six-month Commonwealth tour in 1952. In the event of a political crisis, always possible with such a small majority, it was constitutionally desirable for the king to be in the country.

General election, 1951

The election took place at the end of October. Once again the Conservatives tried to find a Labour bogey man to scare the country with. In 1945 it had been Laski, now it was Bevan. The scare probably didn't work, but the sense of Labour as a divided party certainly did them no good. The Tories emphasised Labour's nationalisation record and the sugar manufacturing company, Tate and Lyle, who feared that they were on Labour's shopping list of candidates for nationalisation, brought 'Mr Cube' into play as a propaganda ploy, the little sugar lump figure denouncing Labour from every packet of sugar. Labour tried to portray the battle as one between the moderate and responsible Attlee and the war-mongering Churchill, their favourite catchphrase being 'Whose finger on the trigger?' The Conservatives entered the election with more money, increased membership and a revamped image of studied moderation. Churchill campaigned on the theme of Labour as the party of the queue, everyone waiting their turn, while the Conservatives were the party of the ladder, offering betterment to those who wished to climb.

Once again it was a close-fought contest with a high turnout. Labour again increased their vote and secured 48.8 per cent of the votes, more than the Conservatives who secured 48 per cent. The Liberal vote collapsed. The British **first-past-the-post system**, however, gave more seats to the Conservatives. Many Labour votes simply piled up in safe northern constituencies giving the winning Labour candidates enormous majorities. The Conservative voters were more evenly spread and the result was Labour 295, Conservative 321, Liberal 6, others 3.

The Conservatives had secured a working majority. Attlee resigned and, at 77 years old, Churchill returned to Number 10. The young Labour MP, Roy Jenkins, was later to summarise the reasons for the result in his memoirs.

Definition

First-past-the-post system

This is the traditional British voting system in which MPs are elected for a particular geographical area and the winner is the candidate with the most votes regardless of whether this is a majority of over 50% or not.

Source P

That Autumn our fears about the mortal blow (Bevan's and the others resignations in April) to Labour in office proved well founded and a general election on the 25 October turned a Labour majority of 6 into a Conservative one of 17. Considering the vicissitudes which the government had suffered, with the loss of Cripps, Bevin and Bevan, the exhaustion of nearly every body else except for Gaitskell, and an election date chosen more in response to that exhaustion than to any tactical game plan, it was a surprisingly narrow defeat.

From Roy Jenkins, *A Life at the Centre*, published in 1991

Assessment of the Labour government

The first majority Labour government had lasted just over six years and in that time had achieved much of what it set out to do. Few governments compare in significance in terms of long-lasting effects. In many ways it set the agenda for the rest of the century and into the next. It made Britain a nuclear power, began the retreat from Empire, joined Britain closely with the United States and created a comprehensive welfare state. If India, the jewel in the crown of Empire was abandoned, the NHS became the new domestic jewel in the crown.

The government has been criticised from both a left and right perspective. From the left's perspective, it did too little. A government of social conservatives left much of British life untouched. In education, it was content to apply the Butler Act of 1944, dividing children at 11 into a majority attending secondary moderns and a minority attending grammar schools. Little was done to promote the technical schools that Butler proposed and it was in the area of technical education that Britain so lagged behind her competitors. Even less was done to end the privileged position of the private schools. The Eton and Harrow cricket match continued to grace the social season of the rich and the wealthiest segments of British society continued with a separate educational system based around public schools. Hunting continued, but then many working-class men indulged in their own version of it. The chance to join more closely with Europe in the Iron and Steel Community of 1950 was rejected and, despite the loss of India, the Labour government still saw Britain as a great world power, not simply as a European power on a par with France and Italy. The death penalty still continued and enjoyed considerable popular support. Judges, barristers and senior civil servants all continued to be drawn from the same upper or upper middle-class families. In so many ways there was continuity.

To right-wing critics, the government tried to build the New Jerusalem without addressing the real problems of Britain in terms of economic modernisation. It cosily accepted a partnership with conservative trade unions, who resisted modern technology and work practices, and continued ways of doing things that in the long-term were not compatible with a modern economy. Money was borrowed from the USA and spent on the NHS. David Low, a cartoonist sympathetic to the government in many ways, drew attention to this as early as 1947 as shown in Source Q.

Source Q

HIGHER STANDARD OF LIFE

UNDER-PRODUCTION

I'LL ATTEND TO THE FOUNDATIONS LATER

3.3 Cartoon by David Low in the *Evening Standard* from 9 October 1946

Yet despite all that it failed to do, the Labour government achieved much. In very difficult economic circumstances, it nursed the British economy back to something like health. It maintained a wide consensus of support, carrying large segments of the middle classes with it in its attempt to build a fairer society. Many historians draw attention to these achievements and feel that overall, judgement on the Attlee Government should be a positive one. Peter Hennessy is one such historian.

Source R

The Attlee years had their failures – refusal to confront the truly harsh reality of diminished world status, a reluctance to modernise the state, a tendency to look back at the problems of the thirties rather than forward to the needs of the fifties. Yet Britain had never – and still hasn't – experienced a progressive phase to match 1945–51. It is largely, though not wholly, the achievement of these years and the wartime experience, the crucial platform on which those advances were built – that 1951 Britain, certainly compared to the UK of 1931 or any previous decade, was a kinder, gentler and a far, far better place in which to be born, to grow up, to live, love, work and even to die.

From Peter Hennessy, *Never Again: Britain 1945–51*, published in 1992

SKILLS BUILDER

Using Sources Q and R, and your own knowledge, what would be your judgement of the successes and failures of the Attlee government?

Unit summary

What have you learned in this unit?

This unit has covered a considerable amount of information. You have learned about how and why Labour tried to deal with an exceptionally difficult financial and economic situation in Britain. In particular, you should appreciate the complex mix of factors causing the problems and how domestic issues were affected by the conduct of foreign policy. The reform and rebranding of the Conservative Party in these years is also an important theme, as well as how and why Labour eventually lost power.

What skills have you used in this unit?

You have encountered a large number of secondary sources relating to this period, as well as some primary ones, and have been asked to consider their strengths and weaknesses as sources of evidence for historians. You have continued to use sources in various different ways. Be aware of the subtle or sometimes not so subtle prejudices of the writers of secondary sources. Peter Hennessy clearly differs in his approach to the Conservative historians John Charmley and Robert Blake.

Exam style question

This is the sort of question that you will find on the examination paper as an (a) question. Use only the sources provided, but none of your own knowledge.

Study Sources M, O and P.

How far do these sources suggest that the Labour Party was weakened by serious divisions in its last two years in power?

Explain your answer using the evidence of Sources M, O and P.

Exam tips

- Remember to examine each source closely. In the question below consider which source most obviously stresses division?
- With regard to the analysis of sources is it necessary to use inference to reach the conclusion that there was division?
- Which source confirms that there was division but lays emphasis on illness and exhaustion as a weakness?

RESEARCH TOPIC

- Examine the workings of the first-past-the-post system in other elections in this period?
- How has the number of seats related to the popular votes cast?
- Why has it been particularly harmful to the Liberal Party?
- What alternative systems are there and what are their strengths and weaknesses?

UNIT

4 Setting the people free: the return of the Conservatives, 1951–56

What is this unit about?

This unit examines the first five years of the Conservatives' return, first under the aged Churchill and then briefly under Eden. The general theme they adopted was 'setting the people free', i.e. unscrambling the many controls put in place during the war and under Labour. Yet they claimed to be a moderate and centrist government and stressed continuity with the former Labour government in many areas of policy. Churchill finally retired in 1955 to be replaced by Eden, who had waited with increasing impatience for the moment. After a brief initial period of success, his premiership turned into a disaster and he retired ill and humiliated in January 1957.

Key questions

- What was Churchill's role and how competent was he as prime minister?
- How far did the Conservatives pursue a policy of consensus politics?
- How successful was R.A. Butler as Chancellor of the Exchequer?
- How effective was the Labour Party in opposition?
- Why was Eden's tenure as prime minister so short lived?

Timeline

1951	26 October	Churchill becomes prime minister
1952	February	Death of George VI
	March	Butler's first Budget – Bank rate goes up
	October	British atom bomb test Tea rationing ends
1953	January	Eisenhower inaugurated as president of the USA
	February	Sweet rationing ends
	March	Stalin dies
	April	Butler's second Budget – Tax cuts
	June	Coronation of Elizabeth II
	July	Armistice ends the Korean War
	September	Florence Horsburgh becomes first Conservative Minister for Education

	November	Announcement that all rationing will end in 1954
	December	Macmillan announces 301,000 houses built in a year
1954	July	Meat de-controlled – all rationing ends
	October	Britain agrees to withdraw troops from Egypt by 1956
1955	April	Churchill finally resigns Butler's tax-cutting Budget
	May	General election – Conservatives increase their majority
	October	Butler's tax-increasing Budget
	November	Cabinet decides not to join the European Common market
	December	Gaitskell replaces Attlee as Labour leader Cabinet reshuffle – Butler demoted
1956	April	Macmillan's first Budget – premium bonds
	July	Nasser nationalises the Suez Canal Company
	September	Eisenhower warns Eden not to use force against Egypt
	October	Anglo-French task force sails from Malta to Port Said – secret deal with Israel
	November	Invasion of Egypt – anti-war demonstrations and pound falls – no US support
	December	British and French withdraw – US/IMF support for sterling
1957	January	Eden resigns – replaced by Macmillan

The new prime minister and his government

Nine years older than Attlee and, at 77, the oldest man to become prime minister since Gladstone in 1892, Churchill was in many ways a Victorian or at least an Edwardian relic. He had entered parliament in 1900 and become a Cabinet minister in 1908. By then, he had already switched parties and he was never a traditional party politician. He was to hold nearly every senior office in government, switching back to the Conservatives in 1924 to become Chancellor of the Exchequer. He was a maverick. His leadership during the war raised him into a unique position, far above his rivals. When his six-year-old grandson managed to get into his study in the 1950s, while the old man was trying to work, he took the opportunity to put a question that was bothering him: 'Grandpapa, is it true that you are the greatest man in the world?' 'Yes,' came the immediate reply, 'Now bugger off!'

Churchill, like most of the country, was aware of the enormous support for Labour, as witnessed in the general election, and also of the widespread support for its reforms. He was anxious to establish a liberal Conservative government that would work essentially within the same fundamental policy areas. He did not want a return to the party-political bitterness of the 1930s. He would be a 'consensus' prime minister, accepting the welfare state, the need for a massive house-building programme, conciliation not confrontation with the trade unions and even a large nationalised segment of the economy. In foreign policy also, continuity would mark the change of government. He appointed notable liberal Tories to all the leading positions and tried to get non-Conservatives like the leader of the Liberal Party, Clement Davies, to join his Cabinet. How far Churchill was fit and able to conduct the government is open to controversy. He had already had a heart attack and a stroke and was to have another massive stroke in 1953, yet he soldiered on to the frustration of his colleagues until April 1955. His doctor, Lord Moran, later published his diaries and these can give the impression of an ailing and unfit national leader. Source A gives the entry for 11 October 1951, just before the election victory that month.

Source A

x When MacKenna, the dermatologist rose to take his leave, Winston asked me to stay.

As the door shut he said that he had a 'muzzy feeling' in his head:

'Oh it's nothing to do with alcohol; it comes on generally before luncheon. Aspirin helps it. If it's due to the circulation in my head, can't you think out something, Charles, that would be more effective than aspirin?'

He sat huddled in his chair, gazing gloomily at the carpet.

'I am not so sure as I was that I shall be able to see things through.'

I was disturbed that he said as much; it was not like him. He knew the incident at Monte Carlo, when his arm suddenly became 'funny' was a notice to quit the world. In a few days he would be 77.

I wondered what was passing through his mind. He has always coveted office, probably he always will, but why does he want to be Prime Minister when as he knows, he is not the man he was.

From Charles, Lord Moran, *Churchill: The Struggle for Survival 1945–60*, published in 1966

However, two other famous diaries of the period might be considered to give different impressions. Source B is Sir Henry Channon's entry for 3 November 1953.

Source B

In the House, Winston, who had not been present at the opening of Parliament this morning, rose amidst the cheers, and it was immediately clear that he was making one of the speeches of his lifetime. Brilliant, full of cunning and charm, of wit and thrusts, he poured out his Macauley-like phrases to a stilled and awed house. It was an Olympian spectacle. A supreme performance which we shall never see again from him or anyone else. In 18 years in this honourable House I have never heard anything like it. Then he sought refuge in the Smoking Room and flushed with pride, pleasure and triumph sat there for two hours sipping brandy and acknowledging compliments. He beamed like a school-boy.

From Chips Channon and R.R. James, *'Chips': The Diaries of Sir Henry Channon*, published in 1996

Churchill had tried to surround himself with the faces of those he had known and liked in wartime, and persuaded John Colville to return as his Secretary. In consequence Colville's diary entries provide as useful a source for these years as they do for the war years. Here is the entry for 16 May 1952.

Source C

Went to Chartwell this evening. Alone with the PM, who is low. Of course the Government is in a trough but his periods of lowness grow more frequent and his concentration less good. The bright and sparkling intervals still come and they are still unequalled, but age is beginning to show.

From John R. Colville, *The Fringes of Power: Downing Street Diaries 1939–1955*, published in 2005

SKILLS BUILDER

How far do Sources A, B and C suggest that Churchill was medically unfit to be prime minister in the years 1951–55? Which of these three sources is the most useful in giving us an insight into Churchill's leadership from 1951–1955?

If there are question marks over Churchill's health, there can be little doubt about the intellectual abilities of his leading ministers. His acknowledged deputy and successor was **Sir Anthony Eden**, the Foreign Secretary. His expertise was almost entirely in foreign policy, but as far as domestic policy was concerned he was a reforming Conservative of liberal

Biography

Sir Anthony Eden (1897–1977)
Eden was from an old gentry family, handsome and clever. He secured a first in Persian at Oxford and was a master of oriental languages. He was appointed Foreign Secretary at 38 and added to his later reputation by resigning in protest at Chamberlain's policies. Churchill appointed him Foreign Secretary again in 1940 and he was acknowledged as the leader in waiting. R.A. Butler was later to observe that he was the son of a mad baronet and a beautiful woman and 'That's Anthony – half mad baronet, half beautiful woman.'

Definition

Greasy pole

This phrase likens political life to the fairground amusement of trying to climb a greased pole and was attributed to Disraeli, who on first being appointed prime minister in February 1868 is reputed to have said, 'Well, I've climbed to the top of the greasy pole.'

views. **Richard Austen Butler** was appointed Chancellor of the Exchequer and had already established a reputation as a highly competent minister with a formidable intellect and capacity for hard work. Perhaps the most radical of all Tory MPS, according to Attlee, was appointed Minister of Housing. **Harold Macmillan** was rather disappointed to be sent to housing, but he used it as an effective launch pad for his ambitions. With his grasp of the 'new economics' of Keynes, he was probably ahead of most politicians in all parties. Beneath these able senior figures was a talented collection of junior ministers marked by intellect and a capacity for independent thought. Iain Macleod was the first of these to reach ministerial office in 1952, but Reginald Maudling, Edward Heath, Edward Boyle and Enoch Powell were beginning to climb the **greasy pole.**

Biography

Richard Austen Butler (1902–1982)

From a well-established academic family, Butler married an heiress and thus had brains, connections and money. He became an MP in his twenties and was rapidly promoted to office. He was the classic 'insider', more concerned with the practical problems of government than abstract principles or party political warfare, which seemed to him crude and destructive. At one and the same time, Butler represented all that was best in the traditions of the English ruling class – intelligence, detachment and a desire to serve, wedded to a failure to appreciate the passions of politics and the pull of the irrational. His natural instincts were to reject Churchill's desire to fight on in 1940 regardless of the apparent hopelessness of the situation. When the visiting Belgian politician, Henri Spaak, trying to persuade Britain to take a more positive attitude to the new European Union, appealed to Butler, who was handling the issue, for an imaginative leap in policy, it is recorded that Butler looked at him 'as if he had taken off his trousers'.

Biography

Harold Macmillan (1894–1986)

A tragic and complex figure, Macmillan was older than either Butler or Eden and, like Churchill, half American. After a brilliant academic career at Eton and Oxford, he served throughout the First World War in the Guards, being wounded five times. Although from the upper middle classes, as the son of a successful publisher, he married Lady Dorothy Cavendish and into the aristocracy. Her sister had married a brewery heir and the old Duke of Devonshire is reputedly said to have reluctantly approved Dorothy's marriage with the words: 'Well at least books are better than beer.' Macmillan became Conservative MP for Stockton in 1924 and developed a real affection for it and a real concern for the plight of the unemployed. He became a genuine Tory radical and, as his firm was Keynes' publisher, developed a real insight into the 'new economics'.

Definition

Consensus politics

This refers to the broad agreement between the two main political parties on most important issues e.g. foreign policy, acceptance of the welfare state, the desire to avoid 1930s style unemployment.

Consensus politics in action

The most obvious area of policy where '**consensus politics**' reigned, was in the government's attitude to industrial relations and the trade unions. Churchill was anxious to avoid the impression of 'union bashing', a policy he had become associated with during the General Strike of 1926. Now in 1951 there was no attempt to restore the *Trade Disputes Act* 1927, which had annoyed the trade unions and been repealed by the post-war Labour government. In some ways the new Conservative government was even more conciliatory to the trade unions than its Labour predecessor had been. There was to be no use of troops to break unofficial strikes such as Attlee had used in 1949. Churchill appointed Sir Walter Monckton as Minister of Labour. Both the following sources, written 30 years apart, tend to agree on the general drift of government policy.

Source D

If Butler's appointment was a sop to Labour, then the decision to place another of Churchill's cronies, Sir Walter Monckton at the Ministry of Labour, was an act of outright appeasement. Monckton was professionally and personally oleaginous [evasive], totally out of sympathy with the Conservative party and his view was that if anything was done 'to rock the boat in our relations with the trade unions I will resign'. There was no need for that. Indeed, so conciliatory was Monckton that there were those that wondered if he was the minister for Labour.

From John Charmley, *A History of Conservative Politics 1900–1996*, published in 1996

Source E

On the wages front a quite deliberate policy of appeasement was adopted. Winston Churchill still had unpleasant memories of the general strike to live down. As Lord Woolton has put it in his memoirs, 'he was determined that there would be no industrial strikes during his period as Prime Minister'. This was the era of Sir Walter Monckton at the Ministry of Labour, when all the Ministry's energies were devoted to bringing the two sides together even at the cost of highly inflationary settlements.

From Samuel Brittan, *The Treasury under the Tories 1951–1964*, published in 1966

SKILLS BUILDER

To what extent do Sources D and E agree about Conservative attitudes towards the trade unions?

Here in its early stages was one crucial aspect of what became known as 'the British disease', the essentials of which were low productivity growth, poor industrial relations and wage demands above the level of economic growth, leading to inflation. Powerful trade unions, their membership steadily increasing, resisted technological innovations in a desire to protect jobs and existing work practices. The reckoning would eventually come but not under the benign management of Sir Walter Monckton. The new Conservative government was quite unprepared to allow the weapon of unemployment to be used to discipline the workforce and the simultaneous pursuit of full employment and peace at all costs with the unions, without an **incomes policy**, was bound in the end to lead to inflation.

The welfare state, including the jewel in the crown of the NHS, was to prove quite safe in Tory hands. As his biographer, Nigel Fisher, who was also a Conservative MP, makes clear, the young new Minister of

Definition

Incomes policy

An attempt by governments to control the rise in incomes and salaries. This could be informal such as under Labour in 1974–79 or statutory (backed up by law), as under Heath in 1970–74.

Source F

Source F

As Minister of Health Macleod was not an innovator. He left the Health Service much as he found it. It was a period of consolidation. The service had survived its teething troubles and was running well. Aneurin Bevan's widow, Jenny Lee, wrote later 'when Iain Macleod became Minister of Health, he was generous enough to tell Nye how little he found it right or possible to change once he had had a close-up of the Health Service as it was at the time'.

From Nigel Fisher, *Iain Macleod*, published in 1973

Definition

Pairing

Usually allowed by the party whips, pairing is a parliamentary convention by which an MP of one party can be allowed to miss a vote in the Commons if his 'pair' in the rival party agrees not to vote, thereby preserving the balance.

Health, Ian Macleod, was not inclined to try to alter Nye Bevan's great achievement.

Macleod tried to fight for more money for hospitals, which he recognised were in need of modernisation, but found himself in a queue very much behind housing. Many Labour MPs appreciated Macleod's efforts and the difficulties he faced. Bevan was initially suspicious of Tory intentions, but eventually became friends with Macleod and the two became '**paired**'.

As far as housing was concerned, the new government was determined to out perform Labour. At its 1950 conference, the Tories had given a pledge to build 300,000 houses a year, a target not met by the Attlee government. Harold Macmillan was the new minister and, although rather disappointed to be placed there by Churchill, saw the possibilities of enhancing his reputation. He acquired an excellent team to assist him, with Evelyn Sharp as his senior civil servant, generally viewed as one of the cleverest women in Whitehall, and Ernest Marples as his junior minister. Marples' background and vowel sounds contrasted sharply with the patrician drawl of Macmillan, but he fully and always acknowledged his debt to Marples.

Source G

As his junior Minister Macmillan brought in a cocky and talkative MP whom he came to admire more than almost any of those whom he promoted after 1957 – Ernest Marples. Almost entirely a self-made man, Marples was the son of a worker. Aged forty five and brimming over with ambition, Marples had burst into Parliament at the 1945 election, often amazing his public school colleagues with his combination of blue suit and orange brown shoes. As Anthony Sampson, another biographer of Macmillan, had put it, 'Between Macmillan with his languid style and Marples with his boasting efficiency, there existed an alliance of mutual advantage, between the amateur and the professional.' Recognising his debt, Macmillan said simply, 'in fact, Marples made me PM: I was never heard of before housing'. One of Marples' many practical contributions was to introduce what Macmillan nicknamed 'the boneless wonder', a form of concrete construction requiring virtually no timber – timber that had to be imported with Butler's scarce dollars.

From Alistair Horne, *Macmillan Volume I 1894–1956*, published in 1988

SKILLS BUILDER

Refer to Source G. What, according to Alistair Horne, was the political significance of Ernest Marples?

In 1952–53, the team at the Ministry of Housing achieved and even exceeded their goal, when 318,750 houses were built. This was partly achieved by reducing the high standards set under Bevan in the 1940s and allowing slightly smaller council houses to be built. Some of the restrictions on private house building and on the use of land imposed by Labour were also relaxed. There was thus an increase in building for private sale, but still 80 per cent were built by local authorities. The alteration to Labour's financial impositions on building land produced one of Macmillan's most unnerving interviews with Churchill, as Macmillan's official biographer records in Source H.

Source H

Macmillan's legislation created one unforeseen, tragic consequence. Early one morning in 1952 he found himself summoned peremptorily [abruptly] to the Churchillian bed chamber, to find the Prime Minister angrily puffing a cigar in bed, with his pet budgerigar perched on his head, and brandishing the *Daily Mirror* at him: 'Have you not heard of Pilgrim's suicide? You are responsible for Pilgrim's death. How are you going to make atonement?' For a moment Macmillan thought the Prime Minister had gone mad, but he discovered that Mr Pilgrim was an Essex smallholder who had bought half an acre of land in 1950 at a price artificially inflated by the Labour government development charges of £400. When he came to sell it under the new Macmillan rulings, all he could get for the land was £65, and having borrowed the money for the original purchase, the financial loss so preyed on his mind that he committed suicide. Always one to rush to the support of the victimised little man, Churchill had been incensed by the potential unfairness of the legislation as it stood.

From Alistair Horne, *Macmillan Volume I 1894–1956*, published in 1988

Macmillan duly atoned by pushing fresh legislation through the Commons in 1954 and Evelyn Sharp commented, 'Your handling of the Bill has been the most brilliant thing I have ever seen. I do not know of anyone else who could have done it.' Macmillan thus added to both his own and the Conservatives' popularity.

Despite the noises made by the Tories, during the general election campaigns in 1950 and 1951, about the iniquities of nationalisation, there was no great attempt to roll back the state and privatise industries. Iron and steel were largely de-nationalised in 1953 and road haulage eventually returned to private hands with the break-up of British Road Services. However, if two areas passed out of direct state control, one important new one moved into it, with the setting up of the Atomic Energy Authority in 1954, to manage and control the new technology of atomic power.

Education

Continuity was thus the dominant theme and this was even true in the one area of government neglect; education. Indeed, education policy remained essentially the same, as laid down by the Education Act of 1944 by Butler.

Both parties ignored the intention of the Act to create a tripartite system with an important role for technical schools, as well as grammars and secondary moderns. As under Labour, education tended to get pushed to the back of the queue for money, behind housing, health and defence. The new Conservative minister, Florence Horsbrough, even disgusted Churchill with her concern for saving money in odd areas of the education budget. The rather plain minister was the butt of one of Bevan's jibes when, as he sat on the Labour benches facing her as she was speaking, he whispered loudly, 'There is the face that sank a thousand scholarships.'

A leading historian of the 1950s, Peter Hennessy, drew attention to the disappointing nature of the period of her stewardship.

SKILLS BUILDER

What two explanations are offered in Source I for the failures in education policy in the years 1951–54?

Source I

School building to house the post-war baby boom came to a halt and pupil–teacher ratios in primary schools declined in 1953–54. At the other end of the process the total of university students fell from 85,000 in 1950 to 82,000 in 1954. Not until a strong-minded minister, David Eccles, succeeded Horsbrough in October 1954 and remade the case for education as a national investment rather than as a taxpayer's burden did matters improve.

From P. Hennessy, *Having it So Good: Britain in the Fifties*, published in 2006

Butler at the Treasury, 1951–55

Among all the consensual politicians mentioned above, perhaps the most important and most consensual was R.A. Butler, who became Chancellor of the Exchequer. So consensual was he perceived to be, that his name gave rise to a new word, 'Butskellism', a compound of Butler and Gaitskell. The word was invented in *The Economist* in 1954 to suggest there were few differences between the two opposing politicians.

Source J

Mr Butskell is already a well known figure in both Westminster and Whitehall and the time has come to introduce him to a wider audience. He is a composite of the present Chancellor and the previous one. Whenever there is a tendency to excess Conservatism in the Conservative Party – such as a wild dash to convertibility, or even for a little more unemployment to teach the workers a lesson – Mr Butskell speaks up for the cause of moderation from the Government side of the House; when there is a clamour for even graver irresponsibilities from the Labour benches, Mr Butskell has hitherto spoken up from the other.

From an article in *The Economist*, 13 February 1954

The Economist was not alone in noticing the similarities. When first appointed in October 1951, Butler was promptly described by the raffish Tory MP Robert Boothby: 'Why that's Gaitskell all over again but from Cambridge.' Certainly there were similarities, but there were differences as Butler himself made clear.

Source K

Despite my friendship with Gaitskell, which became warm, we never discussed the 'doctrine' (Butskellism) that united our two names and each of us would, I think, have repudiated its underlying assumption that, though sitting on opposite sides of the House we were very much of a muchness. I admired him as a man of great humanity and sticking power, and was to regard his untimely death in 1963 as a real loss to the Labour Party, to the country and to the tone of public life. But I shared neither his convictions, which were unquenchably Socialist, nor his temperament, which allowed emotion to run away with him rather too often, nor his training which was that of an academic economist. Both of us it is true spoke the language of Keynesianism. But we spoke it with different accents and with a different emphasis. My key idea could be summed up in a single word: expansion – an expansion I believed capable of achievement only if the fresh winds of freedom and opportunity were allowed to blow vigorously through the economy.

From R.A. Butler, *The Art of The Possible: the Memoires of Lord Butler*, published in 1971

SKILLS BUILDER

1 To what extent does Source K contradict Source J?

2 What does Source K reveal about Butler's personality?

Certainly Butler inherited exactly the same problems faced by Dalton, Cripps and Gaitskell. As soon as he was appointed, Butler was briefed by senior figures in the Treasury about the grave balance of payments situation. The outbreak of the Korean War had raised world commodity prices and exports to the USA had temporarily fallen. The result was another **dollar gap** and a run on Britain's reserves to pay for imports. The reserves were never substantial enough to cover the vast import bill if the terms of trade moved against Britain. The huge defence commitments abroad also drained money from the UK. Butler was told by his officials of 'blood draining from the system and the prospect of a collapse greater than in 1931'. He responded with import controls and cutting travel allowances to £50. The **Bank rate** was also raised. In January 1952, he tried to go further, cutting timber imports, but this cut across Macmillan's housing drive and Butler lost the fight in Cabinet. He then came up with a thoroughly imaginative scheme to let the pound float (as it does today), as opposed to having a fixed exchange rate. This was an attempt to escape from the constant cycle of balance of payment crises and the threat of dramatic devaluation. Once again, this was defeated in Cabinet as it was feared it would damage all those Commonwealth countries who maintained 'sterling balances'.

As it turned out, the scheme was not necessary. The terms of trade swung in Britain's favour with a fall in commodity prices and a surge in exports to

Definitions

Dollar gap

A shortage of dollars earned from exports which were necessary to pay for imports – see balance of payments definition on page 40.

Bank rate

This is the rate at which the Bank of England lends money to other banks and therefore controls the cost of borrowing throughout the economy.

Source L

I passed a quiet solitary evening at the House where the turbulent opposition were deflated by Rab's [Butler's] sudden concession of £17 million per annum on Purchase Tax. He is the ablest Parliamentarian of our time, cold, courteous, suave and seemingly simple, he outwits everyone.

From Chips Channon and R.R. James, 'Chips': The Diaries of Sir Henry Channon, published in 1996

Definition

Purchase tax

An indirect tax on sales and a fore-runner of VAT.

SKILLS BUILDER

Read Source M. What is the attitude of *The Economist* to Butler's work and reforms?

the USA as that country entered a boom. British reserves began to rise. In his first Budget of 1952, Butler had little room for manoeuvre, but he presented it cleverly and made slight changes, reducing some controls. This pleased the Tory back benches as Chips Channon makes clear in his diary entry of 12 May 1952; see Source L.

By 1953, with the currency reserves clearly in a healthier state, Butler was able to do the popular thing and cut both income tax and **purchase tax**. Despite the cut, the standard rate of income tax remained at 45 per cent, far higher than today. Nevertheless, Butler's reputation rose and he appeared very much to be a future leader and in the not too distant future, as Churchill suffered a severe stroke in 1953 and Eden, his acknowledged successor, underwent a very dangerous operation, which nearly killed him. Butler chaired 16 Cabinet meetings in June and August. His reputation remained high throughout 1954, possibly because of a rather dull but responsible Budget that year.

Source M

Mr Butler closed his speech with a brief review of the whole period of his stewardship of the Treasury, where he has now lasted longer than anyone since the war. He was quick to acknowledge that he has enjoyed good fortune, but he can also rightly take credit for what has been achieved. More progress has been made in three and a half years in the restoring British finances and in easing the burden of taxation – not to mention liberating the general economy from the stifling network of controls – than seemed at all probable when the present parliament first met. Politics is the art of the possible, and Mr Butler has done about as much as a Chancellor with so exiguous [very small] a majority could have done.

From an article in *The Economist*, 23 April 1955

However, as always, the British economy was likely to overheat and by 1955 there were signs that the boom was sucking in too many imports and wage demands were fuelling inflation, and another balance of payments crisis loomed. Butler was in a difficult position. A Budget that raised taxes would be unpopular and this was unacceptable with an election likely. Butler decided to take the short-term option and deliver a popular tax-cutting Budget with cuts in income tax and purchase tax. It worked in the sense that it contributed to the election victory in May, but it harmed his reputation for sound finance. In October, he had to return with another Budget, raising taxes on various household objects, which became known as the 'pots and pans' Budget. It looked as if he had sacrificed the economic interests of the nation to short-term political gain and was duly savaged by Gaitskell in a brilliant attacking speech: 'He has behaved in a manner unworthy of his high office. He began in folly, he continued in deceit, and has ended in reaction.'

It was to be an unhappy end to Butler's stint at the Treasury. In December, Eden reshuffled his Cabinet, moving Butler's rival Macmillan to the Treasury and making Butler Leader of the House of Commons and Lord Privy Seal, but deprived him of a big department to run.

The Labour Party in opposition, 1951–56

The Conservative Party, no matter what mistakes were made in the management of the nation's finances, enjoyed an enormous advantage in public perception, the very public division within the Labour Party. Like all parties, Labour was a coalition; an alliance of ex-Liberals, religious idealists, middle-class intellectuals and trade unionists of both conservative and revolutionary persuasion, and simple odd-balls like Tom Driberg. Attlee, backed by the powerful figure of Ernie Bevin, had held the party together. Bevin, through his grip on the most powerful trade union, the Transport and General Workers Union, now under his ex-deputy, Arthur Deakin, delivered the **block vote**. Deakin and the leaders of the other giant unions, the Miners and the General and Municipal workers, supported the right of the party, hating Communists and fellow travellers, against whom they had battled in their unions throughout the 1930s. These union bosses brought their attitude of union discipline into politics; Ernie Bevin had famously ordered a group of striking dockers back to work with the simple words, 'I'll tell you when to **** strike.' The rebellion of the Bevanites in 1951 (see Chapter 3, page 47) outraged Deakin and the union leadership and, with Herbert Morrison, sought the Bevanites' expulsion from the party. Only Attlee prevented this. In many ways, Attlee saw Bevan as his most suitable successor if only the Welshman could learn self-control and self-discipline.

Those who clustered around Bevan were a strange amalgam of the discontented. Some were fellow travelling Communists, deeply upset by Labour's pro-American and anti-Soviet foreign policy. Some, like Michael Foot and Bevan's wife Jennie Lee, were personally devoted to Bevan. Some, like Crossman and Driberg, were alienated public school boys, whom Attlee distrusted for their personal lifestyles. Attlee disliked Crossman's treatment of his own parents, whom Attlee knew well, and Driberg, highest of high Anglicans in religion and most rampant of homosexuals, was a potential embarrassment to any party. The left-wing Ian Mikardo loved conspiracies and plots for their own sake. Barbara Castle and Harold Wilson were lower middle-class grammar school products from the North and very much not part of the high society around Gaitskell and his young acolytes like Roy Jenkins and Tony Crossland. In his memoirs, Jenkins records the bitterness of the party division. He describes Bevan stalking past him in the corridors of the House of Commons, refusing to speak to him as a friend of Gaitskell.

> **Definition**
>
> **Block vote**
> Unions voted at Labour Party conferences with as many votes as they had members, not on the basis of one vote per union. Thus the Transport and General Workers Union had enormous voting power. All the votes from each union would also vote the same way.

Source N

The Labour Party entered a period of tribal warfare which was to last for most of the decade. Within areas controlled by each tribe there was order and even rational government. But each faction was dedicated to fight the other and on the border where the two areas joined there were bitter skirmishes interspersed with periods of hostile watchfulness. Each faction would claim that they were the better at fighting the enemy across the floor of the House of Commons but in reality their minds were occupied with hostility more to each other than to the Conservatives.

From Roy Jenkins, *A Life at the Centre*, published in 1991

Attlee, Morrison and Gaitskell controlled the party through the Trade Union block vote, but increasingly the Bevanites won places on the National Executive Committee (NEC) through the votes of the party members. They were always a minority with six or seven on the NEC, but they did appear to enjoy the support of the party activists. The Bevanites pressed for more nationalisation and a more neutral foreign policy. Many, like Michael Foot, became active proponents of British nuclear disarmament. In this, they were at odds with Bevan himself and as the left-wing biographer of Michael Foot makes clear, the word 'Bevanites' conveys a unity that did not really exist.

Source O

What united the members of the group was personal loyalty to Nye Bevan. Whether Bevan himself actually was or ever wanted to be a Bevanite is debatable. He gave his supporters only intermittent encouragement, and he distrusted both Crossman and Wilson. Barbara Castle recalls that 'he hated teamwork and would sit brooding in his Cliveden Place flat with a few close allies from Tribune, notably his wife Jennie and Michael Foot'. Basically he disliked the whole idea of conspiratorial private groups so beloved of Ian Mikardo. Anyway Bevan was increasingly abroad, with long visits to India, China and even the USA, and unable to keep closely in touch with his followers. And yet his galvanizing presence in the House lent a constant touch of inspiration which kept the Bevanite movement alive.

From Kenneth O. Morgan, *Michael Foot: A Life*, published in 2007

Nevertheless, to the public at large, the impression given of the Labour Party was one of division and weakness. Who were you voting for – safe Mr Attlee or the dangerous Bevan?

Source P

Cummings AND THE
SOCIALISTS' ELECTION POSTER...

YOU CAN TRUST MR. ATTLEE

4.1 Cartoon by Michael Cummings, *Daily Express*, 16 May 1955

SKILLS BUILDER

What impression do Sources N, O and P give of the Labour Party in the mid-1950s?

The Premiership of Eden, 1955–1957

Churchill was finally prevailed upon to resign in April 1955. He had clung onto power despite his stroke and increasing debilities for a mixture of motives. At its most simple, he feared retirement and what he would have to do with the rest of his life. After a life of such richness and excitement, his fears can be understood, even if they do not justify his limpet-like hold on power. He also hoped to finish on a climax of international triumph with a summit that would cool the rivalry with the USSR and reduce the risk of nuclear war. He also feared that his acknowledged successor was not up to it. One of Colville's diary entries is often used to show Churchill's doubts about Eden and, in the light of future events, how insightful the old man was. The diary entry was not dated, but was written shortly after 4 April 1955, when Churchill had entertained the queen at Number 10.

Source Q

When they had all gone, I went up with Winston to his bedroom. He sat on his bed, still wearing the Garter, Order of Merit and knee-breeches. For several minutes he did not speak and I, imagining that he was sadly contemplating that this was his last night in Downing Street, was silent. Then suddenly he stared at me and said with vehemence 'I don't believe Anthony can do it.' His prophecies have often tended to be borne out by events.

John R. Colville, *The Fringes of Power: Downing Street Diaries 1939–1955*, published in 2005

Eden certainly suffered from several deficiencies, not least from waiting for the expected leadership so long. His experience was almost totally in foreign affairs and he was not well. An operation in 1953 had gone badly wrong and he remained in pain and subject to fevers. He was also highly strung, superb at public performances but given to uncontrollable rages in private. He was not 'part of the club' and, in an age when the House of Commons was the ultimate gentleman's club, this was a serious defect, as his biographer makes clear. Robert Rhodes James had served as a Conservative MP for Cambridge and, before that, as clerk of the House of Commons and therefore knew what he was talking about.

Source R

The trouble was Eden's frequent and prolonged absences from the Commons since 1951, either for health reasons or travelling abroad it meant that he had little personal knowledge of present or potential colleagues. The fact that he was not and never had been a convivial House of Commons man proved another disability. His dislike of wearing spectacles meant that he often genuinely did not recognise people, and thereby some over sensitive egotists were offended.

Macmillan, in total contrast, was like Churchill, very much a House of Commons man, revelling in the gossip, banter and companionship of the smoking room and attentive to new members – to all of which Butler in turn was as indifferent as Eden.

From Robert Rhodes James, *Anthony Eden*, published in 1986

General election, 1955

Despite Churchill's doubts and Eden's personal deficiencies, his premiership started well. He decided to go for an early general election in the hope of increasing the slender Tory majority. The election was called three days after Butler's popular Budget (see page 62) and voting took place on 26 May. It was in many ways a personal triumph for Eden, as Sources S and T make clear. They also provide evidence that the election was in some ways both the first of the modern elections of the 20th century and the last of the old style. Now one in three had televisions and the ability to appeal on 'the box' was increasingly more important than the ability to draw and address large crowds in public meetings.

Source S

By common consent the greatest *tour de force* among television broadcasts was the final one by Sir Anthony Eden. Without any tricks or visual devices he talked directly to the viewers for a quarter of an hour in genuinely extempore fashion [with little preparation]. He won universal praise for the way in which he managed to convey a sense of calmness, optimism, decency and competence. Labour fully conceded the supremacy of the Prime Minister's final broadcast.

From David Butler, et al., *British General Elections from 1950 to 1987 (Nuffield Studies)*, published in 1951–88

Source T

When at one open air meeting in London he was asked a question, long forgotten, Eden replied with heat that he would rather lose the election than give a pledge he could not fulfil: he was so patently sincere that it made an immense impression. This was indeed the story of the 1955 campaign, almost a personal and deliberately low key one, admiringly received. Conservative candidates even those with uneasy memories of 1945, found that Eden's name invariably brought applause. But the burden put upon Eden in the last of the old-fashioned general election campaigns, with no daily press conferences, little television and with Attlee, driven hazardously by his wife, jotting speeches on small pieces of paper as he went from meeting to meeting, was excessive.

From Robert Rhodes James, *Anthony Eden*, published in 1986

SKILLS BUILDER

What do Sources S and T tell us about how the 1955 general election was fought?

Labour was badly damaged by the perceived split between the right wing of the party clustered around Morrison and Gaitskell and their opponents, the Bevanite left. The result was a Tory triumph. Their share of the popular vote increased to 49.7 per cent, the highest share achieved by any party since the war. Labour's share fell to 46.4 per cent. The Conservative majority in the Commons was now a comfortable 54. In many ways, the election exorcised a terrible Conservative fear, present since 1945, that Britain was now in the age of Labour and the norm was a Labour government.

In theory, the election opened up a bright new future for Eden and the Conservatives, a comfortable majority and an opposition in disarray. The bitter strife in Labour's ranks was made worse by the retirement of Attlee after the election and the selection of Hugh Gaitskell as leader by the parliamentary party. Yet all was not well for Eden, even before the Suez crisis of 1956. His shortcomings as a prime minister were increasingly exposed and he was facing increasing criticism in the Tory ranks. Some of the problems were purely personal.

- Eden could be charming and a star performer. He was a world statesman and few could rival his knowledge of diplomacy and other world leaders, all of whom he knew. He was where most prime ministers hope to be at the end of their terms.

- He knew little of domestic issues. Economics, finance and the social services were alien territory. Here, he relied heavily on Butler.

- Eden was also highly strung and inclined to fuss. He was given to fits of temper and pointless interference with colleagues, endlessly telephoning them for reports. In many ways, he was unfit for the position of prime minister other than on the odd big occasion.

- His situation was not helped by the suddenly worsening economic situation after the election. Butler, as we have seen, had to backtrack on his giveaway Budget of April. First, hire purchase charges were raised in July and then, in October, taxes were raised in an emergency Budget. It appeared that the giveaway of April had been a cheap election ploy. Gaitskell savaged Butler in the Commons. This attack damaged the prime minister.

- Eden carried through a reshuffle, partly to move Butler but also to get the assertive Macmillan away from the Foreign Office, where he had been since April. Eden wanted a responsive subordinate rather than a strong-minded colleague there. Macmillan moved to the Exchequer and the relatively junior **Selwyn Lloyd** took the Foreign Office, where Butler hoped to go.

By early 1956, there was a growing campaign among Conservative backbenchers that Eden himself must go. Early in the year, the Conservative-supporting *Daily Telegraph* was calling for the 'smack of firm government'. The opportunity to deliver it came in the Middle East and it finally brought Eden down. He failed eventually and spectacularly in the one area of his own expertise; foreign policy.

The Suez crisis, 1956

By 1956, Britain had retreated from India and surrendered its mandate in Palestine, but still clung to the notion of being the dominant power in the Middle East. Two friendly regimes existed in Jordan and Iraq, and Aden was still a British base, as was Cyprus. Eden had negotiated the withdrawal of Britain from her great base near the Suez Canal, but still assumed a friendly and dependant Egypt. In the course of 1956, the assumptions about a friendly Egypt and Britain's dominant role in the Middle East seemed increasingly doubtful. Since access to Middle Eastern oil and the Suez Canal were seen as vital British interests, a diplomatic and eventually a military crisis developed. In Egypt, a nationalist army officer, Colonel Nasser, came to power and began to back radical Arab movements throughout the Middle East and North Africa. This brought him into indirect conflict with France, which was fighting a vicious war to hold onto Algeria. Nasser also tightened the screws on Israel with border incidents and prevention of access to the Gulf of Aquaba. In July, he nationalised the Suez Canal, in which the British government was a major shareholder. Eden decided that Nasser was a posturing dictator similar to Hitler and Mussolini and a threat to British interests throughout the Middle East. He determined to bring him down.

Had Eden been able to act in July, all might have been well. The country, including the Labour Party, appeared outraged by Nasser's action. However, the military were not ready and would not be for some time. Britain also required a moral fig leaf. The French were quite prepared to attack Nasser to promote French interests in North Africa. The British preferred their self-interests heavily disguised with moral principles. Even with a suitable excuse for military action, an insuperable problem began to appear – US hostility to a military solution. Eisenhower, the US president was facing re-election in November and was campaigning as a peacemaker. He made it quite clear to Eden that he did not want any British imperial adventures disturbing the world at such a time. Despite clear US disapproval of military action, a secret deal developed between Israel, France and Britain in October. This would provide the justification the British needed. The French began negotiations with the Israelis and, in a series of secret meetings, the British gave the plan their blessing. Israel would invade Sinai (Egyptian territory) on 29 October and head for the Suez Canal. Britain and France, under the guise of protecting the Canal, would demand that Israel and Egypt withdraw ten miles back from it. The Israelis would accept, since this meant a substantial advance into Egyptian territory and the Egyptians would refuse because it meant surrendering a large amount of their territory.

On 29 October, Israel attacked Egypt and the next day Britain and France issued their ultimatum. Israel agreed and Egypt refused. On 31 October, waves of British Canberra bombers from Cyprus destroyed the Egyptian air force, but there was still a delay before troops landed. On 2 November, the United Nations (UN) General Assembly demanded a ceasefire. Britain and the USA were on opposite sides in the vote. Only Australia, New Zealand and South Africa backed Britain. Britain was nearly isolated in the world. The result of the UN vote was the polarisation of opinion in Britain. Gaitskell was now as fierce in condemning Eden as he had been in July in condemning Nasser. Public opinion was bitterly divided. Many working-class Labour supporters rallied to the patriotic cause and favoured giving Nasser a good hiding. Many of the morally sensitive middle classes, their views expressed forcibly in the *Manchester Guardian*, were appalled at Eden's policy. Two junior Conservative ministers resigned in protest. By 10 November, a clear majority (53 per cent) of the public supported the government.

Fighting on land began on 5 November with a paratroop drop on Port Said. On 6 November, ground troops waded ashore and rapidly gained control of the town and began to push south along the Suez Canal. The military operation had proved a superb success with minimal British and French casualties but heavy Egyptian losses. Unfortunately, Britain now faced heavy pressure from the USA. The pound had been under serious threat since the crisis began with steady selling worldwide. There was the threat of a forced devaluation. In November, the Bank of England tried to prop up the pound by buying it with its precious reserves of dollars. On 6 November, Macmillan, as Chancellor of the Exchequer, appealed to the USA for help and a loan to prop up the pound. He was told very firmly that no help would be forthcoming until the British announced a ceasefire. Macmillan had been a keen supporter of action. He now switched and urged a ceasefire on Eden. Eden was shattered by this time. He had never recovered from his operation in 1953 and lived on a mixture of pills to control pain and enable him to sleep. He was advised by his doctors to rest and took a holiday in Jamaica in the house of Ian Fleming, the creator of James Bond.

Butler and Macmillan were left to mind the shop and negotiate with the USA. A loan was forthcoming, but the price was a humiliating withdrawal. The whole operation had turned into a fiasco. Nasser was strengthened instead of being brought down. Radical Arab sentiment was boosted throughout the Middle East. The imperial British lion seemed a toothless, mangy cat. In Churchill's verdict, 'I am not sure I would have dared to start but I am sure I should not have dared to stop.'

The impact of the Suez crisis

The crisis had much less of a domestic impact than might have been expected. In international terms, it decisively exposed Britain's decline and ensured that in future nothing could be undertaken without the USA. There was little decisive change in domestic politics. The morale of the Tories was somewhat shaken, but there was no massive swing to Labour, who were seen by many working-class families as unpatriotic. *The Guardian* might denounce the venture, but it hardly spoke for the mass of the electorate. Eden retired in January because of ill health. His doctors made it quite plain that if he wished to live he should leave Number 10. His successor, Harold Macmillan, skilfully restored party morale. He began even before he was appointed, at the same time undermining his chief rival R.A. Butler, as Source U makes clear. Here, the historian Dominic Sandbrook describes a crucial address to the **1922 Committee** in December 1956 by Butler and Macmillan.

Definition

1922 Committee
This was a committee of Conservative back-benchers named after the famous revolt by Tory MPs against continuing support for the Lloyd George coalition. Here the bulk of ordinary Conservative MPs had voted against the wishes of the Tory leadership who wished to continue the coalition. The post of chairman of the 1922 Committee was a very prestigious one for a back-bencher (i.e. non-minister) and the committee had considerable influence and acted as a barometer for the feelings of the back-bench MPs.

Source U

After announcing the terms of withdrawal to the House of Commons, Butler agreed to explain the situation to the 1922 Committee, the assembly of Tory backbenchers. That evening he made a vital mistake. He took Macmillan, as Chancellor, with him, turning the occasion into a joint appearance. While Butler made a quiet, low key speech explaining the importance of the terms, Macmillan then followed with over thirty minutes of a 'veritable political organ voluntary . . . pulling out every stop and striking every majestic chord in his well practised repertoire,' dazzling his audience with his dramatic vigour. Enoch Powell, then a young parliamentary secretary at the Ministry of Housing, later wrote that he never trusted Macmillan after that moment. It was one of the most horrible things that I ever remember in politics . . . seeing the way in which Harold Macmillan, with all the skill of the old actor manager, succeeded in false-footing Rab [Butler]. The sheer devilry of it verged on the disgusting.' Powell, however, was in a minority. Most backbenchers had fallen head over heels for Macmillan's rhetorical magic. Their patriotism and pride had been wounded; they did not want to hear the blunt truths that Butler had to tell them; but they responded warmly to Macmillan's mixture of flattery, self pity, anti-American resentment and shameless self-promotion. With his confident guardsman bearing, he even looked more like a statesman than the scruffy, stooping, careworn Butler.

From Dominic Sandbrook, *Never Had it So Good: A History of Britain from Suez to the Beatles,* published in 2005

When Eden handed his resignation to the palace on 9 January, the process of selecting a new leader began. There was no election, but 'soundings' were taken by two grandees of the Conservative Party in the House of Lords, the Earl of Salisbury, known as Bobbety, and Lord Kilmuir, the Lord Chancellor. The two interviewed all the Cabinet in turn.

Source V

There were two light reliefs. Practically each one began by saying 'This is like coming to the Headmaster's study'. To each Bobbety said 'Well, which is it, Wab or Hawold?'As well as seeing the remainder of the ex-cabinet, we interviewed the **Chief Whip** and Oliver Poole the Chairman of the Party. John Morrison, the Chairman of the 1922 Committee, rang up the next morning. An overwhelming majority of Cabinet Ministers was in favour of Macmillan.

From David Patrick Maxwell Fyfe, *Political Adventures: The Memoirs of the Earl of Kilmuir*, published in 1962

Definition

Chief Whip

The Cabinet member responsible for party discipline. They ensure that the government has a majority in any votes by making sure their party's MPs attend and vote as the government wishes.

Exam tips

- The three sources clearly offer a range of reasons and have a different emphasis. A useful starting point would be to note their salient points: support from Cabinet colleagues (Source V); Macmillan's speaking abilities (Source U); and rapport with back-benchers (Source R).
- Defects of opponents – Butler (Sources R and U).
- Remember to consider details that aren't addressed in the sources e.g. Macmillan's record as Minister of Housing.
- What determined the timing? Again this is not really covered in the sources and will require you to use your own knowledge.

Unit summary

What have you learned in this unit?

This unit has covered a considerable amount of information. You have learned about how and why the returned Conservatives tried to govern Britain under Churchill and Eden. You have considered the weaknesses and strengths of these two prime ministers and the crucial position of R.A. Butler. You have studied briefly the election of 1955 and why Eden won and Labour lost. You should understand something of the impact of the Suez crisis and finally why Macmillan, not Butler, emerged as the new Conservative leader and prime minister.

What skills have you used in this unit?

Once again you have encountered a large number of secondary sources relating to this period as well as some primary ones and asked to consider their strengths and weaknesses as sources of evidence for historians. You have been asked to cross reference sources and in the case of Butler's memoirs (Source I) to use the source inferentially. Make sure that you really understand the concept of inference by re-visiting this source and the Skills Builder relating to it.

Exam style question

This is the type of question that you will find on the examination paper as a (b) question. You will use the sources provided, with your own knowledge.

Study Sources R, U and V.

Macmillan, rather than Butler, became Prime Minister in January 1957 because he bothered to cultivate support. How far do you agree with this view?

Explain your answer using the evidence of Sources R, U and V, and your own knowledge.

RESEARCH TOPIC

- The time period you have studied in this unit was the last years of National Service.
- Try to find a neighbour or relative who undertook National Service and ask them about their experiences. Did they resent it? Did they enjoy it? Did they serve in the Korean War, the Malayan emergency or the Suez affair?
- What do you think were the effects on British society of National Service?

5 I'm all right, Jack: Conservative rule, 1957–64

What is this unit about?

This unit seeks to examine the years of the Macmillan government from January 1957 to October 1963 and the one-year premiership of Alec Douglas Home. This involves consideration of Macmillan's remarkable success in restoring Tory morale after Suez and the sweeping Conservative victory in the general election of 1959. There will be an analysis of Conservative economic policy and the degree to which it was successful in boosting living standards and the relative economic standing of Britain in the world. The attempt to adjust defence spending in the light of finance will also be addressed, as will changes initiated by Butler as Home Secretary. The remarkable deterioration in Macmillan's standing in 1962–63 will be the focus towards the end of the unit, with consideration of the rise of satire and the revival of the Labour Party under first Gaitskell and then its new leader Harold Wilson. Finally, the culmination of the party struggle in the election of 1964 will end the unit.

Key questions

- What was Macmillan's role and how competent was he as prime minister?
- Why were the Conservatives able to win the general election of 1959?
- How successful was Conservative economic policy in 1957–64?
- How effective was the Labour Party in opposition?
- Why did Macmillan and the Conservatives come under such attack in 1962–63?

Timeline

1957	January	Macmillan becomes prime minister
	April	Sandys' Defence White Paper
	July	Macmillan's 'Never had it so good' speech at Bedford
1958	January	Resignation of Thorneycroft, Powell and Birch from the Exchequer
	February	CND holds first meeting
	November	Vicky creates 'Supermac'
1959	April	Heathcoat-Amory offers a giveaway Budget
	October	General election – convincing Conservative victory
	November	First section of the M1 motorway opened by Ernest Marples
1960	January	Macmillan makes 'Wind of change' speech
	July	Aneurin Bevan dies

	October	Labour Conference endorses unilateral nuclear disarmament
1961	July	Britain applies to join the European Community
	September	Large CND demonstration in Trafalgar Square
	October	Gaitskell gets the Labour Conference to drop unilateral nuclear disarmament
	November	*Private Eye* is launched as satirical magazine
1962	February	National Economic Development Council set up
	July	Macmillan's 'night of the long knives' – sacks a third of the Cabinet
	October	Vassall spy scandal
1963	January	De Gaulle vetoes Britain's attempt to join the European Community
		Gaitskell unexpectedly dies
	February	Wilson takes over
	March	Profumo lies to the Commons over the affair with Christine Keeler
	April	Maudling's tax-cutting Budget
	June	Profumo resigns
	October	Macmillan resigns
1964	July	Edward Heath's Resale Price Maintenance Act comes into force
	October	General election – slender Labour victory

Introduction

One of the most successful British films of the 1950s was an Ealing comedy starring Peter Sellers as a Communist shop steward. It was called *I'm All Right Jack* and was released in 1959. It captured in comic form many of the crucial traits of Britain, 14 years after the end of the war. It was still extraordinarily class-ridden. Macmillan's Cabinet was filled with old Etonians and his relatives. The prime minister cultivated his grouse-moor hunting image and was indeed an excellent shot. There was growing prosperity for the working classes but not based on a dynamic work ethic such as was found in West Germany and Japan. There was something of a complacent air among both bosses and workers – after all, Britain had won the war. Britain had traditional markets in the Empire. There had been full employment since 1945 and a slow but steady rise in living standards.

The work force was heavily unionised and while there were pockets of Communist influence within the unions, they were not in general particularly militant in the way that French unions often were. The unions were, however, deeply conservative in terms of protecting jobs and work practices. There was little desire to cooperate with management in maximising productivity through innovation. Labour relations often resembled trench warfare as the film *I'm All Right Jack* plays up. Management was regarded with suspicion and came from a different class. Workers sought to gain maximum return for minimum effort. Bosses were reluctant to seek confrontation if the firm could continue to make a steady if unexciting profit and they were left with certain perks and privileges. The nation as a whole seemed to go along with this. There appeared to be no appetite for drastic change. People began to acquire televisions and household gadgets of all sorts, and an increasing number were gaining those badges of middle-class respectability, cars and ownership of their own homes. Eventually this '**embourgeoisification**' would undermine the class conflict and make possible a different approach to industrial relations, but it would be a long time coming.

Definition

Embourgeoisification
This is the name given to the process of more and more people becoming 'middle class' in their lifestyle and attitudes.

Source A

5.1
Peter Sellers as Fred Kite in *I'm All Right Jack*

Source B

5.2
Macmillan on a grouse shoot

SKILLS BUILDER

Study Sources A and B. What images do they present of Macmillan's Britain?

'Supermac': the new prime minister and his government

The new prime minister was not what he appeared. On the surface was a carefully presented image of the unflappable Edwardian gentleman: war hero, classical scholar and crack shot. The image was contrived to hide a lonely, damaged individual who had suffered much pain both physical and mental. His superb performances in the Commons were preceded by pangs of nerves as an essentially shy man forced himself into a role. The image of the upper-class aristocrat concealed a bookish intellectual, well versed in modern economics and genuinely radical in his desire to improve life for all. His taste for the grouse moors helped him relate to a party that still contained a fair number of 'huntin', shootin'' country gentlemen. John Morrison, Chairman of the 1922 Committee of back-benchers, was a fox-hunting fanatic. A very recent assessment of Macmillan in the *New Oxford History of England* draws attention to his complexities and their roots and also to the strengths he brought to the Conservative Party.

Source C

Macmillan's apparent traditionalism was a pose. He was a very unusual Conservative, radical in his inclinations. Behind this stance lay his deeply etched memory of the First World War, which had drawn together officers and other ranks, together with his interwar experience of representing Stockton on Tees, a constituency with serious unemployment. Macmillan could also be ruthless: 'first in, first out' was Wilson's phrase about Macmillan's stance in the Suez Crisis, yet an enthusiast for the venture was specially equipped to repair the damage. Macmillan was radical too, for a Conservative, in so readily keeping abreast of modern publicity devices and throughout his premiership he usually surpassed his party in his personal Gallup poll rating. This together with his flair for phrase making and his unconcealed zest for prosperity, helped the Conservatives to overtake Labour in Gallup polls of voting intentions during 1958–59 and to engineer in 1959 the third successive electoral victory that had seemed inconceivable three years before.

From Brian Harrison, *Seeking a role, The United Kingdom 1951–1970*, published in 2009

Like the prime minister, the image and reality of the government were at odds with one another. On the surface, the government would hardly have looked out of place in the 18th century. The original Cabinet contained six Etonians and all but two of the rest had attended another major public school. There were no women. The wider government was stuffed with Macmillan's relatives through marriage. Early in 1958, 35 out of a total of 85 fell into this category, as did seven out of the 19 Cabinet members. Yet like Churchill's Cabinet, it was a centrist/consensual government, anxious to avoid confrontation with the trade unions, devoted to the idea of full employment and accepting of the welfare state. The most prominent right-winger, the fifth Marquis of Salisbury, known as Bobbety, resigned after three months in protest at what he considered the too-liberal approach to imperial policy. Butler the arch-liberal continued as the most prominent member of the Cabinet, now occupying the post of Home Secretary. He tended to run the government and chair the Cabinet during the many trips abroad that Macmillan made. Occupying many of the middle and junior posts was a generation of talented younger men. Edward Heath was Chief Whip and Enoch Powell number two at the Treasury; both grammar school educated. Iain Macleod held the posts first of Minister of Labour and then Colonial Secretary, where he pushed on the policy of decolonisation, winding down the Empire.

But it was the Prime Minister who set the tone and captured the public's imagination, reassuring the Tory Party and the country that despite the set-back of Suez, all was still well with Britain. She was still a great power and the country was enjoying a steady, growing prosperity. Macmillan has become particularly associated with a speech he delivered at Bedford seven months after he became prime minister.

Source D

Let's be frank about it; most of our people have never had it so good. Go round the country, go to the industrial towns, go to the farms, and you will see a state of prosperity such as we have never had in my life-time – nor indeed ever in the history of this country. What is worrying some of us is 'Is it too good to be true? Or perhaps I should say: ' Is it too good to last?' For amidst all this prosperity, there is one problem that has troubled us ever since the war. It's the problem of rising prices. Our constant concern today is – can prices be steadied while at the same time we maintain full employment in an expanding economy? Can we control inflation? This is the problem of our time.

From a speech by Prime Minister Harold Macmillan to a crowd in Bedford, 20 July 1957

The press and public took from the speech what they wanted to hear – that Britain was prosperous. The key warning Macmillan wished to make tended to be ignored. In the short-term he was lucky in this. Macmillan was equated with prosperity. His warning was forgotten and only later was he blamed for the tarnished economic image of Britain in 1963. Likewise, even in his cartoon critics he was initially lucky. The left-wing cartoonist, Victor Weisz – Vicky – tried to send up the aging prime minister by portraying him as the comic book hero Superman, now redubbed 'Supermac'. It backfired and the public rather took to the representation, which actually enhanced Macmillan's standing.

Source E

5.3 Cartoon by Vicky, *Evening Standard*, 6 November 1958

In the House of Commons he developed an easy mastery. The leader of the opposition, Hugh Gaitskell, was, as Macmillan later pointed out, too much the academic. He asked too many questions at prime minister's question time and Macmillan confessed that it was therefore all too easy to answer one or two easy ones and ignore the difficult ones. Gaitskell never spotted Macmillan's technique and failed to focus simply on one embarrassing question.

Adjusting to reality – but not too much

Macmillan liked to compare the Suez crisis of 1956 to Dunkirk in 1940, a defeat but one from which the country could benefit if it learned the right lessons. While emphasising Britain's greatness, he led the country away from Empire and great power status. There was almost a scuttle from the numerous African colonies as one after another were given their independence. The process was particularly speeded up after Iain Macleod became Colonial Secretary in 1959. There was also a determined attempt to cut the burden of defence spending, which was far higher than any comparable European country. Macmillan appointed Duncan Sandys as Minister of Defence with a clear brief to run down the armed services. Sandys published a Defence Paper setting out the reasons for his policy in 1957.

Source F

Demands on Economic Resources

Over the last five years defence has on average absorbed 10% of Britain's gross national product. Some 7% of the working population are either in the services or supporting them. One eighth of the output of the metal-using industries, upon which the export trade so largely depends is devoted to defence. An undue proportion of qualified scientists and engineers are engaged on military work. In addition the retention of such large forces abroad gives rise to heavy charges which place a severe strain upon the balance of payments.

From the government paper on defence, 1957 quoted in M. Dockrill
British Defence Since 1945 published in 1988

The general thrust of government policy was to reduce conventional forces but to rely on nuclear weapons as a deterrent and as a prop to great power status. Sandys had a long and gruelling battle with the military and some Tory back-benchers. Macmillan gave him uncompromising support but it was a bitter battle as the following extract makes clear.

Source G

Sandys proposed to abolish conscription and devoted himself to the job of reducing expenditure with enthusiasm which appalled the service chiefs. The Hull Committee on manpower needs recommended 200,000 as a minimum number consistent with British defence commitments. Sandys published the figure of 165,000, the total considered possible under voluntary recruiting. Sir Gerald Templar, Chief of the Defence Staff was not pleased: 'Duncan you're so bloody crooked that if you swallowed a nail you'd shit a corkscrew.' Conscription was abolished in 1960.

From Malcolm Pierce and Geoffrey Stewart, *British Political History 1867–1995*,
second edition published in 1996

Another and more serious conflict arose for Macmillan in which he was more directly involved. This time he was defending government expenditure and his opponents, including, his own Chancellor of the Exchequer, Peter Thorneycroft, were pressing for serious deflationary cuts. The problem arose in 1957 as it became clear that a fresh balance of payments crisis was brewing. This time, there was a Treasury team in place willing to call into question faith in the managed economy as it had so far been practised by both parties. Enoch Powell was the key figure behind the Chancellor. He had become convinced that the supply of money in the economy should be restricted to bring down inflation. Between 1948 and 1956, incomes had risen by 75 per cent but output had risen by only 28 per cent. This could spell only rapidly rising inflation. To limit the money supply would impose a discipline on wage demands by causing unemployment. This was the hated evil for Macmillan. Like Dalton before him, Macmillan preferred 'the slight flush of inflation to the deathly palor of deflation'. The Treasury team demanded a halt to increasing government spending and certain cuts, some in family allowances. Macmillan and other members of the Cabinet resisted and the entire Treasury team – Thorneycroft, Powell and Nigel Birch – all resigned. The historian, Kenneth O. Morgan, rightly makes reference to its links to later debates in the Tory Party, which led to what became known as 'Thatcherism'. He also comments on Macmillan's skill in defusing the crisis.

Definition

Monetarism

This is a belief in controlling the money supply as a means of controlling inflation and it is often seen as the most important element in the economic policy of the Thatcher government from 1979–82. It is often used as shorthand for a belief in free-market economics and a rejection of Keynesian demand management as practised by all governments from 1945 to the 1970s.

Monetarism in theory looks easy and uncontroversial but the real problem is measuring the money supply in a modern economy. Is it simply cash in circulation? Is it cash plus money in bank accounts? If so which bank accounts are counted? Does it include building society accounts? The chief weapon of monetarists is controlling interest rates. By raising interest rates they are able to make money more expensive to borrow.

Source H

A later generation of Thatcherites made Thorneycroft an early martyr for **monetarism**. So, to some extent he was. But Macmillan managed to cover the entire episode up with rare political flair. His published letter made it appear that Thorneycroft resigned on a very narrow point, of just £50m additional economies or 1% of national expenditure, with no wider implications. A concerted assault by Butler, Hailsham, Lloyd and other Cabinet ministers made Thorneycroft appear unrealistic and inconsistent, somewhat as Bevan had been when he resigned over NHS charges in 1951. The Prime Minister observed that 'I have watched with some alarm this rigidity of thought descending upon Thorneycroft over the past three weeks and even months'. He breezed off to a Commonwealth Conference in India with the observation that it was merely 'a little local difficulty'.

From Kenneth O. Morgan, *The People's Peace*, third edition published in 2001

Macmillan appointed a more congenial Chancellor in Derick Heathcoat-Amory, who would not be seduced by monetarism but would at the first opportunity put his foot on the financial accelerator and encourage expansion. In 1958, there were modest tax reliefs, but in 1959, with the country basking in economic recovery and increased reserves, Heathcoat-Amory delivered a giveaway Budget with which Macmillan could be well pleased, especially as he hoped to go to the country later in the year. Income tax came down to below 40p in the pound, the lowest it had been since the early days of the war and purchase tax was cut. It was an election-winning Budget.

Butler at the Home Office

At the Home Office, Butler was very much left to his own devices by the prime minister. Butler's instincts were liberal, but it was no accident that he entitled his political memoirs – *The Art of the Possible*. He pushed through a series of important Acts. He inherited a Homicide Bill, limiting the death penalty to certain categories such as the murder of policemen and prison warders. It was suspected that Butler was a sympathiser with abolition, but the time was not ripe and it would certainly not have been popular with the party faithful. He also had to act on the Wolfenden Report. This was the work of a committee of enquiry set up under Sir John Wolfenden to enquire into the law relating to sexual practices. It covered both prostitution and homosexuality. It says something about the delicate sensibilities of the period that, to save the blushes of the lady members, the one category was to be referred to as Huntleys and the others as Palmers, after the famous firm of biscuit manufacturers. Nevertheless, the report recommended tighter legislation regarding street soliciting, which had become a considerable public nuisance in some areas of the bigger cities, and decriminalisation of homosexuality. Butler's instincts were to proceed along these lines, but it rapidly became clear that a liberal move on homosexuality would be unpopular with the Tory back-benches. Again, the time was not ripe.

The Street Offices Act seemed to have had the desired effect of reducing street soliciting by imposing tougher penalties on prostitutes. Butler was told by the police that penalties on their clients were almost impossible to enforce and were therefore not included. The Act therefore attracted the hostility of feminist groups and caused some hurt to Butler as a great nephew of the great Victorian social reformer Josephine Butler, who had done much work for the rights of prostitutes in the 1880s. He also pushed through a *Charities Act*, modernising the administration of charity law, and most controversially the *Commonwealth Immigration Act*, attempting to control the numbers of Commonwealth citizens arriving in the UK. It was denounced at the time by Gaitskell as racist. In fact, as Butler points out in his memoirs, Labour did not repeal the Act when they took power in 1964, but actually tightened the restrictions even more in their own Act of 1965. By 1959, Butler had also produced a White Paper on future Home Office policy entitled *Penal Practice in a Changing Society*, on which all subsequent improvements have been based.

General election, 1959

Labour had gone some way to making themselves more electable. The old guard had either died or retired. Gaitskell won a convincing victory to replace Attlee in 1955. He beat Bevan by 157 votes to 70 with Morrison a poor third with 40. The party then rallied around its new leader, even if the left were suspicious of the new leader's desire to jettison some traditional socialist principles, as the following cartoon by Vicky makes clear in Source I.

5.4 Cartoon by Vicky, *Daily Mirror*, 3 October 1957

Some of the Bevanites, notably Richard Crossman and Harold Wilson, decided to make their peace with Gaitskell, as Source I shows. Wilson became shadow Chancellor and began an effective career in the Commons duelling with Macmillan in 1956 before the latter succeeded Eden. The biggest catch was Bevan himself, who eventually decided to accept the shadow Foreign Office portfolio. There were high hopes that with a younger, vigorous leader and as a less divided party, Labour might recover and defeat the Tories. They underestimated Macmillan as a performer as the television journalist Michael Cockerell makes clear.

Source J

Macmillan's final broadcast drew the highest television audience of the campaign and was generally acclaimed a great success. 'Even the *Daily Mirror* joined the Conservative press in praising it as a real corker and quite the best that had been delivered by a politician of any party,' said John Wyndham. The Prime Minister had made up for the Conservatives' disastrous early campaign broadcasts. In Downing Street on election night, he watched Hugh Gaitskell become the first British party leader to concede defeat on television.

From Michael Cockerell, *Live from Number 10: The Inside Story of Prime Ministers and Television*, published in 1988

By this time, there had been a massive expansion in television ownership from over 4 million in 1955 to over 10 million by 1960. Macmillan and his colleagues had made a poor start with their initial broadcasts, which were stilted and unconvincing, but Macmillan learned quickly and effectively, and eventually made up for it. There were, of course, many other reasons for the Conservatives' success; rising prosperity, enhanced by the recent giveaway Budget, and Macmillan's successful portrayal of himself as a world statesman who had restored Britain's place at the top table. Relations had been restored with the US and Macmillan's personal friendship with President Eisenhower, dating back to the Second World War, had helped. Gaitskell himself had contributed to the defeat of Labour by seeming to promise too much, i.e. increased government spending and tax cuts. For a combination of reasons, the Tories coasted home with an increased majority: Conservatives 365, Labour 258, Liberal 6, others 1.

Macmillan's party had gained 49.6 per cent of the vote to Labour's 44.5 per cent. It was a remarkable achievement for the 65-year-old prime minister.

Managing the economy, 1959–63

In many ways there was a repeat of the situation in 1955, in so far as the Conservatives' management of the economy was concerned. A pre-election give-away Budget in 1959 was followed by panic as the economy began to over-heat, sucking in imports at an alarming rate and thereby threatening the balance of payments. In the course of 1959, exports rose by 4 per cent but imports by 10 per cent. There was a particular surge in November, the month after the election. Appeasement of the unions continued with a 5 per cent pay increase to railway workers. Heathcoat-Amory wanted to deflate and argued for a tough Budget in 1960, as Thorneycroft had in 1958. Macmillan would have none of it. The most he would accept was a stand-still Budget. Heathcoat-Amory obliged, but resigned quietly in June to be replaced by the faithful Selwyn Lloyd, who was transferred from the Foreign Office to the Exchequer, once again protesting his ignorance of his new department. This was Macmillan's third Chancellor in three years.

Selwyn Lloyd as Chancellor

Selwyn Lloyd was appointed for the same reason Eden had placed him at the head of the Foreign Office in 1955. Macmillan wanted a chief of staff and intended to run the Exchequer to all intents and purposes himself. It was to prove an unhappy experience for both men. The pound continued under pressure with the constant threat of an enforced devaluation. Wages rose much faster than productivity. Even Macmillan was forced to agree to an emergency package in the summer of 1961. Purchase taxes were raised and bank rate went to 7 per cent. There was also the announcement of a 'pay pause' in the public sector. This was throwing down the gauntlet to the unions. It was hoped that the private sector would moderate their demands in line with the public sector, but no such thing happened. Non-militant members of the public sector such as teachers, nurses and civil servants fell behind in their standard of living and took out their resentment on the government.

Macmillan and Selwyn Lloyd came up with what was to be one of the standard answers to the nation's economic woes in the 1960s and 70s – indicative planning. In March 1962, the National Economic Development Council (NEDC) was set up, known as NEDDY. It was composed of six trade unionists, six industrialists, two independents and three Cabinet ministers. Meetings were held and reports produced. It was largely useless.

Not surprisingly, a pay freeze, combined with tax increases, produced considerable discontent and NEDDY was hardly the body to restore the government's popularity. Opinion polls showed the Conservatives far behind Labour and there was a surge in Liberal support. In March 1962, the Liberals won a sensational by-election in Orpington in Kent in what should have been safe Tory territory. Selwyn Lloyd didn't help the recovery of popularity with his Budget of 1962. It was a public relations disaster with increased taxes on sweets, soft drinks and ice cream – taxing the children's pocket money, as it was described. Macmillan decided that a major reshuffle was necessary, the chief victim being the loyal Selwyn Lloyd. Butler was consulted and later summarised the process in his memoirs.

Source K

Following the summer of 1961 so marked an economic and political deterioration took place as to cause the Prime Minister to make in July 1962 the most drastic reorganisation of a government ever undertaken within the lifetime of a modern parliament. The end result of this latter-day 'night of the long knives' was the creation of one of the strongest young Cabinets of the century. That to do him justice was Macmillan's aim. But the spilling of so much [political] blood did serious damage to the Prime Minister's hitherto unbroken image of 'unflappability'. The Gallup Poll reported that only 36 per cent of the electorate now expressed approval of his performance.

From R.A. Butler, *The Art of The Possible: the Memoirs of Lord Butler*, published in 1971

Butler himself contributed to the disastrous execution of the reshuffle. He appears to have leaked news of it, forcing Macmillan to dismiss Selwyn Lloyd in a more hasty and sudden fashion than he intended. Macmillan could not manage the terse approach of Attlee and a painful hour-long interview on 12 July left both men emotionally drained. Macmillan then appears to have decided that there was a real possibility of Selwyn Lloyd organising a revolt against him and he proceeded to sack a third of his Cabinet on Friday, 13 July. Lord Kilmuir, the Lord Chancellor, complained that he would have given his cook more notice. Macmillan reflected that cooks were harder to come by than Lord Chancellors. David Eccles, the

Minister of Education, was offered another job, but preferred to retire.
The whole episode made Macmillan look both ruthless and panic-stricken.
In the words of Jeremy Thorpe, the Liberal MP, misquoting the famous
biblical saying, 'Greater love hath no man than that he lay down his friends
for his life.'

The new satirical magazine *Private Eye* ran a front cover with Selwyn Lloyd
apparently expressing his opinion:

Source L

5.5 Front cover of *Private Eye*, July 1962

A less humorous response came from the ex-financial minister, who had
resigned in January 1958.

Source M

Sir,

For the second time the Prime Minister has got rid of a Chancellor of the
Exchequer who tried to get expenditure under control.

Once is more than enough.

Yours truly,
Nigel Birch

Letter from Nigel Birch MP, *The Times*, Saturday, 14 July 1962

SKILLS BUILDER

How far do Sources
K, L and M indicate
that the Cabinet
reshuffle of 12/13
July 1962 was a
political disaster.

The new team Macmillan appointed was certainly more talented than the old one just butchered. Sir Edward Boyle, a liberal intellectual, replaced David Eccles at education and Sir Keith Joseph took housing. The star appointment was **Reggie Maudling** as Chancellor of the Exchequer. Extremely bright, he was like the prime minister – an instinctive expansionist in that he believed in encouraging the economy to grow through lower taxes and easy credit.

Biography

Reggie Maudling (1917–1979)

Maudling was one of the promising young men of the war-service generation to have been brought on in the Tory Party by the modernisers like Butler. He was regarded on both sides of the House of Commons as an intellectual heavyweight with a superb grasp of economics. He was also notoriously self-indulgent and increasingly a heavyweight in the literal sense. Asked by a leading journalist what sort of whisky he liked, he replied, 'large ones'.

Maudling as Chancellor

In the autumn of 1962, Maudling began to try to kick-start the economy. Purchase tax on cars was cut from 45 per cent to 25 per cent. Bank rate was also cut to encourage borrowing. More followed in Maudling's first Budget in April 1963 with tax cuts of £260 million. He was gambling on a dramatic dash for growth. There was, however a very strong possibility that history would repeat itself and a strong 'go' signal would be followed by a shuddering 'stop'.

Audit of success

At one level, the Tories had been remarkably successful in their management of the economy. There had been no return to the mass unemployment of the inter-war years, the security offered by the welfare state had been maintained and living standards had risen steadily. Between 1959 and 1964, the real wages of manual workers increased by 19 per cent. As we have seen, almost every home boasted a television by 1964. Self-ownership of that home had also risen and had reached 44 per cent. The Conservatives were well on the way to creating a property-owning democracy. Vacuum cleaners were no longer the preserve of the middle classes, but were found in 75 per cent of homes. Washing machines were replacing mangles and the fridge was bringing about a revolution in the storage and use of foods. The consumer society had arrived.

Yet in comparative terms, Britain was slipping behind her competitors and was well on the way to becoming the 'sick man of Europe'. It was awareness of this that led the eminent economic journalist, Samuel Brittan, to write a study of the management of the British economy in these years. His conclusions were not comforting.

Source N

The sad story of British export performances is summarised by the following table:

1953–64 (First quarter)

Country	Change in price of manufactured exports (%)	Change in volume of manufactures exported (%)
UK	+ 19	+ 48
USA	+ 18	+ 16
West Germany	+ 7	+ 233
France	+ 3	+ 136
Italy	− 18	+ 303

The table covers a long span and conceals the improvement in the American position and the deterioration of the Italian one near the end of it: but it alas gives a fair picture of the UK over almost the whole of the eleven year period. Even if Britain's competitive position should begin to improve very soon, the eleven year deterioration will have exacted a very heavy toll in lost economic growth.

From Samuel Brittan, *The Treasury under the Tories 1951–1964*, published in 1966

Britain's share of world trade fell from 25 per cent in 1950 to 15 per cent. France, which Britain had clearly passed in the level of economic development in the early 19th century, now began to pull ahead of Britain. Germany and Japan, the defeated in 1945, now surged ahead. What had produced this relative decline fuelled a lengthy national debate. To the right, it was a consequence of the burden of the welfare state and over-powerful trade unions, resistant to changes in working practices. To those on the left of the political spectrum, it arose from complacent, incompetent management, the class structure and bloated defence commitments. Whatever the causes, the reality was beyond dispute. Britain, the third great power of 1945 was now number 6 in economic muscle.

Attempt to join the EEC

Macmillan recognised this, and as well as a belief in the dramatic expansion promoted by Maudling in his Budget, saw the answer to be in joining Europe. It was hoped that access to the dynamic market of Western Europe with over 150 million consumers would revitalise British industry. The prime minister skilfully persuaded his Cabinet colleagues and the bulk of a suspicious Tory Party to back his application to join the European Economic Community (EEC). The decision was announced to the House of Commons on 2 August 1961, by the prime minister in what is often considered one of his finest speeches.

Source O

To sum up, there are, as I have said, some to whom the whole concept of our working closely with other European nations is instinctively disagreeable. I am bound to say that I find it hard to understand this when we have accepted close collaboration on other more critical spheres. Others feel that our whole and sole duty lies with the Commonwealth. If I thought that our entry into Europe would injure our relations with and influence in the Commonwealth, or be against the true interest of that Commonwealth, I would not ask the House to support the step.

I think, however, that most of us recognise that in a changing world if we are not to be left behind and to drop out of the main stream of the world's life, we must be prepared to change and adapt our methods. All through history this has been one of the main sources of our strength.

From a speech by Harold Macmillan to the House of Commons, 2 August 1961

SKILLS BUILDER

What are Macmillan's arguments for joining the EEC in Source O?

The up and coming Edward Heath was selected by Macmillan to lead the British team negotiating entry. It was a tough job. Britain hoped to safeguard her special relationship with the Commonwealth, such as access to New Zealand lamb, and the very different nature of British agriculture compared to that in Europe posed problems. The European Community had been built around the needs of French agriculture and German industry and such a design did not naturally fit British needs.

- Britain had embraced a policy of cheap food in the 19th century at the expense of British agriculture but to the benefit of the majority who lived in cities.
- Europe was built around the principle of expensive food to the benefit of French producers.

Heath worked hard and well, earning the respect of many of the European negotiators. The insuperable obstacle proved to be the French President Charles de Gaulle. De Gaulle feared Britain was too tightly bound to the USA. The slights he had suffered during the war at the hands of the two Anglo-Saxon powers, when they were his patrons and protectors, had not been forgotten or forgiven. The liberation of France by the USA and Britain induced resentment not gratitude. On 14 January 1963, De Gaulle vetoed Britain's entry. Macmillan was furious. The centrepiece of his economic strategy to revive Britain was in ruins.

Source P

5.6 Front cover of *Private Eye*, January 1963

The Labour Party, 1959–64

Defeat in 1959 brought inevitable recrimination and soul-searching within the defeated Labour Party. Two great issues were to divide it during the next two years and relieve the government of the burden of an effective opposition. Labour was too busy fighting itself. Gaitskell and the right of the party decided that it had lost because it was weighed down with out-dated commitments such as 'clause 4', which stated Labour's belief in the 'common ownership of the means of production, distribution and exchange'– in other words mass nationalisation. It had little practical significance, but it was written into the 1918 constitution of the party and to Gaitskell, Jenkins and Crosland and others it was symptomatic of Labour's out-of-date approach. To the left, it was a badge of Labour's left-wing aspirations and sacrosanct. Many in the middle, like Harold Wilson, the shadow Chancellor, privately thought that clause 4 had as much relevance to modern politics as 'building regulations in the Book of Revelation', but that it was pointless to divide the party on something that did not matter.

Unfortunately for Gaitskell, the power balance within the Labour Party had shifted to the left with the arrival of Frank Cousins as the leader of the Transport and General Workers' Union (TGWU) in succession to Deakin. Gaitskell had to accept defeat at the 1960 conference on his attempt to drop **Clause 4**, but he did not accept defeat on another issue, unilateral nuclear disarmament. Since the mid-1950s, there had been a growing movement in Britain to renounce nuclear weapons. Its supporters were very much from the middle-class intelligentsia and contained such

Definition

Clause 4
A clause of the 1918 Labour Party constitution committing the party to the 'common ownership of the means of production, distribution and exchange'. In practice this would mean widespread nationalisation. It was dear to the left of the party but not taken very seriously by most senior Labour politicians.

luminaries as the ancient and eccentric philosopher Bertrand Russell, the historian AJP Taylor and Bevan's friend Michael Foot, the editor of *Tribune*. The Campaign for Nuclear Disarmament (CND) was established in 1957/58 and its marches to Aldermaston, the British nuclear research centre, became part of the left-wing calendar. It suffered from exactly the same delusions as the right-wing proponents of British imperial power, namely exaggerating British influence. In the case of CND it was Britain's moral influence, i.e. if Britain gave up nuclear weapons, others would follow suit.

- There is not a shred of evidence that Chairman Mao in China nor De Gaulle in France would have given up their search for nuclear weapons, if Britain had given up hers.
- It is hard to disagree with Aneurin Bevan's comment, at the Labour conference of 1957, that it was 'an emotional spasm'. Bevan had helped to defeat a non-nuclear policy in 1957, but by 1960 he was dead.
- The supporters of CND were able to get the 1960 Labour conference to endorse unilateral nuclear disarmament, despite the fact that a clear majority of the British public supported British possession of nuclear weapons. Gaitskell refused to accept the policy and in a brilliant speech announced his determination to get the policy reversed.

Source Q

Supposing all of us, like well-behaved sheep, were to follow the policies of unilateralism and neutralism, what kind of an impression would that make on the British people?

I say this to you: we may lose the vote today and the result may deal this party a grave blow. It may not be possible to prevent it, but I think there are a great many of us who will not accept that this blow need be mortal, who will not believe that such an end is inevitable. There are some of us, Mr Chairman, who will fight and fight and fight again to save the Party we love. We will fight and fight and fight again to bring back sanity and honesty and dignity, so that our Party with its great past may retain its glory and greatness.

From a speech by Hugh Gaitskell to the Labour Party conference in Scarborough, October 1960

The speech made an enormous impression and won over many of those there, but the pre-determined block vote of some of the unions, notably Cousins' TGWU, ensured Gaitskell's defeat. It was only temporary and the fight raised his reputation in the party and the country. He easily beat off a challenge from Harold Wilson to his leadership in November and, by the time of the 1961 conference, he had assembled the votes to reverse the commitment to unilateralism. With a reunited party and a strengthened leader, Labour opened up a serious lead over the Tories in 1962. Most commentators now saw Gaitskell as the inevitable next prime minister. He then fell mysteriously ill and died unexpectedly in January 1963.

His successor was the widely distrusted Harold Wilson. His opponent was the brilliant but unstable George Brown, who was from the right of the party and the current deputy leader. It was a contest described as being between a crook and a drunk, and the crook won. Wilson, from the centre-left of the party, was a clever, Oxford-educated economist and a pragmatist. He was likely to be effective in harrying an elderly Macmillan, whose economic strategy appeared in ruins. At the time, one historically minded political journalist pointed out that the last time two Harolds had faced one another in England in 1066, the French won – a reference to the Battle of Stamford Bridge and the Norman invasion.

Decline and fall, 1963–64

1963 was to be something of a nightmare year for the Tory Party, starting badly with the French veto on Britain's entry to Europe. Macmillan was already in trouble with the impression of panic that the 'night of the long knives' in July 1962 had given. Even before this, he was becoming the subject of satire. His created persona of the elderly Edwardian gent was easy to mock and Peter Cook, in the hit review 'Beyond the Fringe', which opened in London in 1961, had savaged him in a spoof political broadcast. Cook gave the impression of an aging incompetent, no longer the respected world statesman but a figure of fun.

Source R

Good evening, I have recently been travelling round the world on your behalf and at your expense, visiting some of the chaps with whom I hope to be shaping your future. I went first to Germany and there I spoke with the German Foreign Minister, Herr . . . Herr and there, and we exchanged many frank words in our respective languages; so precious little came of that in the way of understanding. I then went on to America and there I had talks with the young . . . vigorous President of that great country and danced with his lovely lady wife. We talked of many things, including Great Britain's role in the world as an honest broker. I agreed with him, when he said that no nation could be more honest and he agreed with me, when I chaffed him, and said that no nation could be broker.

From a sketch in 'Beyond the Fringe', 1961–62

SKILLS BUILDER

How does Source R undermine Macmillan's credibility?

The Profumo affair

Late in 1962, the government was embarrassed by a spy scandal involving John Vassall, a homosexual civil servant in the Admiralty, who was relaying secrets to the Russians. There was an outcry in the press and from the opposition and the minister in charge resigned, although completely innocent of any wrongdoing. The image created was of sexual scandal and incompetence. This image received massive reinforcement in 1963, as rumours involving spies, call girls, nude bathing and government ministers began to circulate. Eventually known as the 'Profumo Affair' from the name of the government minister at the heart of the extraordinary series of events, it was a gift scenario for any opposition party. At the centre of the scandal was John Profumo, the minister for the army. He had begun a casual affair with the part-time call girl, Christine Keeler, whom he had met at a house party thrown by the Astor family. She had already had a relationship with a spy, Captain Ivanov of the Russian embassy. As it happens, there was no threat to national security, but Profumo, when challenged about his links with Keeler, chose to deny it, lying blatantly to the House of Commons in March. More and more details of Keeler's colourful relationships emerged and eventually in June Profumo was forced to admit that he had lied and he resigned as a minister and MP. The press had a field day and even the Conservative-inclined *Daily Express* published the following cartoon. Note Harold Wilson lurking in the depths.

Source S

5.7 Cartoon by Michael Cummings, *Daily Express*, 7 June 1963

SKILLS BUILDER

What is the message of Source S?

Macmillan handled the crisis poorly. In the Commons, he admitted to being out of touch with young people and added to his fuddy-duddy image. His persistent critic, Nigel Birch, who had never forgiven the prime minister for the showdown in January 1958, quoted Browning's poem 'The Lost Leader' in a speech:

Forced praise on our part – the glimmer of twilight
Never glad confident morning again.

For Macmillan, it was to be an accurate piece of fortune-telling. Although he seemed to have recovered some of his zest and appetite for political leadership by the early autumn and there were signs that the Maudling stimulus was working on the economy, October brought a fresh tragedy just before the party conference. Macmillan had to go into hospital for a prostate operation. He convinced himself that the condition was more serious than it was and after all the strain of the previous months decided to resign. Later he was to regret it.

What now ensued was a shambolic scramble for the Tory leadership. Butler was the front-runner, as in 1955, but Macmillan thought him unsuitable. Macmillan felt that he lacked the cavalier capacity for risk and excitement, and that the man who did have it was Quintin Hogg, Viscount Hailsham. Hogg was clever with a capacity for colourful phrases and grand gestures but also lacking in those very qualities of measured calculation that Butler had to excess. Hailsham threw his hat into the ring at the party conference, announcing that he would renounce his peerage. The impression given was of a man over-eager for the top job and slightly unbalanced. This should have handed the succession to Butler, but he lacked the ambition and ruthlessness to seize it. Macmillan persuaded his Foreign Secretary, Alec Douglas-Home to offer himself. He did so, very reluctantly. He was 60 and a 14th earl, having left the Commons in 1947 when he inherited his earldom on the death of his father. Utterly decent, he was totally unsuited to the needs of the Tory Party in 1963. Harold Wilson feared that it would be Macleod or Maudling. He could not believe his luck as Alec Douglas-Home 'emerged' as the choice of the party grandees, in reality Macmillan. The queen sent for Douglas-Home, who asked Butler if he would serve under him. Butler could have scuppered Douglas-Home by refusing. He did not, and lost the chance of becoming prime minister. Possibly a man who did not want it so badly was not the man to be prime minister, but then Douglas-Home was not very keen on the job either.

SKILLS BUILDER

Study Source T. What impression do you get of the difference between Alec Douglas-Home and Harold Wilson?

Wilson's opportunity

Wilson, the clever grammar-school boy with the northern accent, now had a dream opponent, as Wilson's authorised biographer, Philip Ziegler makes clear:

Source T

When he heard of the appointment, wrote John Harris, he was 'almost ecstatic with pleasure'. It was not that he underestimated Douglas-Home, still less despised him, but he saw immediately how the contrast between the two men could be exploited. Wilson was lower middle class against aristocratic, innovator against traditionalist, statistician against self-avowed innumerate, golfer against keen shot and fisherman, technocrat against territorial magnate, Montagu Burton against Saville Row or scruffy tweeds, professional against amateur, the future against the past. When Marcia Williams (Wilson's political adviser) found in an *Observer* interview a casual reference by Douglas-Home to the fact that he did his sums with matchsticks, Wilson's cup flowed over. Nothing could encapsulate more neatly his superior claim to be the man who could tackle Britain's economic problems. The white heat of the technological revolution never glowed more brightly than in the months between Douglas-Home's appointment and the election.

From Philip Ziegler, *Wilson: The Authorised Life*, published in 1993

Wilson exploited the situation to the full and came up with a brilliant device to wrong-foot the Tories and unite the Labour Party by avoiding all the many issues on which the Labour Party was divided. He espoused modernisation and the 'scientific revolution'. At the Labour Party conference in 1963, he announced his agenda.

SKILLS BUILDER

Compare Sources Q and U. What image do they present about the contrasting relationship of Gaitskill and Wilson with the Labour Party?

Source U

In all our plans for the future, we are re-defining and we are re-stating our Socialism in terms of the scientific revolution. But that revolution cannot become a reality unless we are prepared to make far-reaching changes in economic and social attitudes which permeate our whole system of society. The Britain that is going to be forged in the white heat of this revolution will be no place for restrictive practices or for out-dated methods on either side of industry. In the Cabinet room and the boardroom alike those charged with the control of our affairs must be ready to think and speak in the language of our scientific age.

From a speech by Harold Wilson to the Labour Party conference in 1963

Over the next 12 months, Wilson dominated the scene, the embodiment of merit, youth (only 47) and cheeky, irrepressible confidence. He constantly ran ahead of his own party and Douglas-Home in opinion polls. The prime minister clung on, hoping that the tide would turn as the economy began to boom under the stimulus of the Maudling package. One development which brought long-time benefits to the consumer was the ending of 'resale price maintenance' i.e. price controls to benefit small shopkeepers. Edward Heath introduced the reform, which was perfectly in accord with Conservative principles of freeing up the market. Unfortunately, it alienated many small shopkeepers just before the election. Nevertheless, the Tories crept closer to Labour in the polls and, when the election took place in October 1964, Labour squeaked home with a majority of four. The Tories lost 60 seats, but they were only 0.1 per cent behind Labour in the popular vote. A surge in votes for the Liberals damaged the Tories even though it produced only nine Liberal MPs. Douglas-Home had done remarkably well, as the historian John Charmley observes:

Source V

When the election came in October the result suggested that Home's counter-attack had very nearly worked, and that those who had been writing the Conservatives off had under-estimated the resilience of the party. The Conservatives had been able to play on fears of Labour's nationalisation plans and upon the party's inexperience, but in the end the Liberal revival scuppered Home's chances.

From John Charmley, *A History of Conservative Politics 1900–1996*, published in 1996

Unit summary

What have you learned in this unit?

This unit has covered a considerable amount of information. You have learned about how the Conservatives recovered after Suez and Eden. You have considered the strengths of Macmillan as prime minister and his developing weaknesses. You have studied briefly the election of 1959 and why Macmillan won and Labour lost. You should understand something of the developments in the Labour Party under Gaitskell and finally why Wilson was able to overturn a large Tory majority in 1964.

What skills have you used in this unit?

You have encountered a large number of secondary sources relating to this period as well as some primary ones and asked to consider their strengths and weaknesses as sources of evidence for historians. This unit has contained a larger number of visual sources than previous ones and it is worth reflecting on both the advantages and difficulties of using such visual sources as evidence. It is always worth noting where a cartoon appears and what is the accepted political bias of the newspaper or magazine in which it appears.

Exam style question

This is the type of question that you will find on the examination paper as a (b) question. You will use the sources provided, with your own knowledge.

Study Sources T, U and V.

Do you agree with the view that it was the contrasting leaders that explain why Labour was able to overturn such a large Conservative majority in the election of October 1964?

Explain your answer using the evidence of Sources T, U and V, and your own knowledge.

Exam tips

- Do remember to cross-reference sources even in a (b) question. In this case note the reference in Source T to the speech that is Source U.
- Note the totally different emphasis in Source V on the Liberals – this clearly needs development with own knowledge.
- What key areas are not addressed in the sources?

RESEARCH TOPIC

Investigate the 'satire boom' of 1962–64 and its impact on the fortunes of the Conservatives.

Two aspects of this boom are used as sources in this unit – *Beyond the Fringe* and *Private Eye*. Try to find out more about these.

The BBC produced a very popular satirical programme, *That Was the Week That Was* that made David Frost's reputation. Try to see some of these and in particular Frost's attack on the appointment of Alec Douglas-Home.

6 A slightly warm technological revolution: Labour in power, 1964–70

What is this unit about?

This unit examines the years of the Wilson government from October 1964 to its surprise defeat in 1970. It involves consideration of the role and personality of the new prime minister and the nature of the team that formed his government. For 18 months, the government struggled to survive with a tiny majority and crushing economic problems, but won through to win a comfortable majority in the general election of March 1966. One of the notable developments was the liberalisation of society under the general guidance of Roy Jenkins as Home Secretary from 1965 to 1967. Fresh economic storms led to a forced devaluation in November of 1967 and thereafter a period of hard slog to improve the nation's finances under the guidance of Jenkins, now Chancellor of the Exchequer. There were notable defence cuts. Finally, the government grasped the nettle of trade union reform, but failed to carry out its policies in the face of widespread opposition. The Conservatives had selected a new leader, Edward Heath, in 1965 and against expectation he won the June election of 1970.

Key questions

- What were Harold Wilson's characteristics as prime minister?
- What problems did the new Labour government face?
- Why was Labour able to win the general election of 1966?
- In what ways was British society liberalised?
- How successful was Labour's economic policy in these years?
- How effective was the Conservative Party in opposition?

Timeline

1964	**October**	Harold Wilson becomes prime minister
1965	**January**	Death and state funeral of Sir Winston Churchill
	February	Prices and Income Board set up
	July	Ministry of Education begins the drive to encourage comprehensive schools
	July	Edward Heath elected as leader of the Conservative Party
	September	National Plan published
	November	Race Relations Act sets up Race Relations Board Abolition of Capital Punishment Act

1966	March	General election. Labour majority of 96
	May	State of emergency in response to seamen's strike
	July	Statutory wage freeze
	July	England win the World Cup
1967	March	Iron and steel renationalised
	July	Homosexual acts between consenting adults legalised
	October	Abortion legalised under certain circumstances
	November	Devaluation of the pound to $2.40 De Gaulle vetoes British application to join the EEC for a second time
1968	January	Major deflationary package – cuts in welfare and defence – Britain withdraws from east of Suez
	March	George Brown resigns as Foreign Secretary
	April	Enoch Powell's 'rivers of blood' speech on immigration
	June	Open University chartered
	August	First civil rights march in Northern Ireland
	September	Lord Chamberlain's censorship of live theatre ends
1969	January	Ulster Defence Force (UDF) founded in Ulster to defend Protestant rights Barbara Castle introduces 'In Place of Strife' to reform trade unions
	April	Voting age lowered to 18
	October	Divorce made easier Department of Economic Affairs abolished
1970	January	Provisional IRA established Conservatives hold conference at Selsdon Park
	May	Equal Pay Act
	June	General election – Conservative majority of 30

The new government

Harold Wilson had excited high expectations of change. His was to be a Britain run by energetic meritocrats not aging aristocrats. His Cabinet certainly was notable for its intellect, filled as it was with a large proportion of men and one woman with first-class degrees from Oxford. Wilson himself was a noted academic high-flyer, having gained some of the highest marks ever awarded in his degree papers. He was an extraordinary mixture of high intelligence and unassuming lower middle-class tastes. Not for him the fine wines and fine food beloved of Roy Jenkins. It was reputed that another of his close Cabinet colleagues, Richard Crossman, also a notable Oxford intellect, offended Wilson's wife by refusing the humble Nescafé proffered to him at Number 10. Wilson, all agreed, was not only highly intelligent but very nice. He was pleasant to all, showing as much courtesy and good humour to his drivers as he did to the queen, with whom he famously got on. There was something of the Boy Scout about him and he was probably more influenced by his happy time as a scout than by socialist theory. He explained his attitude to politics to the BBC political correspondent, John Cole, and socialist theory was pretty low down on his list.

Source A

He said he was pragmatic, because all government was pragmatic. For example, he thought equality of opportunity mattered more than equality. The difficulty was that everybody was different. The idea of a proletariat was nonsense. Marx did not understand people. He himself was interested in people as individuals rather than in the mass. He was interested in the family, because most happiness was family happiness. He was interested in 'Saturdays and Sundays and Bank Holidays'.

This was a preliminary to what was a most radical thought at that time from a man who had emerged from the left of the Labour Party. He recalled that the Labour movement – trade unions as well as the political party – had been born out of the solidarity of labour, the miseries of work. That was a thing of the past. Labour was not now marked by solidarity in any real sense. If there was a bus strike, would the engineers come out in support? No, they would complain about not being able to get a bus:

He added 'I don't like theory. I got an alpha-plus in economic theory, but I never understood it. I think my examiner must have been very kind. Or perhaps he didn't understand it either.' One of Harold Wilson's endearing characteristics has always been his gift for self-mockery.

From John Cole, *As It Seemed to Me: Political Memoirs*, published in 1995

Source B

Wilson's Government, with a majority in single figures, was unusually dominated by electoral considerations, a fact which played alike to the Prime Minister's skills and his inclination. He foresaw 1966 as the moment when he would form his 'real' cabinet, once his interim administration had improvised its way to a more convincing electoral victory, through adroit tactics and clever compromises, designed to keep everyone guessing. The end was duly achieved, but at the price of making the means into a way of life, from which it was subsequently difficult to escape.

From Peter Clarke, *Hope and Glory: Britain 1900–2000*, published in 1996

Wilson's pragmatism could easily develop into a less attractive 'opportunism', for which he was much criticised by colleagues and subsequently by historians. Part of this arose from the circumstances of his government in 1964 with its wafer-thin majority, a point made by the Cambridge historian Peter Clarke.

Wilson became the past master of the short-term fix, out-manoeuvring his Conservative opponents and his would-be rivals in his own Cabinet. He was increasingly given to sensing plots to replace him and surrounded himself with a **'kitchen cabinet'** in Number 10, which encouraged this trend. One of the most powerful influences was his political adviser, Marcia Williams, who exercised an unaccountable hold over him. Within the real

Cabinet, **Barbara Castle** and **Dick Crossman**, both ex-Bevanites, were friends as well as colleagues. The same could not be said of most of the other leading ministers, most of whom were from the Gaitskellite wing of the party and could by no stretch of the imagination be classed as friends to the prime minister. Wilson's technique for managing Cabinet meetings was to allow his colleagues to talk themselves into the ground. The point is well made by Peter Hennessy in his study of post-war prime ministers.

Biography

Barbara Castle (1910–2002) and Richard Crossman (1907–1974)

Both were from the traditional left of the party and had long been friends with Wilson. Barbara Castle shared a similar background to the Wilsons and many of their simple tastes. Crossman, as the son of a judge and a product of Winchester College, was somewhat grander. Both Castle and Crossman, along with Anthony Benn, produced notable political diaries which are major sources for this government. Crossman's was the first to be published and had enormous influence. His own struggles with the civil service head of the Ministry of Housing, the brilliant Dame Evelyn Sharp, were the inspiration for the wonderful television series, *Yes, Minister*. Castle had the services of the very large Sir Andrew Cohen at her first ministry and the pair became known in Whitehall as the 'Elephant and Castle'.

Definition

Kitchen cabinet

This term is used to describe the group of close advisers that a prime minister might choose to serve him or her in Number 10. They are likely to be outside the formal Cabinet and might not even be MPs.

Source C

As a political leader who put party unity on a very high pedestal (it was perhaps, the single consistent aspect of his thirteen years as Labour leader), Wilson had a penchant for letting his Cabinet ramble, encouraging all who wished to speak, doodling as they did so (Ted Short, his Chief Whip, called it the 'doodling Cabinet') and interjecting a little commentary when they finished before catching the eye of the next contributor. Despite his [respect] for the memory of Attlee, Wilson used prolixity [excessive talking] as a weapon, allowing the Cabinet to talk itself out.

From Peter Hennessy, *The Prime Minister: The Office and Its Holders since 1945*, published in 2000

SKILLS BUILDER

What impression do Sources A, B and C give of Harold Wilson's political skills?

Possibly his most hostile colleague was the Labour deputy leader, George Brown who was deeply resentful of Wilson. Brown was an extraordinary individual. He had come up through the trade unions and unlike most of the Cabinet had not been to university. However, all recognised his powerful mind and personality and his very serious defects. Denis Healey, one of the many Oxford firsts in the Cabinet, appointed Minister of Defence, commented in his memoirs (see Source D).

Source D

He had a powerful mind allied to great energy, and could often get to the heart of a problem faster than anyone else. But he was quite unpredictable, and came to depend so much on drink that in the end I tried to avoid seeing him after midday. He was always resigning, sometimes on the most trivial issues.

From Denis Healey, *The Time of My Life*, published in 1989

Another Cabinet member was even more critical of Brown. **Anthony Wedgwood Benn** was to become Minister of Technology and the author of a massive political diary. Here is his entry for 3 February 1966.

Source E

To the Commons to see George Brown. He behaved monstrously to his officials, sending a senior civil servant out for bottles of gin and whisky and five minutes later ringing his own department in Storey's Gate to find out where the poor chap had gone. He really showed off. George is completely erratic and irrational and an impossible old boozer – rarely sober after lunch.

From Tony Benn, *The Benn Diaries*, published in 1995

Wilson appointed Brown to what was meant to be the hub of the new government, the Department of Economic Affairs (DEA), a brand new ministry charged with drafting a National Plan to raise Britain's economic game so that she could compete more effectively. Immediately there was tension between the Treasury and the new DEA, which became known to the Treasury civil servants as the Department of Extraordinary Aggression. As the head of the Treasury (Chancellor of the Exchequer), Wilson appointed one of his other rivals, Jim Callaghan. In this, Wilson demonstrated one of his techniques for managing rivals, setting them against one another. Although quite a good technique for prime ministerial survival, it was not necessarily good for coherent government. Frequent Cabinet reshuffles was also a weapon employed, but again it possibly prevented ministers establishing themselves effectively. Wilson, probably more than any other prime minister, experimented with government restructuring. To be fair this was mainly meant to serve the cause of increased national efficiency, thus a new Ministry of Technology was created, but it also had the effect of creating bureaucratic confusion and Wilson could never fully avoid the temptation to use it as a weapon against his rivals or to serve some other party political aim. As well as wholesale ministry creations, endless Cabinet sub-committees were established, known as MISCs. As one of his Cabinet colleagues, Douglas Haughton recalled, 'He set up MISCs at the drop of a hat. There was a MISC on this and a MISC on that.' The Wilson premiership was thus energetic and dynamic, but whether it was effective in achieving its objectives was another story.

The basic objective was to revitalise the economy and achieve a higher rate of economic growth in line with Germany and Japan. It was hoped that a mixture of judicious planning and the encouragement of technology through colleges and universities would achieve this. From the increased growth would flow all the goodies that a socialist party might desire – increased welfare, greater opportunities for the poor, etc. The intellectual inspiration for this was a brilliant young Gaitskellite, Tony Crosland. He published an influential book in 1956, entitled *The Future of Socialism*. In it he declared that traditional socialism was redundant since its traditional enemy 'traditional capitalism has been reformed and modified almost out of existence'. He rejected the old puritanical socialism of Edwardian socialists: 'Total abstinence and a good filing system are not now the right signposts to the socialist Utopia: or at least if they are some of us will fall by the wayside.' Instead, he embraced the joys of an affluent society. All that was necessary for the new style socialist to do was to redistribute some of the ample riches that the application of modern technology would deliver. The assumption was that Britain could equal France, Germany, the USA and Japan in productivity and its resulting affluence. It was a big and critical assumption.

The struggle to survive, 1964–66

In many ways, the most successful period was the first 18 months when, with a tiny majority, which had shrunk to one by 1966, the new government seemed to be achieving its objectives. George Brown established his new super-department, which proceeded to draft a National Plan, which envisaged 4 per cent growth in the economy. The new Ministry of Technology was established under the TGWU boss, Frank Cousins. He was not a success as a minister, in contrast to his great predecessor Ernie Bevin, but the lack of success was not immediately obvious. Younger, eye-catching ministers were promoted in 1965 to add to the impression of dynamic change. Tony Crosland became Minister of Education and Roy Jenkins a young Home Secretary. Their impact is looked at later (see pages 104–108). Wilson cleverly seemed to manage to maintain good relations with the USA while at the same time avoiding the commitment of British troops to the conflict in Vietnam, no easy task in view of US pressure brought to bear. Britain desperately needed US support in the recurring financial crises, which threatened the pound with another devaluation.

It was, in fact, the almost non-stop financial crises that gave the government its greatest headaches. Here James Callaghan was in the hot seat as Chancellor of the Exchequer. As his predecessor Reggie Maudling was leaving Number 11 Downing Street and Callaghan was seated in his new home and place of work reading the briefs that the Treasury civil servants had prepared, Maudling stuck his head round the door and called

Definition

Devaluation – holding the pound at $2.80

This phrase refers to the attempts of the government to maintain a fixed rate of exchange for the pound sterling against the dollar and other currencies. If large numbers of banks around the world decided that the pound was likely to fall, they would sell their holding of pounds, forcing the value down and fulfilling their fears. Some might speculate against the pound in the hope of making money, i.e. selling pounds to force the value down so that they could then buy them back more cheaply. The government's weapon to prevent this was to get the Bank of England to buy pounds, using its reserves of dollars and other currencies. If it could keep buying for longer than the speculators could keep selling, they would force the speculators into a loss instead of a profit, hopefully teaching them a lesson.

out apologetically, 'Sorry, old cock, to leave it in this shape.' In fact, he left Labour with a severe balance of payments crisis and threatened run on the pound, which could force **devaluation**. Wilson, Brown and Callaghan set their face against devaluation, fearing the political consequences, but holding the pound at $2.80 would mean a constant strain and a certain dependence on the USA for financial backing. When some of Wilson's more left-wing MPs wanted him to take a more condemnatory approach to the Vietnam War, he answered them in homely fashion – 'We can't kick our creditor in the balls.'

Callaghan recalled in his memoirs the strain of '**holding the pound at $2.80**'.

Source F

We had been in office for only three weeks when the first large attack against sterling was launched from the Continent. It was in essence an attack by speculators which I had been half expecting and had believed I was mentally braced to overcome. But in all the offices I have held I have never experienced anything more frustrating than sitting at the Chancellor's desk watching our currency reserves gurgle away down the plug hole day by day and knowing that the drain could not be stopped. I could not even share my misery with others, because the Bank of England insisted that the daily losses should be kept secret so that the speculators would not know how much damage they were inflicting.

Each day turned into a game of bluff . . . It was like swimming in a heavy sea. As soon as we emerged from the buffeting of one wave, another would hit us before we could catch our breath.

From James Callaghan, *Time and Chance*, published in 1987

In fact, the first attack was beaten off with the help of a massive loan negotiated by the Governor of the Bank of England on Wilson's orders. Callaghan tried to cut imports and right the balance of payments with a temporary tax on imports and by deflating the economy by putting up income tax to 41.25 per cent. It seemed to work and by 1966 the economy appeared in good shape with unemployment still low and living standards rising. Prices had increased by 9 per cent since 1964 but earnings were up by 11 per cent. The National Plan and the Ministry of Technology offered hope of better things and government welfare spending had increased. There might be trouble ahead, but there were strong arguments for going to the country and trying to get an effective majority while things looked promising. The Tories had changed their leader, replacing Alec Douglas-Home with Edward Heath, but Heath appeared stiff and ill at ease and was regularly outshone in the Commons by Wilson. When the government won a by-election in Hull in January 1966 (having just announced the building of a new bridge over the Humber), the opportunity seemed too good to miss. A general election was called for 31 March.

General election, 1966

It was very much Wilson's election. Jim Callaghan made this point in his memoirs (see Source G).

Not surprisingly, the authorised biography of Wilson by Philip Ziegler also emphasises his starring role.

Source G

The timing of the general election, eighteen months after the indecisive result of 1964 was faultless, as was Harold Wilson's conduct of the campaign, and Labour cruised to victory. He turned a majority of one at the time of the election into a majority of ninety seven, and we owed our victory to his tactical skill, his determination, his orchestration and the confidence he conveyed to the electorate.

From James Callaghan, *Time and Chance*, published in 1987

Source H

Just by looking prime-ministerial, a Prime Minister can enjoy a head start over a leader of the opposition. Heath featured even more prominently in the Tory campaign than Wilson in the Labour, taking up 70 per cent of the television time as opposed to Wilson's 56 per cent. In direct comparison, however, Wilson fared better: 54 per cent thought he had a 'strong forceful personality' as opposed to 28 per cent for Heath; an astonishingly high 95 per cent of Labour supporters were satisfied with Wilson, only 70 per cent of Tories with Heath. Wilson was far better at handling hecklers, and demonstrated his technique night after night while the Tory leader talked to tamer assemblies confined to the accredited faithful. The approach had its dangers, as was shown when Wilson was hit in the eye by a stink bomb thrown by a boy in Slough. He could have been made to look a fool, but his quick comment – 'With an aim like that, the boy ought to be in the England eleven' – won him respect and sympathy.

From Philip Ziegler, *Wilson: The Authorised Life*, published in 1993

Dick Crossman refers to the same incident in his diary and the entry is revealing about both his character and Wilson's. In the following entry for 27 March 1966, he is referring to events of the previous week.

Source I

It was the morning after the meeting in Slough at which a stink-bomb was flung in his eye, causing a slight injury. Walking across the Park that morning in beautiful weather it suddenly occurred to me that this was a tremendous chance. Why not keep him in bed on Thursday and Friday and make the press report that he was ill? This would create a sag in Labour morale and a sense of suspense in the whole press which would give his Saturday meeting in Manchester enormous psychological importance. When I got upstairs I put this all to him quite impressively; to which he characteristically replied 'But suppose I don't go to Norwich today, how shall I spend the afternoon?' 'Well', I said, 'you can govern the country.' He laughed. 'No, there are no boxes coming upstairs now in Number 10. There is no work for me. I should just sit about.' I laughed and said, 'You being you, Harold, that's something you can't do. If you really feel at a loose end this afternoon I can't really stop you going to Norwich.' So off he went and made one of his best speeches.

Since the stink-bomb had grazed the white of his eye and he still had an appallingly heavy cold, he had every excuse to take the day off. But he wasn't that kind of man, nor does he calculate in that kind of a way. People think Harold a clever opportunist. But when you put to him the idea of a deliberate 24 hour withdrawal he remembers the people who will be waiting for him at Norwich and feels he can't let them down.

From Richard Crossman, *The Crossman Diaries*, published in 1979

The election, as indicated, was everything Labour could have hoped for. Labour gained 48 per cent of the vote and broke out of its traditional strongholds in Wales and the industrial North to take cathedral and university cities. Oxford and Cambridge fell as did York, Lancaster and Exeter. The High Peak in Derbyshire, a traditional Tory seat, fell to Labour for the first time. The Liberal vote fell, but the workings of the first-past-the-post voting system gave them an increase in seats from 9 to 12 (i.e. they had got fewer votes across the country as a whole but more where it mattered in winnable seats). Wilson had triumphed and could now form his 'real' Cabinet and transform the country.

SKILLS BUILDER

1 How many different reasons for Labour's success in the election of March 1966 are provided in Sources G, H and I?

2 How far does Source I support the opinion expressed in Source G of the importance of Wilson as the mastermind of victory?

The civilised society

Much more than the National Plan or even Callaghan's struggles to save the pound, it was Roy Jenkins' encouragement of what he termed 'the civilised society' that made an impact on ordinary people in Britain and certainly excited more debate. There was a dramatic 'freeing up' of society as the state eased regulation of whole areas of human behaviour and softened punishment. In this, the government was both reflecting changes in attitude, but also giving a lead. Most of the reforms had been under discussion for many years, pushed for by activists who were ahead of public opinion, such as Sydney Silverman, the Labour MP and veteran campaigner against capital punishment. The Wolfenden Committee in the 1950s had urged liberalisation of the law regarding homosexuality (see page 81), but no government until the mid-1960s wished to court controversy and possible unpopularity by taking a lead. Indeed, even in the 1960s, almost all the changes came about as a result of **private members' bills**. However, as Roy Jenkins makes clear in Source J, none would have made it onto the statute book without government approval and help.

In 1965, Silverman finally got a Bill that suspended capital punishment for five years passed and in 1969, it was completely abolished. Jenkins carried a Criminal Justice Bill in 1967, which ended the birching of young offenders. It also introduced the concept of a suspended sentence and extended early parole for certain prisoners. The purpose of both these changes was to reduce the growing prison population, but the same Bill sought to increase certainty of conviction by allowing majority verdicts in jury cases. There was much evidence of intimidation of some jurors in trials involving major criminals and the police pressed this change on the Home Secretary as a solution.

Definition

Private members' bills
Draft law introduced into the Commons by a back-bench MP, not by government sponsored legislation which is the norm. Without government support there is little chance of a bill becoming law.

The two big changes of 1967 both aroused controversy and arose from private members' bills.

Source J

The summer of 1967 saw the passage through the House of Commons of the two Bills for which, with approval by some and disapproval by others, my first period as Home Secretary is best remembered: The Medical Termination of Pregnancy (or Abortion) Bill and the Sexual Offences Bill, the latter freeing homosexuals over 21 from the rigours of the criminal law. Neither was a Government Bill, but they would not have got through had not I or someone of similar mind been Home Secretary. I could not have got the cabinet to agree that they should bear the imprimatur [official support] of the government. A substantial majority of ministers were in favour of both, but three or four were opposed, and another larger group wished the issues would go away. The minority were not the same people in both cases (Frank Longford for instance was as strongly in favour of homosexual reform as he was opposed to abortion), but the Secretary of State for Scotland, Willy Ross, who had my responsibility for these matters north of the border, was in each case intransigently part of it.

From Roy Jenkins, *A Life at the Centre*, published in 1991

Leo Abse, a Welsh Labour MP, was responsible for the Sexual Offences Bill. There was growing pressure from the great and the good to legalise sexual practices between consenting adults. Many had noted how the law as it stood encouraged blackmail and that the spy, John Vassall, would probably not have betrayed his country had it not been possible for the Russians to blackmail him for his sexual tastes, which happened to run counter to those of the majority of his fellow citizens. Across much of the country there was a slow but growing toleration of homosexuality.

The issue of abortion excited even more controversy and its criminalisation probably caused more suffering and misery than the penalties attached to homosexual practices. The illegality of abortion makes estimates of its extent difficult, but 100,000 per year in the UK in the 1950s appear likely. This added up to considerable medical risk as well as social stigma and humiliation for many girls and women. David Steel's Bill not only legalised abortion on the grounds of physical harm to the mother, but also allowed her mental health to be taken into account, and it was on these grounds that the majority of abortions were to be undertaken. Another liberalisation sought to cut the number of unwanted pregnancies and the *Family Planning Act* of 1967 removed the restrictions of medical or marital status on women's access to local authority birth control services. This was, of course, dammed by some as encouraging 'immorality' among the unmarried. It was not until 1969, after Jenkins had left the Home Office, that another of his favoured projects finally entered the statute book. The Divorce Reform Act made divorce much easier. To its supporters, it helped to end years of private suffering and domestic unhappiness; to its critics, it encouraged the break-up of the family.

Source K

Did they make the country more civilised as Jenkins and his supporters believed or did they make it coarser and more dangerous as right-wing commentary has alleged? Despite serious rises in violent crime, there is little campaigning for a return to hanging. Censorship too seems something few modern Britons are keen on. Though divorce has become commonplace, causing great unhappiness as well as liberation, tougher laws to force people to remain married are on no political party's agenda. Homosexuals' rights have been increased again, the movement seems all one way. Abortion, affected by changes in medical technology and by the influence of evangelical organisations, is probably the most disputed of the sixties reforms, and the one most likely to be revisited. A fair verdict is that the changes allowed the British to be more openly themselves, and while the results are not always pretty, the apple of self-knowledge cannot be uneaten again and returned to the tree.

From Andrew Marr, *A History of Modern Britain*, published in 2007

Two other important changes encouraged by Jenkins were the abolition of theatre censorship, carried out for centuries by the Lord Chamberlain's office, and two *Race Relations Acts*, in 1966 and 1968, establishing and then extending the powers of a Race Relations Board, designed to investigate complaints against unfair discrimination.

Not surprisingly, Jenkins has become a figure attracting some controversy. Does he deserve to be highly regarded as the patron of the 'civilised society' or the man who opened the floodgates to moral depravity? Andrew Marr gives a historian and a journalist's perspective on the issue.

Two contradictory viewpoints, both from 1970, are also worth considering:

Source L

"PERMISSIVE SOCIETY IS THE CIVILISED SOCIETY"

LAW & ORDER

BLUE FILMS LTD

BLUE PAINTINGS LTD.

DEMO'S UNLIMITED

CRIME

"Help! Our civilised society is being menaced by savages . . ."

6.1 Cartoon by Michael Cummings, *Daily Express*, 6 February 1970

Source M

We no longer terrorise homosexuals. We do not force mothers to bring unwanted children into the world. We have made it easier to end wrecked marriages. We have begun the true liberation of women. Children by and large get a better deal. We do not murder by the rope.

From Paul Johnson, writing as the editor, *New Statesman*, June 1970 (the *New Statesman* was a left-inclined periodical)

SKILLS BUILDER

How far do Sources J, L and M indicate that there was widespread support, at the time, for the liberalisation of the laws affecting criminal justice and social behaviour?

Education and culture

Equally controversial is the Wilson government's record in terms of education. Here the central figure was another Gaitskellite, Tony Crosland. A product of Winchester College and Oxford, he was hardly from an educationally challenged background. In 1965, he was appointed Education Secretary and took up the 1964 Labour Party commitment to further comprehensive education with enthusiasm. In fact, he famously declared war on the grammar schools of England and Wales, despite the fact that they had done much to advance social mobility and give bright working-class girls and boys the chance of competing with children from the type of privileged background he had enjoyed. In her memoir, his wife Susan describes her husband's ringing declaration of intent one evening in 1965 after he had attended a boring, official function with some teachers.

Source N

He stopped at our bedroom door.

'Good evening. You'd better come in the study.'

I put my novel aside and got smartly out of our bed, wondering what had caused this latest vexation.

'If it's the last thing I do, I'm going to destroy every ****ing grammar school in England', he said. 'And Wales. And Northern Ireland.'

'Why not Scotland?' I asked out of pure curiosity.

'Because their schools come under the Secretary of State for Scotland.'

From Susan Crosland, *Tony Crosland*, published in 1982

He was unable to fulfil his pledge entirely, but he speeded up the process, issuing the famous Education Department directive 10/65, tying money for new school buildings to local authorities adopting plans to implement comprehensive schools. Despite the prime minister's less than enthusiastic support, as a notable product of the grammar school system, the Labour manifesto of 1970 boasted, 'Comprehensive reorganisation has been vigorously pursued. In the past six years, 129 out of the 163 English and Welsh local education authorities have agreed plans for reorganising their secondary schools.'

Crosland had also expressed discontent with the attitudes of big business and the private sector back in 1956. The Labour manifesto of 1964 had promised to address the issue, but, apart from setting up the Newsom Commission to consider the problem, nothing was done. It can be argued that the reduction in grammar schools, alongside the continuation of private schooling, actually increased social divisiveness in education by removing the ladder of advancement based on merit and leaving the ladder based on privilege and money in place.

Crosland enthusiastically promoted higher education, a trend already begun by his Conservative predecessors with the setting up of a series of new universities such as Sussex, York and Lancaster. There was a massive expansion of **polytechnics**, brought about in 1967 and designed to close the technology gap between Britain and her competitors. However, it can be argued that Crosland's was a mixed legacy across the educational spectrum as a recent writer on the subject makes clear:

Definition

Polytechnics
These were advanced technical colleges offering a more practical approach to higher education than the traditional universities. Most eventually were re-designated universities and enjoy that status today.

Source O

As busily as the new government built new places of higher learning – thirty polytechnics were commissioned by the Education and Science Department in 1967 – it worked diligently to destroy the solid groundwork of traditional schooling, which would have made these new colleges into intellectual powerhouses. The man who commissioned the polytechnics, Antony Crosland, is known to history for one sentence – his ambition to destroy 'every ****ing grammar school in England'. This is not to say that the development of comprehensive schools (about 60 per cent of British pupils were educated in them by 1970, and about 90 per cent by 1980) was not introduced with the kindliest of motives. Whether standards of numeracy, literacy, scientific knowledge or technological skill arose across the nation, and whether there was more chance for the clever children of the economically disadvantaged than in the old system, will remain a matter of debate. It is hard to imagine Roy Jenkins, Roy Hattersley, Margaret Thatcher, Denis Healey, Edward Heath or Harold Wilson himself having been quite as successful as they were had they not been educated in the despised grammar school tradition.

From A.N. Wilson, *Our Times: The Age of Elizabeth II*, published in 2008

One relatively minor figure in the Wilson government is almost unanimously praised for her impact. Nye Bevan's widow, Jennie Lee, was appointed Minister for the Arts. She oversaw a considerable expansion in funding for the arts and the grants to the Arts Council virtually tripled, adding considerably to the artistic diversity and excellence of the country. Not only a good in itself, it promoted tourism and helped to make Britain a world centre of artistic merit. Perhaps even more important was her campaign to launch the Open University; a campaign vigorously backed by Wilson.

Source P

A particularly valuable innovation was the Open University, which Jennie Lee promoted and in which Wilson himself took a close interest. Finally beginning teaching operations in 1971, it was designed to advance educational opportunities for mature students, working people, housewives and others. Even if the eventual recruitment for the Open University proved to be distinctly more middle class than anticipated, with school teachers in particular taking advantage of the opportunities of gaining a university degree and thereby acquiring professional advancement, the Open University proved to be a pioneering and socially valuable instrument of mobility and cultural inspiration. It also proved to be remarkably innovative in distance learning, instructional techniques, including the use of television, and in developing American-style credit-based modular courses.

From Kenneth O. Morgan, *Britain Since 1945: The People's Peace*, published in 1990

Contrary to the expectations of its creators the expense of the National Health Service rose by leaps and bounds. NHS staff doubled between 1948 and 1979. The number of drugs available proliferated. In 1948 there was only one antibiotic available but in 1968, there was 33. No drugs were available in 1948 for blood pressure or to give it its correct term, hyper-tension; yet eighteen years later, 15 different drugs were available. Developments like this inevitably meant that costs rose and the burden of the NHS doubled between 1950 and 1970. Neither party reacted in this period by suggesting fundamental changes in structures or practice and the money was simply found from increased taxation. The share of expenditure taken by hospitals rose and that given to GPs relatively declined but treatment remained free at the point of delivery. Only in one area did the role of hospitals decline and that was mental health. Here the development of a complex armoury of drugs such as tranquillisers and anti-depressants made it possible for the mentally ill to live more fully in the community. The *Mental Health Act* of 1959 encouraged this development and the policy was enthusiastically pursued by both parties when in office.

Health remained an excellent illustration of consensus politics where it seemed almost impossible to distinguish between the approaches of Labour and Conservative. In terms of preventative initiatives, the Conservatives launched an anti-smoking campaign in 1957 and Labour banned cigarette advertising on television in 1965. Both sought to encourage healthier eating. It remained impossible to foretell how long the consensus could last as costs continued to escalate and hard choices had to be made, but in the 1950s, 1960s and 1970s consensus was the order of the day.

SKILLS BUILDER

How far do Sources O and P indicate that 1964–70 was a period of valuable progress in the provision of education in Britain?

Devaluation and recovery

In theory, the comfortable victory in the election of March 1966 was to usher in a really radical government bent on transforming Britain. There was no longer the excuse of an inadequate majority. In reality, the government now staggered from one crisis to another as it wrestled with the intractable problems of the British economy. It seemed to face failure at every turn. Almost immediately after the victory, a fresh sterling crisis developed. Some of the Cabinet, such as Roy Jenkins, wished to accept the inevitable and devalue and use the fall in sterling as an opportunity to boost exports, but Wilson was determined to fight on with the pound pegged at $2.80. The initial cause of this latest crisis was a strike by seamen, which hit exports. Wilson denounced it as communist-inspired. To defend sterling, a savage deflationary package was pushed through in July. The bank rate was raised, government spending was cut and restrictions were placed on **hire purchase**. Various tax increases were announced and a £50-limit placed as a foreign travel allowance. To control inflation, a Statutory Prices and Incomes Bill was passed, deeply repugnant to the trade unions. There was also a one-year freeze on wage and price increases. The package spelt the end of the National Plan, with its optimistic target of 4 per cent growth in the economy. George Brown initially resigned, but was then appointed Foreign Secretary, a post for which both his drinking habits and personality made him somewhat unsuited. The DEA lingered on for a time with a much-reduced role before being wound up. The Treasury had won. Sterling received a temporary reprieve and the $2.80 rate was held briefly.

One effect of Brown's move to the Foreign Office was to give a boost to all those in the Labour Party who favoured entry into the European Common Market. Brown was as keen as Heath on entry. Wilson agreed that a bid be made and the government's intention to apply was announced in November 1966. Wilson and Brown visited various European capitals in early 1967 and received support from many countries. Unfortunately, this

Definition

Hire purchase

Known traditionally in Britain as the 'never-never', this was buying goods and services on credit. It was a system of purchase widely developed in the United States before the Second World War but only really began developing in Britain during the 1950s.

Source Q

It was this resolute determination to make the best of it that led Wilson into one of his greatest indiscretions. The brief which the Treasury had prepared for the broadcast in which the Prime Minister explained the situation to the nation contained the sentences 'devaluation does not mean that the value of the pound in the hands of the British consumer . . . is cut correspondingly. It does not mean that the money in our pockets is worth 14 per cent less.' Wilson liked the phrase and when Gerald Kaufmann said that a relation of his was worried by the fact that her savings would buy 14 per cent less, he decided to appease the fears of her and many like her by making the Treasury wording a little punchier and reassuring her that 'the pound in her pocket' was not now worth 14 per cent less than the day before. Anyone who listened to the whole of his speech would have realised what he meant, but as a politician of his experience should have known, a telling phrase will always be taken out of context and used in evidence against the speaker. Wilson became stamped as the man who pretended that devaluation would not affect the buying power of the pound; worse still, the man who tried to pass off devaluation as a triumph instead of the economic defeat that it was. Tony Benn referred to his 'absurd broadcast saying the pound in your pocket won't be devalued', and if Benn could represent it in such a way how certain it was that the Tories would have a field day.

From Philip Ziegler, *Wilson: The Authorised Life*, published in 1993 did not include France and De Gaulle was still determined and able to block British entry. The whole bid ended in formal failure in November 1967, 12 months after the intention was announced.

November 1967 also witnessed an even more humiliating defeat for government policy – devaluation. A combination of circumstances determined the timing but the root cause was the overvaluation of a currency whose economy was doing less well than its competitors.

- The outbreak of the Arab-Israeli War in June closed the Suez Canal and harmed British trade, but additional harm was done by a series of dock strikes in London and Merseyside.

- October 1967 saw the worst monthly trade deficit in British History.

- Across the world, dealers were selling sterling. The bank rate was raised to a crisis 16 per cent. A key treasury adviser, Sir Alec Cairncross, persuaded first Callaghan, his political boss at the Treasury, and finally Wilson that sterling would have to be devalued by 14 per cent.

It was reduced to $2.40. As always Wilson was determined to put on a brave face and make the best of it and this was to lead him into one of his most serious political mistakes as his official biographer, Philip Ziegler makes clear (see Source Q).

Callaghan resigned as Chancellor at the end of the month and did a straight swap of jobs with Roy Jenkins, who now gave up the Home Office for the Treasury. Jenkins was determined to tackle the balance of payments issue and return the national accounts to the black. The result was a period of stringent budgets not unlike those of Stafford Cripps. Government spending was cut and reforms like the raising of the school leaving age postponed. This latter provoked the resignation of Lord Longford from the Cabinet. Taxation was raised to try and cut down the national propensity to consume imports the country could not really afford. The consumer found that petrol, cigarettes and drink were all to cost more and currency restrictions meant that foreign travel became even more difficult to undertake. Jenkins presented it as unpleasant but necessary medicine. For a time it seemed that it was not working and plans for even further devaluations and stronger deflationary medicine were drawn up. However, by the autumn of

Source R

In the last financial year, 1969–70, our national surplus was £550 million, the largest we have ever had.

Only five years ago, the outgoing Tory government left the largest deficit ever recorded in our history – running at minus £800 million and this was only the culminating year of a long period of economic decline. So in just five years, Labour has registered an improvement of more than £1300 million.

We have got out of the red in our national accounts. We are now strong and solvent and we intend to remain so.

From 'Now that Britain's strong lets make it great to live in', the Labour Election Manifesto, 1970

1969, as an upswing in world trade began, a balance of payments surplus was recorded. Jenkins' two years hard slog seemed to be paying off. The Labour election manifesto of 1970 made much of the achievement.

Jenkins prudently did not do what many chancellors have been tempted to do before an election, namely increase spending and cut taxes in a bid for temporary popularity. He maintained a careful posture of responsibility and fiscal rectitude, and public opinion appeared to be impressed. After a considerable period of unpopularity and lost by-elections, by 1970 the government appeared to be pulling ahead of the Conservatives, hence Wilson's decision to go for an election in June.

Denis Healey and defence

One of the most impressive ministers in the Wilson government stayed in one job for six years. Denis Healey brought a powerful intellect and a somewhat bullying personality to a very difficult job. Even before the stringency of the Jenkins period at the Treasury, Healey was determined to reduce Britain's defence commitments and expenditure in line with a shrunken economic power in the world. He brought in tough cost-benefit analysis and produced a clear new defence review. The decision was taken to scrap the British built TSR2 aircraft, being designed at vast expense to deliver Britain's nuclear bombs on Russia. No more aircraft carriers were to be built for the navy and expenditure on the territorial army was slashed. Despite much US pressure to stay, British military commitments east of Suez were run down from 1967. The defeat of the long-running Communist insurgency in Malaya enabled more and more troops to be withdrawn. Following the devaluation crisis, the pressure was on for further cuts, some of which Healey himself resented. Jenkins forced Healey to accept the cancellation of another British aircraft, the F111. Defence expenditure was to fall from 6 per cent of GDP to 4 per cent by 1971. The decision was made to withdraw altogether from Asia. Aden was abandoned and, despite protests from Malaya and Singapore, all British troops were to leave by 1971. Britain was no longer a world power. The poet Philip Larkin wrote a bitter epitaph on British decline.

Taming the unions (but not very much)

In March 1968, George Brown resigned as he often tried to do; this time his resignation was accepted. Various stories were told within the Foreign Office of his eccentric behaviour. It was said that at one diplomatic reception in South America, somewhat the worse for drink, he approached a figure, gorgeously attired in red and purple and suggested they dance. 'No', came the riposte, 'and for three reasons. One, this is the national anthem; two, I do not dance with drunks and three I am the Cardinal Archbishop.' If Brown's addiction to drink had not abated, neither had Wilson's addiction to reshuffles and George Brown's resignation gave him the opportunity for a major one. Michael Stewart moved back to the Foreign Office, which he had exchanged with Brown for the DEA in 1966. Two

Source S

Next Year we are to bring
    the soldiers home
For lack of money, and it
    is all right.
Places they guarded, or
    kept orderly,
Must guard themselves,
    or keep themselves
    orderly.
We want the money for
    ourselves at home
Instead of working. And
    this is all right.

From the poem,
Homage to a
Government by Philip
Larkin, published in
the anthology *High
Windows*, 1971.

friends, the diarists Barbara Castle and Richard Crossman were promoted. Crossman became Lord President and Leader of the House of Commons and Barbara Castle was named First Secretary of State and sent to head the newly reorganised Ministry of Labour, now renamed the Department of Employment and Productivity. Here, she heroically set about tackling what most people acknowledged was a major obstacle to Britain's economic advance, the behaviour of the unions and the chaos of industrial relations.

It was a brave decision and one in which she was whole-heartedly backed by Wilson. First the strike by the Seamen's Union in 1966 and then the dock strikes a year later had convinced him that it was necessary to act. Both the dockers and the seamen could have a particularly devastating effect on trade and the balance of payments as their striking could prevent goods and commodities from being imported and exported. A further spur was provided by the Conservatives, who produced proposals for reform in April 1968, entitled 'Fair Deal at Work'. These proposals included compulsory cooling-off periods before strikes and other reforms, and were well received. It appeared that public opinion was moving in favour of regulating union power. The problem lay in the whole history and traditions of unions and industrial relations in Britain. In 1906, a Liberal government had granted the British trade unions an extraordinary legal position, where they could exist within the law for all the benefits that brought but were outside the law with regard to any negative consequences, i.e. they could not be sued. Lawyers at the time had protested at the unfair situation that created but had been overruled by political calculation. The result was that there was a deep resentment

Source T

6.2 Barbara Castle holding up 'In Place of Strife', the government White Paper published on 17 January 1969

within the trade union movement of any suggestion to impose legal restraints and regulations, which ran counter to 60 years of legal immunity.

Barbara Castle's biographer sets out the issues at stake at the beginning of the crucial chapter on 'In Place of Strife':

Source U

The decision to legislate on industrial relations destroyed Barbara's career. Taken in a matter of weeks in the late autumn of 1968, it was a bold attempt to deliver to her patron Wilson the Holy Grail of industrial peace and the simultaneous humiliation of the Tories. She had set out to produce a policy that would be more eye catching than the Conservatives, to prove that in 1968, 'the year of the strike', the government still governed. Yet where she intended to restore the government's standing, she succeeded only in bringing it lower; and where she sought a personal triumph, she ended by being vilified throughout Labour circles. The circumstances that made legislation desirable also made it almost impossible to achieve.

From Anne Perkins, *Red Queen: The Authorised Biography of Barbara Castle*, published in 2003

The White Paper proposed to set up an Industrial Relations Court, to which the unions would be subject in certain circumstances. The minister was given powers to impose settlements in inter-union disputes, which had created anarchy in some industries, and could order a strike ballot before a strike. It was also proposed that there be a compulsory 28-day 'conciliation pause' before a strike took place. These proposals were vehemently disliked by the union leadership, who encouraged resistance within the Labour Party and even within the Cabinet. The result was an increasingly bitter struggle, which ended in the defeat of Castle and Wilson. Callaghan took the lead within the Cabinet in stopping the Bill and, as time went on, it became increasingly clear that the measure could not be got through. Jenkins, an initial supporter, wavered and then ran up the white flag. An angry Cabinet meeting in June finally put paid to the proposed legislation. Tony Benn described the scene in his diary entry for 17 June 1969:

Source V

It was a very, very tense meeting and Harold and Barbara had evidently taken the future into their own hands, relying on the fact that we couldn't get rid of them. But I'm not sure that if it had come to a choice between Harold and Barbara and the survival of the Labour Movement and Government, people would not let them go; and I think Harold knew that and that was why he was so angry. But he did emerge as a small man with no sense of history and as somebody really without leadership qualities. My opinion of Harold Wilson, if I haven't set it down in my diary recently, is very low indeed.

From Tony Benn, *The Benn Diaries*, published in 1995

This Cabinet meeting was followed by a long meeting with the TUC the next day at Number 10 in an attempt to find a face-saving formula. It emerged eventually under the title of 'A Solemn and Binding Agreement' by which the TUC promised to monitor strikes and labour disputes and use its influence to settle them. The prime minister tried to sell it as a major achievement and in his memoirs of his government wrote:

Source W

The year from the agreement of 18 June 1969, to the General Election of June 1970, was too short to show what the TUC could have achieved. But in case after case where it did intervene, in conditions where no Government, no legislation, could have had any assurance of success, they were successful. The reason why the TUC was involved was because the Downing Street undertaking, itself the direct result of In Place of Strife, had created a new and hopeful dimension in industrial relations.

From Sir Harold Wilson, *The Labour Government 1964–70:
A Personal Record*, published in 1971

Most commentators are more cynical about the agreement and the Labour-supporting historian, Kenneth O. Morgan, created a Labour life peer in 2000, wrote of it:

Source X

A virtually meaningless 'solemn and binding' covenant procedure was cobbled together by the government and the TUC: journalists ridiculed the phantom figure of 'Solomon Binding'. A Labour government had caved in abjectly to union power. At the same time, it was clear that Barbara Castle was a Pandora who had opened an ominous box. The shelf life of Solomon Binding could not be lengthy. Some form of industrial legislation to control the unions, perhaps from a future Tory government carrying out the terms of the right-wing Selsdon Park programme of January 1970, appeared inevitable.

From Kenneth O. Morgan, *Michael Foot: A Life*, published in 2007

SKILLS BUILDER

1 How far do Sources U, W and X agree that the attempt to reform the unions in 1969 was essentially a failure?

2 Compare Sources V and H regarding the personality and political style of Harold Wilson. Suggest why they might produce such differing pictures of the man.

Developments within the Conservative Party

Source Y

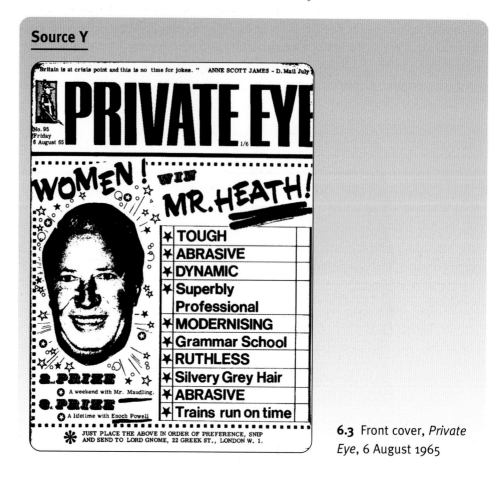

6.3 Front cover, *Private Eye*, 6 August 1965

The Conservatives had chosen a new leader in 1965. Alec Douglas-Home had stepped down and, for the first time, in a conscious attempt to avoid the controversy surrounding his appointment in 1963, there was an open election by all Conservative MPs. Edward Heath, who had much in common with Wilson, beat Reggie Maudling and Enoch Powell. Heath came from a similar social background to Wilson, had been born in the same year, 1916, and had attended a grammar school and then Oxford. He had had a 'good war', finishing as a lieutenant colonel, and had been spotted as a talented young Conservative hopeful. Macmillan had promoted him to the Cabinet and placed him in charge of Britain's bid to enter the European Community. Heath, in contrast to Wilson, was a seriously committed 'European'. He was also, however, in contrast to Wilson, often stiff and unrelaxed. He was unmarried and came across as humourless and unfriendly. In the House of Commons, Wilson was able to run rings round him, rather like Macmillan had with Gaitskell. Heath was in fact a very private person, a first-class musician and yachtsman – in this sense different from Wilson, who had few interests outside politics. Despite the differences in personality and style, in many respects they shared the 'consensus politics' that marked British political life in these years. Heath was sympathetic to the unions and had a notably good relationship with

Jack Jones, the new leader of the TGWU, whom he had met during the Spanish Civil War back in 1938. He was likely to give his policies a more free-market spin, such as that associated with the **Selsdon Park conference** in 1970, compared to Labour, but he essentially believed in the welfare state and government management of the economy to deliver full employment. Of his two opponents for the leadership, Maudling was even more centrist and 'liberal' than Heath. The other was a very different kettle of fish.

Enoch Powell was acknowledged as possibly the best speaker in the House of Commons and possessed of a mind of extraordinary if eccentric brilliance. Douglas Hurd, no friend to Powell, a close associate of Edward Heath and later Foreign Secretary under John Major, paid tribute to Powell's charisma:

Source Z

I never came close to understanding Enoch Powell. He was the only adversary in the House of Commons who ever seriously worried me. Others were nimble and could disconcert me for a moment, but Powell, by his appearance, voice and choice of words, radiated an authority which I had no immediate resources to match.

From Douglas Hurd, *Memoirs*, published in 2003

Macmillan, as prime minister, had found the intense face of his Minister of Health so disconcerting that he asked the Cabinet Secretary to move him from his normal place facing Macmillan across the Cabinet table. Powell was beginning to question 'consensus politics' and had resigned from his position in the Treasury in 1958 (see page 80) in protest against increased public spending. He became an increasingly vociferous critic of the role of government in managing the economy. He opposed nationalisation, prices and income policies and seemed to be becoming a supporter of an unfettered free market. The only role for the government was to control the supply of money and its own spending. In this sense, he looked forward to the Conservatism associated with Margaret Thatcher in the 1980s. Yet it was not his abandonment of consensus politics as far as economic policy was concerned that brought him notoriety but his foray into the issue of immigration and race relations.

Immigration and race relations

Immigration had slowly emerged as a political issue in the 1950s as Commonwealth citizens first from the West Indies and then from the Indian sub-continent began to settle in Britain. This tended to be in certain areas such as London, the Midlands and parts of Lancashire and West Yorkshire. The front benches of both parties operated a 'consensus' approach. They condemned racism, but sought to restrict the inflow. Labour had initially condemned the Conservative actions to do so when in government, but in 1965 tightened access to Britain even more, although

Definition

Selsdon Park conference
This conference was a meeting in January 1970 of Heath and his shadow Cabinet. The communiqué issued afterwards gave the impression of a shift to the right in Conservative thinking, i.e. a smaller role for the state and an emphasis on law and order. Wilson seized on it with the image of 'Selsdon Man', a wild right-wing extremist tearing up consensus politics. In reality, the communiqué was a last-minute improvisation. Heath had forgotten that he was holding a press conference to catch the Sunday papers and, when reminded one was about to happen, in desperation cried to his colleagues, 'What on earth am I going to say to them? We haven't decided anything.' Iain Macleod, a liberal in the Macmillan mould, responded, 'It's quite easy, Ted, you just tell them we believe in law and order.' The newspaper reports then carried a story of a shift to the right.

seeking to sweeten the pill with the setting up of a Race Relations Board to tackle discrimination against those already here. This process was to be repeated in 1968 with a new act. There was evidence of a 'white backlash against immigrants'. There had been riots in Notting Hill in 1958 and an overtly anti-immigration Conservative had defeated a Labour Cabinet minister in the supposedly safe Labour seat of Smethwick in 1964. Race and immigration were becoming issues, but issues that both front benches were anxious to keep out of the spotlight. Powell, sitting for a seat in Wolverhampton, found the issue raised by his constituents. He had been much affected by the terrible conflict in India in 1947 when as many as half a million may have died in communal conflict between Muslims and Hindus. He feared the arrival of what he termed 'communalism' in Britain. The growing tension in the USA over race in the 1960s added to his fears. He decided to raise the profile of debate.

Source AA

We must be mad, literally mad, as a nation to be permitting the annual inflow of some 50,000 dependants, who are for the most part the material of the future growth of the immigrant descended population. It is like watching a nation busily heaping its own funeral pyre.

As I look ahead, I am filled with foreboding. Like the Roman I seem to see 'the River Tiber foaming with much blood' that tragic and intractable phenomena which we watch with horror on the other side of the Atlantic but which there is interwoven with history and the existence of the States itself, is coming upon us here by our own volition and our own neglect.

From a speech by Enoch Powell delivered in Birmingham, 20 April 1968

He did not seem to have anticipated the furore it would cause. Heath immediately sacked him from the shadow Cabinet for what were seen as the racist implications of the speech. To many working-class voters, he became an overnight hero. A thousand London dockers marched out in support, Smithfield meat porters and Heathrow airport workers demonstrated in his favour and by the next day he had received 20,000 letters largely approving his stance. It brought him a degree of populist fame he had never enjoyed before, but destroyed his career as a governmental player. Michael Foot, left-wing Labour MP and future leader of the Labour Party, was to comment on the event to this effect:

Source BB

I believe it is the tragic irony of Enoch Powell's political life that the issue which made him famous is also the one which has barred his path to the highest office in the state. Without the Birmingham speech, the Tory kingdom would sooner or later have been his to command, for he had all the shining qualities which others lacked. Heath would never have outmanoeuvred him; Thatcher would never have stepped into the vacant shoes. It was a tragedy for Enoch, and a tragedy for the rest of us too.

From Michael Foot, *Loyalists and Loners*, published in 1986

The satirical magazine *Private Eye* was to produce one of its wittiest covers later in the year:

Source CC

6.4 Front cover, *Private Eye*, 6 December 1968

General election, 1970

An election was not due until 1971 and it appears that Wilson's decision to go for one in June 1970 was a last-minute one brought about by the improving economic situation and trade figures and good results for Labour in the May local elections. The weather was sunny and the country had high hopes of England repeating its football World-Cup victory of 1966, this time in Mexico. The election campaign was a rather lack-lustre affair. Wilson campaigned as a 'safe pair of hands' rather than as the begetter of radical change. The Tory, Willie Whitelaw, accused him of going round the country, stirring up apathy and Powell expressed the opinion that the election was about nothing more than the choice between a 'man with a pipe and a man with a boat', Wilson and Heath respectively. The weather deteriorated and England was knocked out of the World Cup. The man with a boat won to the surprise of all but himself.

Source DD

The campaign proper began on a First of June of glorious weather, and began for me about as badly as it could have done. In the morning I recorded a major interview for that evening's Panorama programme on the state of the economy. My interview was neither very good nor very bad, and Macleod's balancing one was about the same. The net effect of the programme was however damaging, for Cromer, ex-Governor of the Bank, spoke sceptically, partisanly and in my view dishonestly about the reality of our balance of payments turn-around, and was in no way balanced by Kearton who was supposed to be his left-of-centre counterpart.

After that unsatisfactory morning things proceeded to get much worse. I took John Harris (Labour press chief) to lunch at Brook's. On arrival he went into a telephone box to get the May export figure, which was due in at noon. As soon as he came back into the hall I could tell from his face that something was seriously wrong. Exports were down by £45 million on the previous month. As we knew that there had to be absorbed into the import figure the big lump sums of two Jumbo jets which had arrived for British Airways in May, the outlook for the trade figures, due out three days before polling day, was bleak. I proceeded gloomily to Preston, where I had my opening meeting of the campaign and delivered a desultory speech to an audience of 400 in a hall for 1200.

From Roy Jenkins, *A Life at the Centre*, published in 1991. Jenkins was Chancellor of the Exchequer at the time of the election.

Source EE

On the Sunday before the poll our lead in the opinion polls varied from 2.5 to 12.4 per cent. So our defeat four days later was as big a surprise for the Conservatives as it was for us: even George Brown lost his seat at Belper.

It is not easy even now to say what brought about this last reversal of public opinion. The newspaper polls were certainly unreliable, as the wide variety of their findings suggested. Moreover, as public opinion becomes steadily more volatile, impulsive decisions to change one's vote or to abstain become more common: even the more sophisticated techniques used nowadays cannot track such movements of opinion which may be occurring in millions every day. Bad trade figures in the last week may have given credibility to Heath's final attack on Labour's handling of the economy.

In any case there is no doubt that the 1970 general election was lost by the government rather than won by the opposition. The Wilson government of 1966–70 was not regarded as a success even by the Labour movement. It can now be seen as the turning point which started a long decline in Labour Party's fortunes.

From Denis Healey, *The Time of My Life*, published in 1989

Unit summary

What have you learned in this unit?

This unit has covered a considerable amount of information. You have learned about how the Labour government tried to transform the country and solve some of the problems associated with the nation's lack-lustre economic performance and how it was blown off course. There were spectacular and humiliating failures like the reluctant acceptance of devaluation, the failure to enter Europe and, most important of all, the inability to reform the trade unions. Against these were the liberalisation of everyday life and new educational opportunities associated with such new creations as the Open University.

What skills have you used in this unit?

You have encountered a large number of sources relating to this period which is particularly rich in both the number of important diaries it has given rise to and the number of high quality memoirs. It is important to realise that the three most famous diaries, those of Anthony Wedgewood Benn, Barbara Castle and Richard Crossman were all written for publication. Memoirs can often be defensive and self-serving. They therefore need approaching with care but not necessarily cynicism.

Exam style question

This is the sort of question that you will find on the examination paper as an (a) question. Use only the sources provided, but none of your own knowledge.

Study Sources R, DD and EE.

How far do the three sources suggest that it was the sudden deterioration in the trade figures during the election campaign that explains Labour's unexpected defeat in the general election of June 1970?

Explain your answer using the evidence of Sources R, DD and EE.

Exam tips

Like all (a) questions all three sources are primary and here it is essential to cross-reference them. Clearly the Labour Manifesto, Source R, makes great play of Labour's achievement in turning around the balance of payment deficit and both the other sources make reference to the apparently bad figures just before the election.

The implication of this might reasonably be 'inferred' that this was therefore very damaging. Certainly Jenkins writes extensively on the issue but then he was Chancellor of the Exchequer (use the attribution here). Healey, another Cabinet minister, thinks it important enough to mention but gives more emphasis to general disappointment with the Labour government.

RESEARCH TOPIC

In view of the number of published diaries and memoirs available, it would be an interesting exercise to research a particular event of a particular day and compare the differing viewpoints. Five or six individuals may have attended the same Cabinet meeting but when reading their individual accounts it can seem at times that they were attending different meetings.

7 Ted, Harold and Jim: Ruling an ungovernable nation, 1970–79

What is this unit about?

This unit examines the troubled years of the 1970s, recently described in the title of a book on the decade as 'When the Lights went out'. Ted Heath and the Conservative government came to power in June 1970, promising a no-nonsense solution to the national ills so clearly on display in the 1960s. Unions would have to abide by new laws, Britain would join Europe, government would be tidied up and made more efficient and all would be well.

Britain did join Europe, but all was not well. Northern Ireland seemed to be dissolving into anarchy, the unions refused to play by the new rules and took on the government. A new Arab-Israeli War threatened western oil supplies and induced an economic crisis. Inflation took off to hitherto unknown levels. Serious questions were asked about whether Britain, already the 'sick man of Europe' really was becoming ungovernable. Heath called a crisis election in February 1974, questioning who governed Britain – the elected government or the unions. The answer was unclear with no majority for either party. Clearly the country didn't know the answer or at least were divided as to what was the right answer. Wilson returned to power but was a shadow of the dynamic Wilson of 1964.

In 1976, he handed over to Callaghan, a man four years older than himself. For three years Callaghan wrestled with economic crisis and no majority. The Conservatives had selected a new leader, Margaret Thatcher, in 1975 and in the aftermath of the so-called 'winter of discontent', which again seemed to emphasise the problems of irresponsible and over-powerful unions, she won the election in May 1979. Not only was she the first woman to be prime minister, her government seemed to mark the end of consensus politics.

Key questions

- What were characteristics of Heath's Conservative government?
- What problems did the new government face?
- Why did Heath call and lose a crisis election in February 1974?
- How did the Wilson government cope with the problems of 1974–76?
- How successful were Labour under Jim Callaghan?
- How did the Conservative Party in opposition change?

Timeline

1970	June	Edward Heath becomes prime minister
1971	January	First British soldier killed in Ulster in the new outbreak of the 'Troubles'
	April	Barber Budget – big tax cuts and cuts in government spending
	August	*Industrial Relations Act* becomes law
	October	Heath wins the vote in House of Commons for entry into Europe – Tories joined by 69 Labour MPs
	November	NUM begins over-time ban
1972	January	NUM begins national strike
	March	Direct rule of Ulster imposed
	November	Statutory wage and pay-freeze – return to prices and incomes policy
1973	January	Britain joins EEC
	October	Arab-Israeli War sparks oil crisis
	November	Miners begin second over-time ban
1974	January	Three-day week to ration electricity
	February	Miners' strike and general election
	March	Wilson returns as prime minister – ends miners strike
	October	Second general election – Labour majority of 3
	August	First Civil Rights march in Northern Ireland
	November	IRA pub bombing in Birmingham – 21 killed
1975	February	Thatcher defeats Heath in Tory leadership election
	June	Referendum on British membership of Europe
	August	Annual inflation rate almost 27 per cent
	November	Opening of first British North Sea oil pipeline
1976	March	Wilson retires as prime minister, replaced by Callaghan
	September	Sterling crisis – Britain appeals to the IMF for help
	December	IMF loan on condition of cuts in government spending
1977	March	LIB-LAB pact
	June	Mass picket in Grunwick dispute
1978	January	Annual inflation rate drops to below 10 per cent
	July	LIB-LAB pact ends
	September	Callaghan decides against general election that was widely expected
	November	TGWU goes on strike – 'winter of discontent' begins
1979	January	Callaghan's 'Crisis. What Crisis?'
	February	Exceptionally cold weather and wave of strikes
	March	Government loses vote of confidence in Commons
	May	Thatcher wins general election with majority of 43

'HeathCo': the new government and its problems

The new Conservative government of Edward Heath came in with a bustle of no-nonsense efficiency that reflected the style and personality of the new prime minister. Short on smalltalk and often appearing ill at ease with his own back-benchers, he seemed only to relax and express himself freely through music. There was no 'kitchen cabinet' as there had been under Wilson. There were trusted assistants, such as the young ex-Foreign Office civil servant Douglas Hurd, but nothing like the gossipy, plot-sniffing coterie that surrounded Harold Wilson. Heath seemed most at home with two other civil servants, Sir William Armstrong, the Cabinet Secretary, and Robert Armstrong (no relation), Heath's personal secretary.

Heath was prickly and could take offence easily, when in Roy Jenkins' famous phrase he 'flapped around like an affronted penguin'. Jenkins, who had known him since they were students together at Oxford, also refers to his 'grumpy integrity', which he respected. There was something open and honest about him, which, after the duplicitous Harolds (Wilson and Macmillan), was refreshing but could be unnerving. Here was a prime minister who was likely to do what he said he was going to do and for the reasons he said he was doing it. He was firmly in charge of his Cabinet and the whole government came over as the board of a company, with Heath as the assertive chief executive. The satirical magazine *Private Eye* immediately picked up on this and in place of the spoof 'Mrs Wilson's Diary' of the Labour years introduced a column 'Heathco – a message from the Managing Director'.

Source A

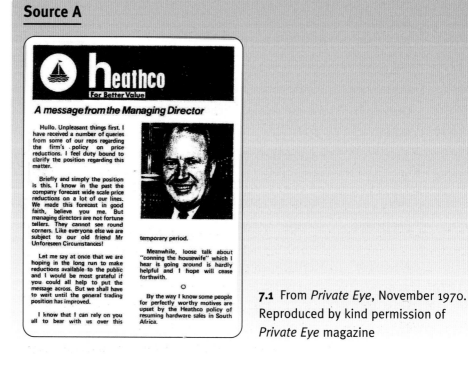

7.1 From *Private Eye*, November 1970. Reproduced by kind permission of *Private Eye* magazine

It was unfortunate for the Conservatives that the government came over as a one-man band. Enoch Powell had been relegated to the back-benches. The other outstanding Tory, Iain Macleod, was appointed Chancellor of the Exchequer but died five weeks later, to be replaced by the little-known Anthony Barber. Reggie Maudling, the other major figure on the Tory front bench, became Home Secretary but was becoming detached from the day-to-day work of a minister and eventually resigned in 1972, following accusations of improper financial associations. There was a younger assortment of talented Tories: Margaret Thatcher at education, Peter Walker at housing and Jim Prior at agriculture, but none could challenge the managing director of the firm who laid down the framework of policy.

Heath had a very clear idea of what was wanted and what was not wanted. Not wanted were some of the **quangos** established by Labour and the Price and Incomes Board. This was part of the necessary slimming down of government to make it more efficient. What was wanted was a new framework for industrial relations, established by legislation similar to that proposed by Barbara Castle. A new Industrial Relations Court would see fair play for workers and employers and end the industrial anarchy that bedevilled the country. Central to the whole Heath solution was Britain's entry to the EEC. However, the scale of the problems he faced more than matched the determination he could summon to carry his policies through. Despite the improvements made in the national finances under Jenkins, Labour handed over a situation that any government would find difficult to cope with. John Cole, the BBC political commentator, draws attention to these in his memoirs.

Definition

Quangos

Quasi-autonomous Non-governmental Organisation, or quangos for short, were bodies that, whilst funded by government and controlled by government appointees, were meant to act with some degree of independence from the government.

Source B

Ted Heath began with a real problem in retaining public confidence. There was never any chance that he could deliver his decisive election promise: to reduce the rise in prices 'at a stroke'. After only five months in office, the Organisation for Economic Co-operation and Development was warning him that inflation was becoming dangerous. Wage increases were running ten per cent ahead of productivity. Britain was in its all-too-familiar state of crisis.

The government's inherited difficulty was that, although some Labour people blamed Roy Jenkins for losing the election by introducing a 'responsible' budget, this puritanical stance did not extend, in Labour's dying months to wages. So Ted Heath came to office with wage inflation accelerating.

There was an added difficulty. The government was committed to bring in an Industrial Relations Bill, to control the unions. In this, it had much support from a public which was fed up with wildcat strikes. But this legislation forced the TUC, fresh from its victory against Harold Wilson and Barbara Castle over In Place of Strife, into opposition to Ted Heath. It was therefore unwilling even to consider the voluntary wage restraint which was so obviously needed.

From John Cole, *As It Seemed to Me: Political Memoirs*, published in 1995

The problems of Northern Ireland

In Cole's birthplace, on the other side of the Irish Sea, another seemingly intractable problem festered. A Roman Catholic civil rights movement had developed in the province of Ulster, the only part of Ireland still under the British Crown and therefore part of the UK. Since the early 1920s, it had enjoyed its own parliament, but was dominated by Protestant loyalists, fiercely resistant to being integrated into Roman Catholic Eire, with its government in Dublin. The large Roman Catholic minority in Ulster was viewed as potential traitors and a system of effective apartheid operated. Catholics married Catholics and attended Catholic schools. The two communities lived side by side but in mutual distrust and incomprehension.

Catholic protests in 1967 and 1968, partly stimulated by the American Civil Rights Movement, produced a Protestant backlash. The Labour government, in the shape of Jim Callaghan as Home Secretary, acted firmly and in August 1969 sent in units of the British Army to protect the Catholics, who initially welcomed them. By 1970, this honeymoon had ended and Catholic attacks on British troops, as a hated ancient enemy, were taking place. The almost defunct Irish Republican Army (IRA) was revitalised and a breakaway group calling itself the Provisional IRA was established in Londonderry and Belfast and began to wage a guerrilla war. Arms paid for in the USA seeped across the border from the Republic. Violence escalated throughout the province and spilled over into England. In Ulster, 16 civilians were killed in 1970. In 1971, 61 civilians and 43 soldiers died violently. Here was another mess requiring the attention of the 'managing director'.

A promising start, 1970–71

Despite the scale of the problems, for just over 12 months all seemed to be going according to plan, as another BBC journalist relates:

Source C

1971 was the high point of Heath's premiership. He won a parliamentary majority of over a hundred in favour of Britain's entry into the Common Market. In August he skippered *Morning Cloud* [his yacht] to victory in the Admiral's Cup, the foremost ocean-racing trophy in the world, and allowed a young Granada producer, John Birt, to make a special television documentary about his sailing. The programme depicted Heath as the great helmsman steering the nation to victory. 'If you are going to helm effectively, you can never let your attention waver for a moment', Heath told Granada, 'what is important is sailing to win.' Heath was using television to cultivate the image of the strong leader.

From Michael Cockerell, *Live from Number 10: The Inside Story of Prime Ministers and Television*, published in 1988

Undoubtedly for Heath, the great achievement was getting French, then parliamentary approval for Britain's entry into the European community. Heath himself played a large part in winning over the French President Pompidou in May. Thereafter, the struggle shifted to Westminster and the difficulties in getting it through parliament. Enoch Powell was resolutely opposed as were a small band of Conservatives following his lead. Labour had swung overwhelmingly against and Heath was only able to carry the day with a group of Labour rebels led by Roy Jenkins. Heath's triumph in October was made all the sweeter by the knowledge that it left the Labour Party weakened and divided.

1971 was also marked by a popular tax-cutting Budget from Tony Barber in April; designed to stimulate the economy. The standard rate of income tax was cut by 2.5 per cent. Some of the associated cuts in government spending were less popular, notably the ending of free school milk. Here, it was the Education Secretary, Margaret Thatcher, who got the blame, appearing in the public eye as 'Thatcher – milk snatcher'. In other ways, Thatcher's supervision of the Education Department was non-controversial and marked more by continuity than dramatic reversal of Labour policies. She launched the new Open University, backing it against some Conservative critics who thought it a typical Wilson gimmick. She withdrew Crosland's famous circular encouraging local authorities to push forward with comprehensives, but approved the vast majority of schemes sent to her by local authorities and the pace of the 'comprehensivisation' of the nation's secondary schools continued unabated. One of the most talented of Heath's lieutenants, Peter Walker, pushed through a radical overhaul of local government and his Local Government Act of 1972 swept away historic boundaries in the name of increased efficiency. Tiny but independent Rutland disappeared, merged in with Leicestershire and new authorities like Cleveland and Humberside were created. It horrified traditional Conservatives.

Labour relations

The other great plank of the Heath programme, a new framework for industrial relations was also achieved in 1971. A hugely complex Bill was laboriously pushed through parliament by the Employment Secretary, Robert Carr, assisted by a young Tory lawyer, holding the post of Solicitor General, **Geoffrey Howe**.

Biography

Geoffrey Howe

A major Conservative politician of the 1970s and 1980s. He served as Chancellor of the Exchequer from 1979 to 1983 and then as Foreign Secretary. His resignation speech in 1990 was devastating to his erstwhile leader Margaret Thatcher. It was not what was expected from the politician whose powers of attack in the Commons Denis Healey famously likened to being 'savaged by a dead sheep'.

Source D

So the Bill, as published on 3 December 1970, was for me a particular disappointment. It was a most complex piece of legislation. It was going to be hard to sell, in Parliament as well as to the trade union movement. Its value as a foundation for the 'law with a human face', for which we yearned, was sharply reduced. We settled down for the long parliamentary battle ahead. . . . One aspect of this particular confrontation had struck me as particularly sad. That was the uncompromising bitterness with which Barbara Castle opposed every aspect of our Bill. The problems we were facing were exactly the same as those that she had tried to tackle. So too were many of the solutions. How I wished then that she could have seen her way to joining us in the task of shaping them! But our reaction to her own earlier efforts might be seen as equally unconstructive.

From Sir Geoffrey Howe, *Conflict of Loyalty*, published in 1994

Blown off course

Heath might have enjoyed a seafaring triumph in 1971, as Source C points out, but by the end of the year it was clear that the political weather was increasingly dangerous. A Conservative government intent on reducing the role of government was forced to nationalise one of the most prestigious companies in the country. Rolls Royce, maker of prestige cars and even more important as the maker of aeronautical engines, faced bankruptcy. It could not be allowed to collapse. Likewise in Scotland, the threatened termination of Upper Clyde Shipbuilders, with the loss of 4000 jobs, was politically unacceptable and the government stepped in with a large subsidy. There was also a new spirit of violence in the country, not confined to Northern Ireland. Geoffrey Howe recorded an example of this shocking development in his memoirs.

Source E

It was at about that time that we had a particularly disagreeable foretaste of the worst kind of violence, from a self-styled anarchist group calling itself the Angry Brigade. They bombed the home of the Employment Secretary, Robert Carr, and my name was found to be on their hit list. We received a number of telephone threats, and a twenty-four-hour police guard was mounted on our home. It is surprising how quickly such things become part of the routine. When I arrived home early one evening, Amanda spoke up brightly, 'Oh, by the way Daddy, I took another threatening phone call for you this afternoon.' It was a strange world in which our children were having to grow up. The hazards have not grown any less since then.

From Sir Geoffrey Howe, *Conflict of Loyalty*, published in 1994

In Northern Ireland, Heath's trusted lieutenant, the amiable Willie Whitelaw, wrestled with the intractable problem of centuries-old sectarian hatred. The violence continued to grow with four bomb explosions and thirty shootings a day on average. In August 1971, Whitelaw agreed to the request of the Northern Ireland government for internment of IRA suspects, i.e. detention without trial. It was a disaster. No senior IRA figure was caught and a third of those arrested were released within two days. It merely infuriated the Roman Catholic community and brought the IRA additional support. Worse was to follow when, in January 1972, a banned civil rights meeting went ahead and 14 unarmed Catholics were killed by the British Army. 'Bloody Sunday', as it became known, was a triumph for the IRA. Money for weapons poured in from North America's Irish communities. In the course of 1972, 223 civilians and 103 soldiers died. Loyalist paramilitaries now killed Catholics and tit-for-tat violence became commonplace. In March, Heath decided to suspend the Stormont Parliament and rule Ulster directly from London. It marked the end of a 50-year experiment. Secret talks were held with the IRA, but got nowhere, and the IRA decided to extend the bombing to mainland Britain.

The miners

At home, other horrors were brewing for the Heath government, escalating inflation and pay claims and ultimately confrontation with one of the most powerful unions, the National Union of Miners (NUM). It was soon clear that the *Industrial Relations Act* was not working as was hoped. The new Industrial Relations Court, which had powers to enforce ballots before a strike and a cooling-off period, could only act if unions registered under the Act. Most unions simply refused to register as the TUC advised and most employers, not wanting trouble with their workforce, also ignored the court. It found that it had little to do. When it did act, as in a controversial case in the London Docks in 1972, ordering the arrest of five shop stewards in an unofficial dispute, a national dock strike was threatened. The government sent in a hitherto obscure government official, the Official Solicitor, to secure the men's release. An attempt was made to use the Act in the rail strike in May 1972. The membership of the National Union of Railwaymen (NUR) simply voted 6 to 1 to continue the strike. The Act was clearly a failure and was bringing government into contempt as being unable to enforce its policy.

The government found itself confronted with a wage explosion with pay increases running ahead of inflation and fuelling further inflation. The miners, in a declining industry, had accepted moderate pay settlements over the past 15 years in return for job security and a policy of voluntary redundancies as uneconomic pits were closed. Now they demanded a catch up. In 1971, they gained 14 per cent when inflation was 7 per cent. The government, as the ultimate paymaster in the nationalised industries, felt that wage demands should be moderated. The miners, traditionally moderate since 1945, were increasingly under the influence of more extreme leaders. The Scottish Communist, Mick McGahey, became

Definition

Flying pickets and picketing

Picketing is the placing of striking workers outside their place of employment with the object of persuading other workers not to go in to work but to support the strike. The law since 1875 allowed 'peaceful picketing' such as persuasion, but this often became blatant intimidation and the forcible prevention of working, which was illegal. Flying pickets are small bands of strikers that can quickly move to any workplace associated with the strike. They would often intimidate rather than 'peacefully persuade' other workers.

vice president of the NUM and, in Yorkshire, the militants were becoming more influential. The Coal Board offered 8 per cent for 1972. This was rejected by the union and a national strike by the miners began in January.

The strike was to bring to prominence a young Yorkshire activist of militantly left-wing views, one Arthur Scargill. Scargill had already established a local reputation in two unofficial disputes in 1969 and 1970. The 1969 strike witnessed the first widespread use of '**flying pickets**'. Using cars and minibuses, hundreds of miners could descend unexpectedly on the chosen target to close it and swamp any police cover. The tactic was widely adopted by the NUM in the 1972 dispute. A coke depot belonging to the West Midland Gas Board at Saltley, near Birmingham, became the focus of a battle of wills and tactics between the miners and the government. Thousands of miners arrived and, under the direction of 'General' Scargill, the depot was successfully closed. The Home Secretary, Reggie Maudling, explained his sense of helplessness in his memoirs.

Source F

The numbers of strikers involved was so great, and feelings were running so high, that any attempt by the relatively small body of police who could be assembled to keep the depot open by force could have led to very grave consequences. Some of my colleagues asked me afterwards why I had not sent in troops to support the police, and I remember asking them one simple question, 'If they had been sent in, should they have gone in with their rifles loaded or unloaded?'

From Reginald Maudling, *Memoirs*, published in 1978

Saltley closed its gates on 11 February. Coal stocks at power stations were rapidly running down and power cuts occurred. The government decided to surrender. The NUM secured almost everything they could think of asking for. Miners got a settlement more than twice the rate of inflation. It was, in **Douglas Hurd**'s words, a 'public and disastrous defeat' for the government.

Biography

Douglas Hurd

A Conservative MP from 1974, he initially had been a career civil servant in the Foreign Office and there was always something of the civil servant rather than the committed party politician about him. Despite this he became Home Secretary under Margaret Thatcher and challenged for the Party leadership as a compromise candidate in 1990. He came a poor third but served the winner, John Major, as Foreign Secretary until 1995.

The growing economic problems of 1972 forced the government into what became popularly known as a U-turn. Two problems confronted the government, growing inflation and growing unemployment, which reached over a million in 1972. The inflation had complex causes. Partly, it was international, arising from the depreciation of the US dollar as a consequence of the Vietnam War. Partly, it was a result of government policy to stimulate the economy, the so-called Barber boom. Cuts in taxation, combined with low interest rates led to a splurge of borrowing and an explosion in house prices. It may, in part, have been caused by the introduction of the new decimal currency, when such historic coins as the half-crown (12.5p) disappeared. It was certainly caused by spiralling wage increases. In the three full years from 1971 to 1973, prices increased at an annual average of 9 per cent. Male industrial earnings were increasing by almost 14 per cent without the necessary increase in productivity to justify it. The result was even greater inflation.

The miners' victory of February 1972 encouraged other workers to press for bigger and bigger increases. The answer, it seemed to Heath, other than allowing galloping unemployment to discipline the workforce, was to return to a government prices and incomes policy. Throughout the autumn of 1972, talks were held with the TUC and **CBI** to see if a voluntary wage agreement was possible. The unions, already incensed by the Industrial Relations Act, and the TUC, being quite incapable of disciplining their members, broke off the talks in November. Heath promptly introduced a three-stage prices and incomes policy, beginning with Phase 1, a six-month pay freeze. A pay board was introduced in 1973. Phase III followed in the autumn of 1973. The policy actually favoured the less well off with flat-rate increases, but this did not save it from union denunciation as oppression of the working class. The adoption of an incomes policy, in direct contradiction to the very public dropping of it in 1970, was the real essence of the U-turn, made so much of later by so-called Thatcherites. In reality, Heath was always an interventionist and 'Selsdon Man' (see page 117) was largely a product of Labour Party propaganda and Thatcherite mythology. At the time, only Enoch Powell, among Tory MPs, denounced the return to an incomes policy. Thatcher herself, Keith Joseph and Geoffrey Howe, all later to be associated with the return to 'market forces' and the damning of government intervention, voted with and supported Heath.

To begin with in 1973, it looked as if the policy might work, but a fresh disaster hit the country. The outbreak of a new Arab-Israeli War in October led to a reduction in oil supplies to the West from the Middle East. The price of oil on the world market suddenly rocketed, undermining much of the cheap energy base of western prosperity. The price multiplied by a factor of five between January 1972 and January 1974. Suddenly British coal became more important.

Definition

CBI
The Confederation of British Industry (CBI) is a pressure group representing the interests of the boards of directors of companies in Britain.

Source G

During November 1973 the earth began to move under the Government's feet. Our oil supplies were going to be cut by the producers. There was an immense confusion of information and much hectic diplomacy, so no one could yet tell how harshly we would have to cut our consumption. At the same time the Government was being drawn into a struggle with the miners on incomes policy. The Conservative Party, its leader, its ministers, its backbenchers and its supporters in the country had already been beaten on this very ground in 1972. Most of us had dreaded, beyond anything else, a further engagement with the miners. Yet here we were being manoeuvred once again towards the same fatal field, still littered with relics of the last defeat.

From Douglas Hurd, *Memoirs*, published in 2003

Hurd and other Tories close to Heath were right to fear a further confrontation with the miners. Joe Gormley, the moderate president of the NUM, was only too happy to avoid a confrontation and an open challenge to the government's pay policy, but the open and straightforward behaviour of Heath made a confrontation inevitable as Cambridge historian Peter Clarke relates:

Source H

Heath nonetheless sought an unofficial deal with NUM, the union of which he was most fearful. Again, Gormley himself was appreciative of Heath's good will, and he tipped the wink that a payment for 'unsocial hours' might be enough to appease the miners. What made a second coal strike inevitable was the fact that Heath guilelessly wrote this provision into the general guidelines for phase three, instead of keeping it up his sleeve as a special treat for the miners alone. The NCB therefore made its full and final offer at once, only to find it summarily rejected by the NUM, which began an overtime ban in November. Thus the government became locked into a further conflict with the miners, this time with the complication that stage three had statutory backing. This meant that the miners could be represented as taking a political stand, challenging the government itself.

From Peter Clarke, *Hope and Glory: Britain 1900–2000*, published in 1996

To some in the NUM, such as Scargill, the strike was political. Trade union power could be used to bring down the capitalist system. The government was better prepared this time and introduced a three-day week in December to save power and the demand for coal. The introduction of the three-day week, where work only took place for three days not five days in the week, cut 40 per cent from productive activity, but produced only a 5 per cent fall in output, a fact raising serious questions about the normal productivity of British industry. In February, Heath decided to strengthen his hand by fighting and winning a general election on the theme 'who governs Britain?' Despite the question, the prime minister was anxious not to polarise the country and avoided a union-bashing campaign which was probably his best hope of success. Both Labour and the Tories were less than exciting and many felt that the small Liberal Party was the most interesting thing on offer. Enoch Powell probably damaged Heath's chances by leaving the Tories and standing as a Unionist in Northern Ireland. He urged the voters in Britain to vote Labour as the best option for getting out of Europe. A quiet election at the end of February produced a **hung parliament**, perhaps the very worst of results. The Liberals did exceptionally well, gaining 19 per cent of the popular vote but only 14 MPs as a result of the British first-past-the-post system. The Tories, with 38 per cent, gained 297 and Labour, with a similar share of the popular vote, 301. Heath sought a deal with Jeremy Thorpe, the Liberal leader, but in the end failed to get one. Harold Wilson was called to the palace to become prime minister for a second stint. Once again it appeared a triumph for union power as this cartoon of March 1974 makes clear:

Definition

Hung parliament
This is a parliament in which no party has an overall majority.

Source I

7.2 Cartoon by Cummings, *Daily Express*, 8 March 1974

Whether the Heath government should be seen in a positive or a negative light divided Conservatives, as the two following extracts make clear. Julian Critchley was a liberal Conservative MP of many years standing.

Source J

To his intimates Ted Heath was both warm and friendly but his intimates did not include the great majority of Tory backbenchers, some of whom at least still carried scars inflicted by Ted when he was the party's chief whip at the time of Suez. He was a highly competent Prime Minister (Reggie Maudling told the 1922 committee in my hearing that Ted was the most effective of the three Tory Prime Ministers under whom he had served) with none of the dictatorial characteristics that Margaret Thatcher would show when she was in office.

From Julian Critchley, *A Bag of Boiled Sweets: An Autobiography*, published in 1994

SKILLS BUILDER

Using Sources H, J and K and your own knowledge, how far do you agree that Edward Heath was a highly competent prime minister?

Source K

Heath lost the ability to control events paradoxically because he tried to control too much: all the complex machinery of prices and incomes control – the Pay Board, the Price Commission and the rest – left the government still helpless in the face of soaring imported food and commodity prices on the one hand and the industrial muscle of the miners on the other. The lesson Mrs Thatcher took from the Heath government was not so much monetarism which she grasped later as a useful technical explanation, but rather a compelling affirmation of an old Tory article of faith – the self-defeating folly of over-ambitious government.

From John Campbell, *Margaret Thatcher*, revised edition published in 2009

Wilson as centre half, 1974–76

Wilson returned to office, less the irrepressible 'smart-arse' of 1964 and more the experienced and slightly wearied statesman. He announced that he would play in a less prominent position, no longer the main striker but a centre half, playing from the back. His colleagues found him less interfering and less concerned with Cabinet plots. He almost seemed to be working out his time to retirement. He was not old by prime ministerial standards, a mere 58, yet he seemed older. Peter Hennessy, in his study of the office of prime minister, comments:

Source L

In gearing up for his last great political fix, Wilson, too, had to overcome serious health problems. From the beginning of the last premiership, fellow ministers had detected a lassitude that could not be explained away by the Prime Minister's increasing fondness for brandy. He rambled in Cabinet and sometimes failed to sum up. His deputy, Ted Short, recalls 'a Cabinet meeting one afternoon, an awful Cabinet meeting when we were going to alter the secrecy laws and it got into the most hopeless confusion. Everybody was absolutely exasperated and angry and furious about it. Nothing emerged from it at all.

From Peter Hennessy, *The Prime Minister; The Office and its Holders since 1945*, published in 2000

Despite his age and increasing fondness for brandy, Wilson was still capable of dominating prime minister's question time, running rings round Heath and then out-smarting the young Margaret Thatcher, Heath's successor in 1975. He could still display a pretty wit as this memo sent on 1 April 1974, by him to the head of the Cabinet 'Think Tank', the Central Policy Review Staff, illustrates:

Source M

In view of the current crisis, I would be grateful if you would give consideration to the following figures

Population of the United Kingdom	54,000,000
People aged 65 and over	14,000,000
People aged 18 and under	18,000,000
People working for the Government	9,000,000
The Armed Forces	2,300,000
Local Government employees	9,800,000
People who won't work	888,000
People detained at Her Majesty's pleasure	11,998
Balance left to do the work	2

You and I, therefore must work harder, especially you, as I have felt no evidence of your considerable weight since I took office

1 April 1974   HW

From Peter Hennessy, *Whitehall*, published in 1999

Source N

For month after month, the Government had sat back watching inflation rise; frightened apparently of the political cost of confronting the unions with the inflationary consequences of their actions, listening uncomplainingly to the self justifying nonsense emerging from the lips of one union leader after another . . . It is difficult to imagine greater irresponsibility.

From Edmund Dell, *A Hard Pounding: Politics and Economic Crisis, 1974–76*, published in 1993

Wilson, however, had no ready answers to the mounting economic crisis. He had no appetite for confronting the unions, as the new junior treasury minister made clear in his memoirs, see Source N.

Party unity and Europe

Source O

7.3 Cartoon by 'Trog' Wally Fawkes, *Observer*, 23 March 1975

SKILLS BUILDER

Study Source O. Try to identify the different Labour Cabinet members in the boat. What is the message of the cartoon?

Wilson's real priority appeared to be the saving of party unity, seriously threatened by the issue of Europe. Since the Labour bid to join Europe in 1968, the party had overwhelmingly swung round to an anti-European stance. Many from the British left saw the European Community as a rich man's club devoted to capitalism and there was a growing mood within the party to reject the whole European idea and withdraw. However, a substantial minority of Labour MPs, led by Roy Jenkins, still believed that membership was good for Britain. Wilson had never been a Euro-enthusiast like Jenkins and Heath, but he was increasingly convinced that withdrawal would be a disaster. His Foreign Secretary, Jim Callaghan, tended to share the same view. Both of them worked closely together to see if they could salvage Britain's continuing membership and party unity.

It was a tall order and some have argued that it was Wilson's greatest achievement in this, his final government. He adopted Benn's idea of a referendum as an alternative to a party policy of outright withdrawal. He claimed that he and Callaghan would try to renegotiate terms but if this failed, the government would recommend withdrawal. He drew out the procedure, not giving either side the chance to take an irrevocable stand against one another and shatter the party. He was able to gain sufficient minor concessions from the Europeans to persuade a majority of the Cabinet to back staying in. However, it was agreed that Cabinet members could campaign on either side in the referendum. Benn and Foot campaigned enthusiastically for a 'No' vote along with Enoch Powell. Jenkins and Heath campaigned enthusiastically for a 'Yes'. Wilson supported the 'Yes' campaign which meant staying in Europe, but kept a low profile. The result of the referendum on 5 June 1975 was a clear majority for staying in, in almost all parts of the UK. Tony Benn's judgement in his diary was that 'Harold has scored a tremendous triumph'.

There was no shortage of talent in the Wilson government.

- Callaghan went to the Foreign Office and mended fences with the USA. He was much more in favour of good relations with the USA, in the consensus tradition, than Heath had been.

- The cheerfully energetic Denis Healey went to the Treasury, the most important and challenging job. As Chancellor of the Exchequer, he served for five gruelling years.

Wilson, Callaghan and Healey were very much the managing inner team. Roy Jenkins returned to the Home Office, but his stock had fallen as a leading pro-European and he was no longer seen as a likely leader. The diarist Richard Crossman died of cancer in April 1974, but the two other notable diarists Barbara Castle and Tony Benn (born Anthony Wedgwood Benn) continued in the Cabinet. Benn was increasingly the standard bearer of the far left. He had become a vigorous opponent of Britain's membership of the European Community and now at the Department of Industry pushed for much greater state ownership, somewhat to the embarrassment of Wilson. He was a leading member of the Labour Party's National Executive, the hero of the left-leaning party activists. He had pushed for a commitment to nationalise the top 25 firms in the country. The NEC agreed, but Wilson did not. Benn was to have a very unhappy relationship with the prime minister, who seized the first opportunity to clip his wings and in 1975 reshuffled him to the Department of Energy.

Note: interesting figure of speech. Kenneth Morgan, in "Britain since 1945" (1992), uses the same phrase when describing Benn's transfer to the D. of Energy (p. 377). Lynch the tbh's authors for plagiarism? Yes, indeed we should! I'd strongly recommend them to use footnotes to reference sources (even if stylistical ref. only).

— R. B.
Mar 2014

Source P

"Damn thing's STILL trying to kick me!"

7.4 Cartoon by Paul Rigby in the *Sun*, 4 June 1973 (nisyndication.com)

SKILLS BUILDER

How is Tony Benn (cracking the whip) portrayed in terms of his effect on the Labour Party?

The other leading left-wing figure in the Cabinet was **Michael Foot**, also an opponent of EEC membership but increasingly a crucial member of the government. He was sent to the Department of Employment and became the key linkman with the trade unions.

As well as seasoned talent, there were up and coming young figures of promise such as David Owen and Shirley Williams. For all their abilities, Wilson and his team would have their work cut out in view of the scale of the problems.

Britain from 1974 to 1975

The two years of the Wilson government were among the most crisis-ridden in modern British history. Violence in Ulster escalated and spilled over into mainland Britain with bomb scares in many major cities. In Wales and Scotland, separatist parties began to do well, threatening the very existence of the UK. There seemed to be no answer to the power of the trade unions, which had now humiliated governments of both parties. Only slavish appeasement of union demands seemed an option and with this came escalating inflation, reaching 27 per cent in 1975. Shares tumbled and foreigners withdrew their money. The FTSE index fell from 544 in May 1972 to 146 in December 1974. Living standards were actually falling

Biography

Michael Foot (born 1913)
A traditional left-wing rebel, he had never served in government before 1974. He was an ex-Bevanite and CND supporter of many years standing and a writer and journalist of talent. He could be a brilliant speaker, but his careless dress sense led to the press nicknaming him Worzel Gummidge after the figure of a television scarecrow.

Source Q

The British government is now so clearly headed towards a policy of total confiscation that anyone who has any wealth left is taking any chance to get it out of the country. The price can only be slower economic growth and still lower living standards for all the British, rich and poor. Goodbye, Great Britain, it was nice knowing you.

From *Wall Street Journal*, 29 April 1975

for the first time in 40 years. Inflation ate away into savings and house prices fell 13 per cent in 1974 and 16 per cent in 1975. Even the population fell as more and more sought to emigrate. Britain appeared to be washed up. On 6 May 1975, an American commentator on CBS stated, 'Britain is drifting slowly towards a condition of ungovernability.' A week before, the prestigious *Wall Street Journal* commented on the latest Budget. Taxation had reached frighteningly high levels with the highest rate of tax on earned income at 83 per cent and on 'unearned income' at 98 per cent.

Some immigrants were trying to settle in Britain, but their endeavours elicited this comment in the *Daily Mail*:

Source R

'No, we're not police—we're psychiatrists.'

7.5 Cartoon by 'Mac', *Daily Mail*, 16 January 1974

SKILLS BUILDER

Compare the image of Britain given in Sources Q and R.

There was a growing extremism in political life, symbolised by the greater prominence in the NUM of such committed political activists as Arthur Scargill. A new group of left-wing activists were coming to the fore in universities and in some urban areas. They looked to the memory of Trotsky for inspiration, rather than Stalin. Some of these sought to take over local Labour parties, shouting down the traditional moderates, who had been the bastion of the party often for decades. In many areas the process was easy as badly attended meetings could be dominated and key local positions occupied. Resolutions were passed calling for extensive nationalisation and confiscatory taxation. There was a frightening loss of grip on reality. Consensus politics was being challenged as never before since 1945.

Almost symbolising the state of Britain was the official residence allocated to Jim Callaghan as Foreign Secretary, see Source S.

Just about surviving

The most urgent matter was to settle the miners' dispute. The new government's strategy was simplicity itself – give in. Miners received enormous pay increases with the wage bill of the industry increasing by 32 per cent. This clearly was likely to ratchet up the pay demands of other workers and inflation was already rising dangerously. The other early requirement was to enlarge the governments' hold on power with another election. Wilson stuck it out until October 1974 and then fought a quiet campaign on the grounds that Labour was more likely than the Conservatives to preserve social harmony. There was talk of a 'social contract' with the unions by which, in return for various concessions in welfare and legislation on work practices, the unions would behave responsibly when it came to wage demands. Basically, Wilson promised peace and quiet or at any rate more peace and quiet than Heath. The electorate just about believed him. Labour's share of the popular vote increased and their seats rose from 301 to 319, giving them an overall majority of 3. There were 13 Liberals, 11 Scottish Nationalists, 3 Welsh Nationalists and 1 SDLP member from Northern Ireland. In effect, the working Labour majority was stronger than it looked as many of the MPs of the smaller parties were likely to vote with Labour.

Michael Foot at the Department of Employment was responsible for building bridges to the trade unions. He enjoyed a friendly relationship with Jack Jones, the leader of the TGWU, still the biggest union in the country. Foot was new to government and opinion is divided on his handling of the department. He was a broad-brush politician with a gift for the telling phrase, but his work habits were somewhat eccentric. His sympathetic biographer, Kenneth O. Morgan, paints a charming picture of his work style.

Source S

It was a grand address and the house contains some elegant rooms, in which the Foreign Secretary may entertain visiting foreign ministers and other dignitaries, with a flat at the top of the house overlooking St. James' Park. Alec Douglas-Home, my predecessor, had lived in the flat, but when he moved out his wife Elizabeth warned Audrey that it had its drawbacks. The roof leaked so badly that she had been forced to place a bucket at the right spot in the bedroom to catch the drips when it rained; the house was infested by dry rot and the external stone parapets were dangerous.

From James Callaghan, *Time and Chance*, published in 1987

Source T

Some civil servants might have had their reservations about Foot's performance as a minister. One or two felt , that unlike Callaghan or Healey, he never learned how to run a department, and that as a result things could get out of control. But in general officials found Foot's informal, almost post-modern style as Secretary for Employment attractive and refreshing. They liked the volumes of Rousseau, Montesquieu and Montaigne on the minister's office shelves. They liked his sneaking off from all his hard grind to write the odd book review for the Observer or the Standard, and the bottles which emerged from his drinks cabinet at unexpected times. They were amused by his habit of leaving a television on in his office with the sound turned down during Test matches. Serious discussions on complex legislative issues would be interrupted by cries of 'He's got him!'

From Kenneth O. Morgan, *Michael Foot: A Life*, published in 2007

Foot pushed through a series of measures designed to placate the unions. This was a key element in the 'social contract'. One civil servant described his policy as finding out what the unions wanted and then giving it to them. Heath's legislation was repealed. A *Health and Safety at Work Bill* was passed. The *Trade Union and Labour Relations Act* got rid of the National Industrial Relations Court and restored trade union immunity from civil claims for damages. Foot was prevented from extending the rights of pickets by pressure from Cabinet colleagues, notably Roy Jenkins. Jenkins was appalled at the proposal to give pickets the same rights as the police to stop vehicles on the road.

Foot was instrumental in establishing the Advisory and Conciliation Service (ACAS) to bring the two sides of industry together and settle disputes. It was a pet project of Jack Jones. An *Employment Protection Bill* was pushed through extending workers' rights and it led to fresh disputes in Cabinet about the **closed shop**. Foot and the unions did not get all that they wanted here in the face of determined opposition from Roy Jenkins again. A new *Sex Discrimination Act* was also put through. In all, the trade unions had received considerable concessions.

The growing economic crisis, with raging inflation and a falling pound, forced the Treasury to press for a statutory incomes policy. Foot made it clear that he would resign if one were adopted. In the end, Jack Jones was able to deliver something in return for the concessions, a voluntary maximum increase of £6 a week. He got the proposal accepted by his own union in March, by the TUC General Council in June and the whole TUC conference in September 1975. Foot stayed in the Cabinet and it did something to rescue the government.

Source U

Henceforth the centrepiece of the government's anti-inflation policy was Jack Jones' £6 a week pay limit. It would involve an enormous amount of monitoring by the Department of Employment, working with the TUC. The measure was not as powerful in reducing inflation as the Treasury had hoped, since in 1976 the retail price index fell only from 25 per cent to 15 per cent, not to the hoped-for 10 per cent. But it was the only show in town. It was also powerfully egalitarian, since it would erode wage differentials.

From Kenneth O. Morgan, *Michael Foot: A Life*, published in 2007

Tony Benn at the Department of Trade and Industry tried to push through a real hard left agenda of growing state control. He hoped to use the National Enterprise Board (NEB), forcing companies into planning agreements and taking a growing state share of the ownership. In fact, circumstances forced him into various rescue operations of 'lame ducks' such as that of the Norton Villiers Triumph motorbike factory at Meriden and Kirby Engineering in Liverpool. This involved the promotion of worker's cooperatives. They were not a notable success and became known as 'Benn's follies'. Eventually much of the department's budget had to go into rescuing Britain's biggest car manufacturer, British Leyland. Most of the Cabinet proved hostile to Benn's approach and Harold Lever, who Wilson had appointed to a non-departmental Cabinet post with a roving brief on the economy, was particularly critical.

Source V

Lever strengthened Wilson's non-interventionist impulses and was a powerful debunker of Tony Benn's push for economic planning from the Department of Industry. Many years later, speaking of 1974–75, Lever told me (in between doing deals on the telephone from his dazzlingly luxurious Belgravia home) 'I had a very sceptical view about most of our programme. I did not believe in the social policy [the Social Contract with the unions – social improvements in return for voluntary wage restraint] and I did not believe in the so called industrial strategy ... all this crap about Benn and his industrial planning ... the NEB. I knew it was going to be a dud and the investments would be no good.'

From Peter Hennessy, *The Prime Minister: The Office and its Holders since 1945*, published in 2000

SKILLS BUILDER

Refer to Sources N, U and V, and your own knowledge. How far do you agree that the Labour government's handling of the economy in the period 1974–75 was largely unsuccessful?

Sunny Jim – holding the fort

In March 1976, the country was stunned by the news that the prime minister was to retire. He was only 60 and, given his reputation for intrigue and crooked plots, speculation was rife about the motives. In fact, he had given out hints for a long time that he would not serve a full term. Callaghan had been informed by Wilson's crony, Harold Lever, just after Christmas 1975 that Wilson would go in March. Clearly Jim Callaghan was the favoured successor, although he was four years older than the retiring prime minister. The explanation of the change is probably the obvious one – ill health. Harold Wilson was increasingly burnt out. The fabled memory was failing and the appetite for power flagging.

The succession was smooth and relatively painless. Michael Foot stood as the leading candidate of the left of the party and won the most votes on the first round. On the second ballot, when other candidates dropped out, Callaghan won the votes of 176 MPs to Foot's 133.

Jenkins chose to leave British politics for the time being to serve in the well paid and prestigious post of President of the European Commission in Brussels. Michael Foot became Leader of the House of Commons and Lord President in charge of managing government business. Healey continued as the Exchequer and these three were clearly the dominant figures.

The only real victim of the change was Barbara Castle, who had never got on with Callaghan. She was fired, much to her annoyance. Her diary entry

Source W

Jim could not have been more matey, insisting on standing us wine though he only had a modest glass of beer himself. He couldn't have been nicer. But as I looked at him I thought once again how dull his virtues are. He looked more like a neutered Tom than ever. I longed for the sparkle of wit and the touch of devilment of a Nye Bevan, a Michael Foot – or even a Harold Wilson.

From Barbara Castle, *The Castle Diaries 1964–1976*, published in 1984

for 3 April 1977, nearly a year later, still expresses some of her anger towards Callaghan, see Source W. She and many other leading Labour figures were attending a Socialist conference in Oslo.

Yet, even Barbara Castle had to admit that Callaghan was an effective prime minister, as her diary entry for 15 December 1977 in Source X shows.

Source X

Jim has kept his cool brilliantly: it is a late flowering in a man who flopped as Chancellor, made no mark as Foreign Secretary and was a reactionary Home Secretary. But it is not just a case of the office making the man, but of the hour making him. Jim got his chance to give the kind of calm, conservative leadership natural to him at a moment when the unions had been frightened out of their wits by the fear of a Thatcher government and Labour MPs were ready to follow anyone who would save their seats.

From Barbara Castle, *The Castle Diaries 1964–1976*, published in 1984

Both Healey and Benn felt that Callaghan was a considerable improvement on Harold Wilson. He was a firm but fair leader of a team. There was disciplined debate in Cabinet and on the whole a masterly and kindly control of parliament. He dominated prime minister's question time, almost patronising the rather strident Margaret Thatcher, who appeared to be trying too hard. He was a reassuring figure on television. Sufficiently working class in origin to appeal to traditional Labour voters, he also appeared solidly patriotic, as a naval officer in the Second World War and a man of conservative personal tastes. As such, he did not frighten the middle classes. He expressed concern to Tony Benn abut the growing Trotskyite influence in local Labour parties and was determined to defend the Labour Party of Attlee and Bevin, into which he had come so many years before. Yet Callaghan was to need all his skills as a politician to guide the country through the next three years.

Crisis and recovery

By 1976, government spending as a percentage of GDP had increased by nearly 6 per cent in two years. It seemed that it was out of control. As indicated already, taxation had reached punitive heights, no longer afflicting the rich alone. In 1949, a married man with two children on average earnings escaped income tax altogether; now a man earning half the national average paid income tax. Unemployment was climbing to reach more than a quarter of million more than the million that had caused Heath's U-turn in 1972. Annual inflation was at 16 per cent despite the so-called pay restraint. Interest rates were at 15 per cent and the pound was sliding downwards, despite a vast loan from a combination of countries at the end of 1975. There was a balance of payments deficit on Britain's trade of £1,000,000,000 (one billion). In September, the selling of sterling threatened a collapse of the currency and Healey and Callaghan decided that they needed another massive loan, this time from the International Monetary Fund (IMF). The IMF usually dealt with failing third world economies. It was in some ways a national humiliation. Tony Crosland, as Secretary for the Environment, had already announced in 1975 that the 'Party is over' as far as local government spending was concerned. Now Healey realised that he would have to make more savage cuts in central government spending to secure an IMF loan. Such a policy would be deeply unpopular with left-wing activists in the Labour Party.

Callaghan swung behind his Chancellor and, in a bold speech to the party conference in September 1976, seemed to announce the death of Keynesian economics, a key plank in the post-war consensus.

Source Y

For too long, perhaps ever since the war, we have postponed facing up to fundamental changes in our society and in our economy. . . . The cosy world we were told would go on for ever, where full employment would be guaranteed by a stroke of the chancellor's pen – that cosy world is gone . . . We used to think that you could just spend your way out of a recession and increase employment by cutting taxes and boosting government spending. I tell you, in all candour, that that option no longer exists and that in so far as it ever did exist, it only worked on each occasion since the war by injecting bigger doses of inflation into the economy, followed by higher levels of unemployment as the next step.

From a speech by James Callaghan to the Labour Party conference, September 1976

SKILLS BUILDER

What makes the speech in Source Y so significant?

Healey and Callaghan forced the Cabinet to accept £2 billion in cuts and the IMF agreed to a $3 billion loan. In many ways, it was a national turning point. It marked not the end of consensus politics but the beginning of a new consensus no longer based on an absolute faith in Keynes. Thatcher and Geoffrey Howe were to take over from where Callaghan and Healey left off. Healey also began the process of privatisation with the sale of £500 million government-owned BP shares.

Not surprisingly, the cuts and the crisis brought unpopularity on the government. By-elections were lost, threatening its slender majority. Callaghan skilfully negotiated a pact with the Liberal Party and its new leader David Steel. This lasted from the spring of 1977 to the autumn of 1978. The Scottish and Welsh Nationalists were kept on side with the prospect of devolved parliaments in Edinburgh and Cardiff, which, happily for Callaghan, proved a lengthy business to accomplish. In the meantime, recovery began to take place, aided by the steadily increasing flow of oil from the North Sea. This aided the balance of payments as Britain ceased to be a net oil importer and boosted government revenue. The pound began to climb again, reaching $2 to the pound. Healey's job became easier and, not surprisingly, he records the success and recovery in his memoirs.

Source Z

The Pound grew stronger month by month. Interest rates began to fall faster than we wanted – they were only 5 per cent in October 1977. When I attended the annual meeting of the IMF that month, even British correspondents described me as walking on water. The Labour Party Conference which followed gave me a standing ovation. The leading American financial monthly, *Institutional Investor*, produced a cover story showing me as first among the six best finance ministers of the day. Since none of the other five had to operate in a democracy, I took this as high praise; it is much easier to manage an economy if you can use electrodes on the most sensitive parts of those who refuse to cooperate.

From Denis Healey, *The Time of My Life*, published in 1989

Refuse to cooperate is what many were to do in the winter of 1978–79, which came to be known as the 'winter of discontent'. By the summer of 1978, Labour had recovered in the opinion polls and there was a chance of winning an election in the autumn of that year. Many of his colleagues wanted Callaghan to go to the country, but he decided to soldier on. Private party polls suggested that the Labour lead was not strong, particularly in marginal seats. As it turned out, it was a mistake not to call an election. The Liberals decided to end their pact with the government and the two devolution Bills had finally passed, so there was little to keep the nationalists loyal to a Labour government. Worst of all, the trade unions decided to cease to cooperate and, as Denis Healey pointed out, the option of using electrodes was not available.

By the late 1970s, half the work force was unionised with 13 million being members. The giant TGWU had 2 million members. The retirement of Jack Jones as leader was a blow to Callaghan. His successor, Moss Evans, showed no interest in cooperation. The prime minister was determined to bring inflation down further than the 8 per cent of 1978 and decided to try and sell a 5 per cent pay limit as a means of achieving it. The unions refused point blank and 1978–79 became one of the worst periods for strikes of the century.

Trouble began in the car industry at Ford where the TGWU backed a pay rise of £20 per week, which totally smashed the 5 per cent guidelines. They got 17 per cent. Firemen got 22 per cent. A nationwide strike of lorry drivers was declared in early January. They gained 17–20 per cent. Public sector workers now entered the fray. Health service workers, dustmen and even grave diggers went out on strike. Rotting rubbish piled up in the streets in February. Each strike produced a breach in the 5 per cent limit, and damaged Labour. The Tory lead in opinion polls shot up to 20 per cent. Callaghan was privately appalled by the behaviour of the unions, rounding on Tony Benn in one Cabinet meeting for defending them – 'What do you say about the thuggish act of a walk out without notice, from a children's hospital?' Callaghan himself was pilloried for apparent indifference.

7.6 Piles of uncollected rubbish litter the streets during the strikes of the 1978–9 'winter of discontent'

Source AA

Returning from an economic summit in Guadeloupe, Callaghan was asked at the airport, 'What is your general approach in view of the mounting chaos in the country at the moment?' His answer was 'Well, that's a judgement that you are making. I promise you that if you look at it from outside, and perhaps you're taking a parochial view at the moment, I don't think that other people in the world share the view that there is mounting chaos.' That very week, the lorry drivers achieved a pay rise of 20 per cent. Public sector unions such as NUPE [National Union of Public Employees] and NALGO [National Association of Local Government Officers] called for a twenty-four hour general strike.

The *Sun* newspaper, recently acquired together with *The Times* by the American-Australian tycoon Rupert Murdoch summarised this waffly speech in the devastating headline: CRISIS? WHAT CRISIS?

From A.N. Wilson, *Our Times: The Age of Elizabeth II*, published in 2008

The end of the government came not at a time of its choosing. For the first time since 1841, a government was brought down by a vote of no-confidence at the end of March. On 1 March, Wales had voted decisively to reject devolution in a referendum and in Scotland only 33 per cent of the electorate approved, not the 40 per cent required by the Act. The Nationalists and Liberals voted with the Tories to bring Labour down. The government lost by one vote. An election followed in early May where Callaghan fought back. The Tories played on the 'winter of discontent' and unemployment with an effective election poster showing a long queue of the unemployed with the caption: 'Labour isn't working.' Unemployment was 1.3 million. Healey offers his explanation of the result:

Source BB

By March Jim was exhausted and dispirited. I believe that if we had struggled on a little longer we might have cut Mrs Thatcher's majority by a few seats for each week we moved further away from the Winter of Discontent. But exhaustion is sometimes a decisive factor in politics; it also led the Attlee Government to defeat in 1951. Even so, the Tories fell from an initial lead of 13 per cent to as low as 2 per cent at one stage in the campaign; but we never overtook them.

From Denis Healey, *The Time of My Life*, published in 1989.
Denis Healey was Chancellor of the Exchequer from 1974 to 1979

The television journalist Michael Cockerell records an exchange between Callaghan and ITN's David Rose on the eve of polling. It reveals something of the strain that the prime minister had been under.

Source CC

Rose: On industrial relations and picketing, what about the TUC putting its house in order?

Callaghan: The media is always trying to find out what's wrong with something. Let's try and make it work.

Rose: What if the unions can't control their own militants? Are there no circumstances where you would legislate?

Callaghan: I didn't say anything of that sort at all. I'm not going to take the interview further. Look here, we've been having five minutes on industrial relations, you said you would do price. I am just not going to do this . . . This programme is not to go out. I am not doing the interview with you on that basis. I'm not going to do it.

From the transcript of an interview between David Rose of ITN and the Prime Minister, James Callaghan in early May 1979

Margaret Thatcher, leader of the opposition since 1975, tried to broaden the appeal of the Conservatives, as this extract from her final election broadcast makes clear:

Source DD

A lot of things we take for granted seem to be in danger of disappearing. Money that keeps its value; real jobs that last; paying our way in the world; feeling safe in the streets – especially if you are a woman; schools that give children from modest backgrounds like my own the chance to get on in life as far as we are able.

From a transcript of the final election broadcast of Margaret Thatcher, leader of the Conservative Party in May 1979

Her appeal seemed to have worked, at least in the south of England. Here, there was a large swing from Labour to the Conservatives. Overall, Labour's share of the popular vote fell to only 37 per cent, its lowest since 1931. The Conservatives gained 43.9 per cent, overall considerably less than Heath had gained in 1970. If Thatcher's victory with a majority of 44 marked a sea-change, as is often argued, then it was a change largely limited to England, and the southern half of England at that.

Unit summary

What have you learned in this unit?

This unit has covered two governments under three prime ministers, each wrestling with seemingly intractable problems, posed by the balance of payments and British trade and the power of trade unions. Yet important developments took place which were to really re-shape Britain and her place in the world. Britain finally joined the EEC and later voted in this country's only referendum to stay in. Within both parties there were serious doubts beginning to develop about Keynesian economics, but by the end of the decade the prospect of North Sea oil looked like bringing some economic relief.

What skills have you used in this unit?

As in all units you have encountered a large number of secondary sources relating to this period as well as some primary ones and asked to consider their strengths and weaknesses as sources of evidence for historians. It is interesting to reflect on how many of these sources reflect the general pessimism of a country in apparent decline.

Exam style question

This is the sort of question that you will find on the examination paper as an (a) question. Use only the sources provided, but none of your own knowledge.

Study Sources BB, CC and DD.

How far do the sources suggest that it was the 'winter of discontent' that was the decisive factor in the loss of the election in May 1979 by the Labour Party?

Explain your answer using the evidence of Sources AA, BB and CC.

RESEARCH TOPIC

This period was notable for the high quality of its comedy programmes on television and it is an interesting exercise to try to see what the particular appeal was in the context of your new knowledge of the period.

Dad's Army which began in 1968 ran until 1977 and centred upon a heroic but bungling Home Guard platoon during the Second World War. It can be seen, in part, as representative of a growing nostalgia for a disappearing world.

Monty Python began in 1969 and ran until 1974 with massive acclaim. Finally Fawlty Towers also starring John Cleese appeared in 1975 with a second series in 1979. Some have seen the hotel as a metaphor for contemporary Britain.

8 The Iron Lady: the breaking of consensus politics, 1979–83

What is this unit about?

This unit examines the controversial years of Margaret Thatcher's first term as prime minister. It is necessary to understand what was new about her approach but also how much of a cautious politician she was. The Budgets of 1980 and 81 and mounting unemployment generated much criticism. The impact of the unexpected war with Argentina in 1982 is assessed, as well as the wave of popular enthusiasm it generated for the government. The Labour Party swung radically to the left on the resignation of Callaghan and in many ways this was more of a challenge to consensus politics than the policies of Thatcher. The resulting split in the Labour Party and the emergence of the Social Democrats in alliance with the Liberals contributed to the Conservative electoral triumph in 1983. Thatcher's second term was dominated by the confrontation with the miners and the strengthening of Thatcher's hold on government, with the growing influence of the **'drys'** in place of the traditional Tory **'wets'**. Privatisation gathered pace and it appeared that the state was being rolled back and the economic pattern established by the post-war Labour government, the economic foundations of consensus politics, was being overthrown.

Key questions

- What were the characteristics of Thatcher's Conservative government?
- What problems did the new government face and how had it coped by 1983?
- Why did the Labour Party do so badly in these years?
- What was the impact of the Falklands Conflict?

Timeline

1979	**May**	Margaret Thatcher becomes prime minister
	June	Howe's first Budget – VAT doubled – direct taxes cut
		Abolition of Price Commission
		Exchange controls abolished
1980	**January**	Steel strike begins
	March	Howe's second Budget – £900 million cut in government spending

	October	'The Lady's not for turning' speech at party conference
	November	Michael Foot becomes Labour leader
1981	January	Gang of four call for realignment of British politics
	February	Government gives in to miners
	March	Howe's third Budget SDP formed
	April	Riots in Brixton
	July	Riots in Liverpool and Birmingham
	November	SDP wins safe Tory seat of Crosby
1982	January	Unemployment reaches over 3 million for the first time since 1932
	April	Argentinian troops occupy the Falkland Isles
	June	Port Stanley liberated – crushing victory over Argentina achieved
1983	June	General election – Conservative majority of 144

Margaret Thatcher

In February 1975, the Conservative MPs elected Margaret Hilda Thatcher as their leader, in place of Ted Heath. There was now the prospect of Britain having its first woman prime minister. It was a surprising development to everyone concerned, including Margaret Thatcher. Like so much about the career of this remarkable woman, luck, or chance, played an enormous part. It was clear to everyone, apart from Ted Heath, that he would have to step down after the second defeat in 1974. Enoch Powell had ruled himself out by leaping over a political precipice and leaving the Tory Party to become an MP for Northern Ireland. The other candidate from the political right who had embraced free-market ideas and condemned the post-war consensus was Sir Keith Joseph, an intellectual and utterly honourable Tory, but hopelessly unsuited to leadership. He agonised over decisions and his pained expression and tortuous wrestling with ideas brought him the nickname of the 'mad monk'. All the other leading members of Heath's Cabinet were 'consensus politicians' loyal to their chief. Margaret Thatcher decided to stand. When she informed Heath of her decision, his typically brusque response was, 'You'll lose.' He was wrong. She strongly beat him on the first ballot but with not quite enough to secure outright victory. Heath stepped down and now the obvious successor came forward, the upper-class gentleman from the traditional party and Heath's number two, Willie Whitelaw. It was too late. Thatcher had established her credentials by her courage and she beat Whitelaw on the second ballot. Many Tory MPs could not quite believe what they had done.

Definition

Wets and drys
These became terms used to describe the two wings of the Conservative Party in the 1980s. Wets were traditional consensus Tories anxious to avoid confrontation with the unions and supportive of a large economic management role for the state. Drys were suspicious of Keynesian economic policies which they feared had led the country to disaster. They believed the role of the state should be slimmed down and union power disciplined by both legislation and the impact of higher unemployment.

The new leader marked a change in every way from the traditional Tory grandees, firstly as a woman but equally importantly as middle or even lower middle class. Her father had been a shopkeeper in Grantham. Brains and hard work had got her to Oxford and an advantageous marriage to a rich divorcee brought financial independence. With gritty determination, she eventually gained the chance to stand for the safe Tory seat of Finchley, which she won in 1959. She impressed all with her thoroughness and rose as a junior minister. Heath made her his token woman Cabinet minister in 1970. Although she served Macmillan and Heath loyally, she was different to them in the fervour of her beliefs. She was interested in ideas and was, in contrast, ideologically committed to the pragmatic approach that marked almost all Tory leaders of the 20th century.

Source A

You had only to talk to her in the couple of years before the election, when the Labour Government's popularity had gone, to savour her self-confidence. In part this was ideological: all over the world, she told me, the long night of collectivism was receding. 'Impoverishment' and 'socialism' went together in her conversation, with the hammer-beat of a doctrinaire non-doubter. With Margaret Thatcher, Keynesian orthodoxy had been abandoned. She came nearer to laissez-faire liberalism than any Tory leader in this century.

From John Cole, *As It Seemed To Me: Political Memoirs*, published in 1995

Source B

One of her remarkable characteristics which stamps her as a superb politician, is her ability to put up with things and go along with them, even though she doesn't agree with them, until the time comes when they can be dealt with. Now, not possessing that quality myself – having the loquacity which always impels me to say: 'I don't agree' – I admire this.

From Enoch Powell, speaking in 1989

She was very much conditioned by the Cold War, with a complete and uncomplicated view of the evils of Communism. Western Socialism, it appeared to her, was only a watered-down version of full-blooded Marxism. Both, in the end, deprived human beings of responsibility for their lives and diminished them. Freedom worked. Like many of her generation who grew to political maturity during and after the war, she was heavily influenced by the work of Professor F.A. Hayek's *Road to Serfdom*, published in 1944. Hayek attacked the pursuit of equality as likely to undermine freedom, a much more desirable goal for humanity.

Yet, if Margaret Thatcher was a believer, she was also an astute politician. Timing was important. Enoch Powell comments on this in Source B.

Many of her colleagues commented upon her caution and almost nervousness in launching an initiative. Geoffrey Howe refers in his memoirs to 'the ambivalence which Margaret often showed when the time came to move from the level of high principle and evangelism to practical politics'. In this, of course, she was a practical politician and politics is, as R.A. Butler entitled his memoirs, *The Art of the Possible*. Nevertheless, she was not a Harold Wilson figure where opportunism clouded the objective and could lead to the abandonment of the ultimate goal. She knew where she wanted to end up but would bide her time to get there. In this sense, she was one of those rare politicians who make the weather. Her vision was of the need to revitalise a tired and dispirited country by injecting a large dose of free enterprise, to roll back an oppressive state which had crushed the initiative out of a great people. In her forward to the 1979 manifesto, she had written: 'There has been a feeling of helplessness, that we are falling behind and that it is too late now to turn things round, I don't accept that.'

Thatcher, then, had brains, determination, a crucial sense of political timing and a vision. She was also lucky throughout her period of office. As she gained power, North Sea oil was coming on-stream, relieving her government of many of the economic pressures faced by her predecessors. In 1980, Britain was self-sufficient in oil and became a net exporter. She enjoyed remarkable support in the popular press not just in traditional Tory papers like the *Mail*, *Telegraph* and *The Express*. Rupert Murdoch had acquired *The Times* and, more importantly, the populist tabloid the *Sun*. By 1979, the *Sun* had overtaken the Labour-leaning *Mirror* as the most popular daily in Britain and it gave Thatcher its support. The legacy of the 'winter of discontent' was a bonus. The gravediggers may not have buried the dead in February, but in a sense they dug the grave of popular trade unionism. Finally, the Labour Party entered a period of internal warfare and embraced a series of policies that took it further to the left than at any time since the early 1930s. It broke the consensus of British politics in its manifesto for the 1983 election. In this, it was a gift to the 'Iron Lady', as the Soviet Union had christened Margaret Thatcher.

Her foreign affairs adviser from 1984 to 1990, Sir Percy Cradock, a career diplomat, was to sum up her singular characteristics as prime minister:

Source C

She was different. It was partly that she carried with her into No. 10 a greater baggage of ideology than her predecessors. It was partly that she was a scientist by training, not for once a product of the humanities. It was partly that she was a woman. She was also intensely serious. The camaraderie, the relaxed jokey, allusive style, the affectation of doing things well without trying, the view of politics and most other things as a game, these expressions of the ruling male culture, which with Harold Macmillan had been carried to extreme lengths, all these were alien to her.

From Percy Cradock, *In Pursuit of British Interests*, published in 1997

SKILLS BUILDER

How far do Sources A, B and C agree on the characteristics that marked Margaret Thatcher as a politician?

The new government

From the word go, the new government was different in style compared to its predecessor and this was very largely due to the new prime minister. One of the most praised biographies of her, which came out before she fell from power, was by the journalist Hugo Young. He took as his title her much-used phrase, which described those in the government who fundamentally agreed with her approach.

Source D

For those who saw [her approach] first and at close quarters this experience was not unlike being struck about the head by a very purposefully whirling dervish. The staff of private secretaries at No. 10, who were the cream of the middle ranks of the civil service, had grown accustomed to a different regime. Jim Callaghan was a prime minister who kept his distance from minor events. His style was very much that of the chairman of the board, concerning himself with strategic questions and issuing instructions that cabinet papers should normally occupy no more than two sides of a page. Callaghan was a good chairman, and a prime minister well suited to the compromise and permanent negotiation which is the condition of a minority government. But a leisurely air, naturally associated with a government that could do little, undeniably permeated Downing Street.

The new prime minister was something completely different. From the first hour she established her desire to see everything and do everything. At the end of the first week, one of her officials told 'She reads every paper she gets and never fails to write a comment on it. "Nonsense", "Needs more briefing", "Do this again" are what she's constantly writing.'

From Hugo Young, *One of Us: Life of Margaret Thatcher*, published in 1989

Within Downing Street, she surrounded herself with a loyal team of professionals. Surprisingly she took Robert Armstrong, Heath's ex-private secretary, as Cabinet Secretary and a very promising young civil servant, Clive Whitmore, as her private secretary. These were from the cream of the civil service, a group of whom in many ways Thatcher was suspicious, as being too much associated with consensus politics and national decline. Her press secretary was an ex-Labour supporter from Yorkshire, Bernard Ingham. He developed an uncanny ability to present her views to the press and guess her reaction to events. Perhaps the most important person in Downing Street on whom she could rely totally was her husband Dennis. She could retreat upstairs to the flat to moan to him about the feebleness of her Cabinet colleagues who, for the most part, were patently not 'one of us'.

It was almost a sign of her weakness within the Tory Party that her Cabinet, as first constituted, was filled with traditional Conservative moderates. These rapidly became known as 'wets'. They favoured a moderate approach to trade union reform and the economy. Willie Whitelaw was the most important of these, now appointed as Home Secretary, and his intense sense of loyalty to her was invaluable in heading off revolt. Other 'Heathites' were Jim Prior at employment, Lord Carrington and Sir Ian Gilmour at the Foreign Office, Peter Walker at agriculture and Francis Pym at defence. Those who were 'one of us' were a clear minority. The most important initially was the lawyer Sir Geoffrey Howe, appointed Chancellor of the Exchequer. His two deputies at the Treasury were John Biffen as Chief Secretary and Nigel Lawson, as

Financial Secretary to the Treasury. All were perceived as 'monetarists.' The other vitally important member, to whom she owed a great debt, was Sir Keith Joseph, placed as Secretary of Industry. Thatcher hoped that the small band of true believers would be able to control economic policy and thus revitalise the economy.

Setting the country to rights, 1979–82

Margaret Thatcher's prescription for the country was relatively simple – it was to get the government to do less. Her recent biographer John Campbell explains it clearly, in Source E.

To carry out this policy required three or four big decisions early on. These were, on the whole, done in 1979. Pride of place went to Geoffrey Howe's first Budget in June.

- The minimum lending rate was raised to 14 per cent to control the money supply.
- The standard rate of income tax was cut from 33 to 30 per cent and the highest rate from 83 to 60 per cent. This clearly favoured those earning more, but the idea was to provide incentives. Hard work should be encouraged and its rewards not confiscated by the government.
- To cover the lack of revenue, the government raised VAT, indirect taxes on goods and services that all consumers would have to pay. VAT went up from 8 to 15 per cent. These changes in taxation marked a major shift in the philosophy behind taxation – consumption not effort should be penalised.

This might produce long-term gains but, in the short-term, increase in VAT would push up inflation. In fact, inflation practically doubled by the end of 1980 to 21.9 per cent. Cuts were imposed on government spending and attempts made to reduce the subsidies to nationalised industries. In both cases, these were more limited than the government hoped. Thatcher had promised to increase defence expenditure and to honour pay awards in the public sector promised under the Callaghan government.

Two other free-market changes announced early on were the abolition of the Price Commission and exchange controls on the movement of currency. These, with the Budget changes, amounted to a bold strategy. The value of the pound increased with the removal of exchange controls, which harmed exports, adding to unemployment. The government found that it was having to borrow more as unemployment rose and more was spent on benefits but less tax revenue was coming in. Interest rates were raised to 17 per cent in November, further squeezing business and increasing the number of the unemployed. By 1980, many were denouncing the monetarist experiment as dogmatic stupidity. Many in the Cabinet were unhappy. Norman St John Stevas, the leader of the House of Commons, referred to the prime minister (not in her hearing) as the 'immaculate misconception'. One notorious 'wet', Julian Critchley, a Tory back-bencher, denounced his own leader in an anonymous letter to the *Observer*.

Source E

Her fundamental philosophy of anti-socialist economics prescribed a number of broad objectives: the government should cut public spending, cut taxes, keep tight control of the money supply, refrain from detailed intervention in the economy and generally trust the operation of the free market. But very little of this required legislation. Most of it simply involved not doing things which previous governments of both parties had believed it their function to do.

From John Campbell, *Margaret Thatcher*, revised edition published in 2009

> ## Source F
>
> It is a matter both of policy and personality. Mrs Thatcher is didactic, tart and obstinate. Her economic policies are 'Thatcherite' rather than Conservative for her treasury team to have placed the Public Sector Borrowing Requirement upon a pedestal.
>
> We are suffering from A-level economics. In consequence of this new ideology economics have been elevated above politics in an almost Marxist fashion and it cannot be long before the Conservative Party pays a price.
>
> From 'Why the Tories must halt the charge of Margaret's Light Brigade' by a Tory, *Observer*, 17 February 1980

Despite doubts among her colleagues, Geoffrey Howe's second Budget produced more of the same with a further £900 million taken out of public spending. There were heavy cuts in higher education. Social security payments to those on strike were reduced and made liable to income tax. Prescription charges were raised, as were taxes on petrol and drink. Unemployment continued to rise, reaching 2.8 million by the end of the year. Whole areas of the country were being de-industrialised as companies went bust. To Thatcher, Howe and Lawson this was a necessary evil as the weak and inefficient were allowed to collapse. This was made more easy for the Conservative government to bear as it tended to be in the North and in traditionally Labour-voting areas. When unemployment had reached one million under Ted Heath in 1972, the famous U-turn had resulted, now there would be no U-turn. At the Conservative Party conference in October 1980, Thatcher uttered her ringing challenge to the wets in her party: 'You turn if you want to – the Lady's not for turning.'

Far from a U-turn, 1981 brought more evidence of prime ministerial determination to press on with the same policies. The first sign of this was the removal of St John Stevas as Leader of the House in January. His sacking enabled Thatcher to move Francis Pym from defence, where he had been resisting cuts, to take St John Stevas' place. It was, however, Geoffrey Howe's third Budget that really rubbed in the abandonment of Keynesian economics and the fact that this was a government of a very different approach to its predecessors. In the middle of the worst economic downturn since the war, instead of increasing spending, the government proposed to cut it further and squeeze the economy by raising £4 billion in extra taxes. By this means, it was hoped inflation would be squeezed out of the system. However, it was rather like giving a man with pneumonia a cold shower. Howe himself entitles his chapter on this Budget, 'The most unpopular budget'. It produced mutterings of disapproval on the Tory back-benches and resentment in the Cabinet, which was given no time to influence it. Most notable was the denunciation it received from 364 eminent economists, including 76 professors and 5 ex-Chief Economic Advisers to the Treasury, in a letter to *The Times*.

Source G

A) There is no basis in economic theory or supporting evidence for the Government's belief that by deflating demand they will bring inflation permanently under control and thereby induce an automatic recovery in output and employment.

B) Present policies will deepen the depression, erode the industrial base of our economy and threaten its social and political stability.

C) There are alternative policies.

D) The time has come to reject monetarist policies and consider urgently which alternative offers the best hope of sustained recovery.

From a letter to *The Times*, 30 March 1981

Not surprisingly, Geoffrey Howe was not impressed and in his memoirs comments:

Source H

Their timing could not have been more apt. The fall in national output came to an end in that very quarter. Over the next eight years real GDP grew by an average of 3.2 per cent p.a. and the 364 economists found themselves immortalised. For my Mansion House speech that year I deployed for the first of many times the line that an economist was a man who knows 364 ways of making love – but doesn't know any women.

From Sir Geoffrey Howe, *Conflict of Loyalty*, published in 1994

Howe's Cabinet colleague, Francis Pym, was less enthusiastic about the Budget and wrote in his memoirs:

Source I

The 1981 budget was rigidly deflationary and thus highly controversial at a time of deep recession, yet the strategy behind it was never discussed in Cabinet and was only revealed to the full Cabinet on Budget Day itself. One can guess the reason is the Chancellor and the Prime Minister concluded that the Cabinet might well insist on some changes. But that is why Cabinet exists – to make collective decisions on important issues that face individual Departments, and thus affect the Government as a whole. Collective responsibility is based on collective decision making. Margaret Thatcher is not the first Prime Minister to circumvent her colleagues, nor will she be the last, but this habit is not the sign of a happy or healthy Government.

From Francis Pym, *The Politics of Consent*, published in 1985

SKILLS BUILDER

In what ways do Sources G, H and I differ in their attitudes to the 1981 Budget?

As Sources G, H and I show, controversy rages around this Budget. To Howe and Thatcher, it marked the turning point when a determined minority took a tough but essentially correct stance in the face of wrong-headed prejudice and ushered in real economic recovery. Certainly there were to be eight years of growth, and inflation fell to 4.5 per cent in 1983. To the critics, the squeeze was unnecessarily severe and delayed recovery and laid waste much of Britain's traditional manufacturing. It is impossible to get agreement among historians or economists. A recent study by a historian, basically not sympathetic to Margaret Thatcher, concluded that it was the political significance of the government's economic policies that really mattered.

Source J

There was a touch of the tribal war dance in its early economic policies. The aim was to illustrate the government's determination as dramatically as possible. In this sense, government economic policy was remarkably successful. At the end of 1982, most people did not understand the details of government economic policy, and many people who did were not impressed. However, the British people had a general sense of a new kind of economic policy – one that made the government responsible for lowering inflation – and absolved it of responsibility for unemployment and most importantly, one that would be pursued ruthlessly beyond the point at which earlier governments had backed down.

From Richard Vinen, *Thatcher's Britain: The Politics and Social Upheaval of the Thatcher Era*, published in 2009

In contrast to the government's Budgets, which might seem uncompromising, Jim Prior at employment was notably gentle in his handling of the trade unions. He decided to adopt a softly-softly approach and his Employment Act of 1980, while outlawing secondary picketing and tightening the rules regarding the 'closed shop', did not amount to a full frontal assault on union power. Growing unemployment would sap their strength and militancy. When Norman Tebbit took over from Prior, a tougher Act was pushed through in 1982 and further changes followed, which collectively weakened the very privileged position trade unions had held since 1906.

Even the theoretically 'super dry' Keith Joseph at the Department of Industry was forced by the realities of British nationalised industries to retreat from cutting government spending to actually increasing it. Inefficient nationalised giants queued up for more subsidies and Joseph could not allow them to collapse. The British Steel Corporation was losing £7 million a week by the end of 1979. It suffered from over-manning and chronic inefficiencies. It was Joseph's first big test. He tried to get the Corporation to cut its losses by closing inefficient plants, with the loss of 50,000 jobs, and getting those left in work to accept a 2 per cent pay rise. This led to a massive strike in January 1980, which lasted until April. It ended with the union gaining a 16 per cent pay increase but accepting plant closures. Joseph installed a tough American manager to return the Corporation to profit. He turned it into the most efficient steel producer in Europe within two years and almost into profit but at the price of losing nearly half the workforce.

British Leyland was another inefficient giant soaking up government subsidies since it was nationalised in the 1970s to save it from bankruptcy. It was a byword for inefficient practices and unofficial strikes. Tough new chairman, Michael Edwardes, held out the prospect of change and improvement, but £990 million was needed from the government to keep the plant open and launch new models like the Metro and Maestro. Joseph could not face the prospect of massive redundancies in the Midlands, with its large number of marginal seats, and stumped up the money. The biographer of Mrs Thatcher, Kenneth Harris, draws attention to the extraordinary lengths to which Joseph was driven to embrace policies diametrically opposed to those which he and Thatcher believed in.

Source K

To the surprise of many, the Government also disbursed £9 million to save the Meriden Motor Cycle Corporation, a co-operative workers enterprise that had been the cherished child of Tony Benn from his days at the Department of Industry; for Keith Joseph to be bailing it out seemed most incongruous. Similarly, £200million was given to the computer giant ICL to prevent liquidation, £13 million was assigned to write off the debts of the National Film Finance Corporation, and most controversially of all, the government gave a hefty grant to the American car producer John DeLorean to start making sports cars in Belfast. These hand-outs were glaringly at odds with the declared policy of encouraging competition rather than using public money to lengthen the life of lame ducks.

From Kenneth Harris, *Thatcher*, published in 1988

SKILLS BUILDER

In what ways do Sources J and K differ in their views of the economic policies of the Thatcher government in its first two years?

Riots and resistance

Those who feared that government economic policies would threaten social cohesion seemed to have their fears realised by the events of April to July 1981. The journalist John Cole makes this point in his memoirs:

Source L

An already turbulent political year became more turbulent when riots broke out in the inner cities, first in Brixton in April then in Southall, the Toxteth district of Liverpool, and the Moss Side district of Manchester in July. Margaret Thatcher strenuously denied that these had anything to do with unemployment, but in both the opposition and the discontented sections of her own party this view was contested. Immediately after the budget, I had written a leader in the Observer arguing that to pile deflation on existing recession was to risk jeopardising the social cohesion of a nation that was now multiracial. The riots all too soon seemed to confirm that fear.

From John Cole, *As It Seemed To Me: Political Memoirs*, published in 1995

Although the riots seemed to fit with unemployment as a cause, Cole himself admits that the causes were complex and bad race relations and insensitive policing were probably more important. Whitelaw, the Home Secretary, a noted 'wet' and as such worried about rising unemployment, still observed that many of those arrested for rioting were in steady jobs. The prime minister was largely unmoved and her sympathies as the daughter of a corner-shop grocer were very much with the 'poor shopkeepers'. She pressed Whitelaw to ensure that the police had the latest American anti-riot equipment. The streets were not going to be surrendered to thugs.

Probably more upsetting to her was a specially troublesome Cabinet meeting on 23 July. Howe, Thatcher and Joseph were isolated in discussions regarding future cuts. Had Whitelaw given a lead to the wets, it could have ended Thatcher's premiership. He stayed loyal and urged loyalty on others. In consequence of the meeting, she was determined to reshape her Cabinet. Some of the moisture needed squeezing out of it. Sir Ian Gilmour was sacked, as was Lord Soames the leader in the Lords. Jim Prior, a 'wet' Secretary of Employment was humiliatingly demoted to Northern Ireland and his place taken by the very dry, Norman Tebbit. Cecil Parkinson, very much 'one of us', was made Chairman of the party. The sacking of the Education Secretary, another Heathite wet, enabled Keith Joseph to escape from industry to the department of his choice. The new Cabinet was much more 'Thatcherite'.

However, the prospects of the government were not good. The government's approval rating was down to 18 per cent and Mrs Thatcher was reckoned the most unpopular prime minister since polling began. In March the Labour Party had split, a process dealt with in more detail later (see pages 162–163). Out of it emerged the Social Democratic Party (SDP), led by the so-called Gang of four. One of the four, the personable Shirley Williams, stood in the 'safe' Tory seat of Crosby in a by-election in November 1981. It produced a political earthquake when she won it with a majority of 18,000. On these figures, not a Tory seat in the country was safe. It was no wonder that there were mutterings on the Conservative back-benches about the need for a change in direction and a change in leadership.

General Galtieri to the rescue

In terms of foreign policy, Margaret Thatcher was vey much aware of her inexperience and was largely prepared to leave it to her aristocratic Foreign Secretary, Peter, Sixth Baron Carrington. He handled her skilfully, even teasing her in a way few other members of her Cabinet would dare. The one area that she did concern herself with seriously was Britain's contribution to the EEC. By 1980, Britain was paying in £1000 million more than the country was getting out. Britain, with a smaller economy than Germany or France, was the largest net contributor to the community. Thatcher was determined to have 'our money' back and went about getting it in a way that shocked professional diplomats and Roy Jenkins as president of the European commission. She lectured and hectored the other European leaders and established a thoroughly bad relationship with the French President Giscard D'Estaing. He snubbed her at an official dinner in Paris by being served first and she responded at an official dinner for him in Downing Street by seating him facing full-length portraits of Nelson and Wellington, who had defeated the French respectively in 1805 and 1815. Eventually, she got most of what she demanded and established a reputation in Europe as a troublesome battleaxe.

This reputation was to be massively reinforced by totally unexpected events in the South Atlantic. They were to rescue her premiership and make her almost unassailable. Yet she was partly responsible for the trouble. Britain had occupied the Falkland Islands, 400 miles off the coast of Argentina, in the 1830s. They became thinly populated by British sheep farmers and fishermen, and the capital, Port Stanley, was a port and communication centre for the Royal Navy. Argentina had always claimed the islands and referred to them as Las Malvinas, but while Britain remained a great power, they accepted the status quo. As Britain became progressively enfeebled and her navies melted away, so the Argentinians became more strident in asserting their claims. A small British garrison of marines was stationed on the islands, but the only naval ship in the area was the Antarctic exploration vessel, *Endurance*. There had been the threat of invasion in the late 1970s when Callaghan was prime minister. He had dispatched a hunter-killer submarine to the area and told MI6 to discreetly let the Argentinian government know it was there. Nothing happened. The Thatcher government seemed to have little interest in the islands and as part of defence cuts proposed to withdraw *Endurance*. The military dictatorship of General Galtieri took this as a sign of weakness or indifference on Britain's part. As a bid to boost its popularity in Argentina, where a vicious repressive campaign had left many opponents tortured and dead, Galtieri and his military associates decided to seize the islands in April 1982. They gambled that Britain lacked both the means and the will to respond. It was a serious error.

Initially the occupation of the islands seemed to be yet one more national humiliation, part of a process that had continued since the Suez crisis of 1956. Yet again Britain would appear to the world as the once great lion now mangy and toothless. The Tory MP and diarist, Alan Clark, recorded his feelings on 2 April 1982:

Source M

'We've lost the Falklands' I told Jane [his wife] 'It's all over. We're a Third World country, no good for anything.

I have a terrible feeling that this is a step change down, for England. Humiliation for sure and, not impossible, military defeat.

From Alan Clark, *Diaries*, published in 2001

Source N

So ends the Falklands Affair – which began in such despair and humiliation. How well I remember that first emergency debate and looking down the bench at The Lady when Enoch was speaking, at how low she held her head, how knotted with pain and apprehension she seemed as he pronounced his famous judgement . . . 'in the next few weeks the world, the country and she, herself, will discover of what metal she is made'.

I only hope he is generous enough to recall that moment when he speaks today.

From Alan Clark, *Diaries*, published 2001

Source O

Is the Right Honourable Lady aware that the report has now been received from the public analyst on a certain substance recently subjected to analysis and that I have a copy of the report? It shows that the substance under test consisted of ferrous matter of the highest quality, and is of exceptional tensile strength, is highly resistant to wear and tear, and may be used with advantage for all national purposes.

From a speech by Enoch Powell in the House of Commons, 15 June 1982

Margaret Thatcher rose magnificently to the challenge. Initially shaken and surprised when it became clear at the end of March that the Argentinians were about to invade and US pressure could not stop them, she cast about for a solution and grasped the lifeline offered by the First Sea Lord, Sir Henry Leech. The navy, he assured her, could put together a task force and re-capture the islands. The risks were enormous, with a very real chance of military disaster. She gave the go-ahead. She was determined to restore the islands to British control. It was vital that aggression be defeated for the sake of Britain's self-respect and the rule of law in the world. In these feelings the prime minister seemed to have articulated the response of the majority of her compatriots. Galtieri couldn't be allowed to get away with it. It was a simple case of right and wrong.

Over the next few weeks the stress was enormous, first in dealing with various peace initiatives which threatened to reward Galtieri in some ways through a negotiated settlement, then when the fighting began as the task force arrived, the nerve-racking weeks of war. Controversy surrounded the sinking of the Argentinian cruiser *General Belgrano* with the loss of 368 sailors. Thatcher had given her approval to a naval request as the ship posed an obvious threat even though it happened to be steaming away from the islands at the time of its sinking. She was later accused of deliberately doing it to torpedo a negotiated settlement. The reality was that it was on very sound military grounds. The Argentinian navy stayed safely in port thereafter. The criticism both at the time and subsequently, points up the difficulties of a liberal democracy conducting a war.

The war ended in total victory but not without considerable luck and key mistakes by the Argentine military. Crucial help in the form of sidewinder missiles for the British Harriers and intelligence reports was supplied by the USA. Almost all commentators agree that it was the prime minister's finest hour. She impressed the military with her decisiveness, patience and a grim determination, despite the tears as she heard of British casualties. Not surprisingly, the right-wing Tory MP, Alan Clark, was full of enthusiasm, as shown by his diary entry for 15 June 1982 (Source N).

Clark was not to be disappointed, as shown in Source O.

Source P

Just as defeat would have destroyed her, victory elevated Mrs Thatcher to a new level of pubic esteem, hitherto untouched. It was an event of stunning political impact all over the world, and not least on her personal reputation. This was true even in Argentina. Not long after the war was over, an unnamed woman in Buenos Aires told a reporter from the *New Yorker*: 'Thatcher deserves a statue in white marble here on the Plaza de Mayo'. She had broken the hated junta, at whose hands thousands of people, including the woman's son, had disappeared. At home, the prime minister's ratings in the opinion polls, which stood at rock bottom in late 1981, soared to 51 per cent in June 1982.

From Hugo Young, *One of Us: Life of Margaret Thatcher*, published in 1989

However, there were some negative effects for both Thatcher and the country, as one of her more recent biographers points out.

Source Q

The Falklands War was a watershed in domestic politics, leading directly to the unprecedented domination that Mrs Thatcher established over the next eight years. As well as hugely boosting her authority and self confidence, the experience of war leadership encouraged autocratic tendencies which had hitherto been contained. In particular the speed and convenience of working through a small War Cabinet led her increasingly to by pass the full Cabinet in favour of decision making through hand-picked ad hoc committees and her personal advisers. Meanwhile, the conviction that it was only her firmness which had brought victory encouraged her belief that a refusal to compromise was the only language foreigners understood.

Victory in the South Atlantic exacerbated her worst characteristics not her best. After 1982 she used her augmented authority to pursue more self-righteously than before her particular vision of British society and to trample on those groups, institutions and traditions which did not share it.

From John Campbell, *Margaret Thatcher*, revised edition published in 2009

Source R

8.1 The Royal Navy Falklands Task Force is escorted back to Portsmouth by a flotilla of small-craft

The Labour Party abandons consensus politics

The antics of the Labour Party in these years could have been scripted by Conservative Central Office. If Thatcher and Keith Joseph felt that the trusted policies of post-war Britain had failed the nation and new initiatives were called for, within the Labour Party there was a similar mood, but here the case was being made for full-blooded socialism. Compromises with capitalism, membership of the EEC and even NATO were increasingly denounced. Constituency parties were moving further to the left as members of the Militant Tendency infiltrated poorly attended branches and bullied long-standing party activists into silence. Endless resolutions calling for widespread nationalisation were passed by constituency parties and funnelled up to the party conference. Callaghan was 70 in 1981 and chose to retire. He hoped that by going before the activists could change the rules for the election of leader, Denis Healey would inherit the crown. On a first ballot Healey came first, beating Michael Foot by 112 to 83. When the other two candidates withdrew, however, Foot beat Healey by 139 to 129. An old campaigner of the left had become leader. Foot was a long-time supporter of CND, a republican and an avowed atheist; it appeared that Labour had surrendered to the extremes as this Cummings cartoon indicates.

Source S

8.2 Cartoon by Michael Cummings, *Daily Express*, 14 January 1981

Definition

Gang of four

This was a reference to four leading Labour politicians: Shirley Williams, Bill Rodgers, David Owen and, most prestigious and famous of all, Roy Jenkins, newly returned from being president of the European commission. Jenkins was often satirically referred to as the 'prince from over the water' or in view of his pronounced lisp, 'the pwince'. The phrase 'gang of four' had become famous in the 1970s from Chinese politics.

In reality, Foot's years in government in the 1970s had induced a certain realism. The real leader of the left was now Tony Benn and, since Foot was already 67, it looked likely that he would soon inherit the crown. This was particularly so as a special Labour conference in January 1981 agreed to change the rules for the election of future leaders. From now on there would be a tripartite system with MPs counting 30 per cent, constituency parties 30 per cent and affiliated trade unions 40 per cent. It was a triumph for the left. Immediately a group of right-wing Labour MPs, led by the **Gang of four**, issued the Limehouse Declaration.

8.3 The Gang of four

Initially the Council for Social Democracy was to be a pressure group within the Labour Party, but in March 1981, 12 Labour MPs withdrew from the party whip and the Social Democrat Party was born. It resolved to form an alliance with the Liberal Party under David Steel and this became generally known as the Alliance. It was initially a massive success. A string of by-elections revealed its potential and the unpopularity of the two major parties. Roy Jenkins chose to stand in the safe Labour seat of Warrington and nearly won. Shirley Williams, standing in the Merseyside suburbs of Crosby, which had returned a Tory in 1979 with a 19,000 majority, won with 5000. Roy Jenkins did then return to parliament with a by-election win in Glasgow Hillhead in March 1982. Eventually, 29 Labour MPs joined the new party, but despite the discontents of the Conservative 'wets' with Thatcher, only one Tory crossed the floor to join Roy Jenkins. Christopher Brocklebank Fowler was described as being 'so wet you can shoot snipe off him'. Appropriately enough he came from the fenlands of Norfolk. Despite the disappointing number of defections from the Conservatives, it really did look as if the Alliance would change the face of British politics. Then came the Falklands War.

General election, 1983

As Source P indicates, the prime minister's approval ratings leapt and the Tories crept into a comfortable lead. Not surprisingly, Margaret Thatcher decided to cash in on her new-found popularity and in 1983 called an election for June. The role of the 'Falklands factor' has been debated by historians, as this recent study, Source U, makes clear.

Source T

The conference disaster is the culmination of a long process by which the Labour Party has moved steadily away from its roots in the people of this country and its commitment to parliamentary government.

We propose to set up a Council for Social Democracy. Our intention is to rally all those who are committed to the values, principles and policies of social democracy. We recognise that for those people who have given much of their lives to the Labour Party, the choice that lies ahead will be deeply painful. But we believe that the need for a realignment of British politics must now be faced.

From the Limehouse Declaration, 25 January 1981

Source U

Her political opponents were bitter about exploitation of military victory for internal ends and made much of the ways in which the Falklands allegedly benefited the Tories in the 1983 election.

In fact, less than a third of Conservative candidates referred directly to the Falklands during the 1983 campaign, though many of them made more general remarks about the restoration of British prestige, and few voters admitted that the Falklands had exercised any influence over them. The point about the electoral significance of the Falklands, however, was precisely that it mattered only when mixed with other ingredients. One of these was defence. The election was fought at a time when tension between the Soviet Union and the West was high and when the Labour Party supported unilateral nuclear disarmament.

From Richard Vinen, *Thatcher's Britain: The Politics and Social Upheaval of the Thatcher Era*, published in 2009

Clearly there were other developments favouring the Tories. Inflation had fallen rapidly and economic growth was beginning to spread a sense of affluence, particularly in the South and Midlands. New high-tech industries were springing up in places like Cambridge and the so-called M4 corridor, stretching from London down to South Wales. The suffering of the economic blizzard of the early 1980s had largely been confined to the North and Scotland. Spring had arrived in the South. There were plenty of seats for the Conservatives to hold and gain.

The Labour Party drafted an election manifesto, which was described by Gerald Kaufman, a front bench member of the party, as 'the longest suicide note in history'. Withdrawal from the EEC had the support of a sizeable minority, but unilateral nuclear disarmament was widely unpopular. In his memoirs, Roy Jenkins spelled out what it meant to support Labour in 1983, see Source V.

Source V

It should not be forgotten what was involved in accepting the Labour ticket at the election: withdrawal from Europe, unilateralism, the reduction to a mockery of membership of NATO, massive further nationalisation, the forbidding by law of private education or private health care, the almost total surrender to trade union power.

From Roy Jenkins, *A Life at the Centre*, published in 1991

The Labour Party had abandoned consensus politics and British voters abandoned them. Labour did worse than at any time since 1918, securing only 27 per cent of the vote in June. Labour still won 209 seats in its northern and Scottish heartlands.

It might be expected that the SDP would do well. A formal deal had been negotiated with the Liberals but only after much acrimony, which damaged both parties. It was agreed that if they won, Roy Jenkins would be prime minister. In the event, the Alliance secured 26 per cent of the vote, only just behind Labour. The first-past-the-post system ensured that these popular votes did not translate into seats won. They secured only 23 seats, 17 Liberal and 6 SDP. Jenkins would not be prime minister.

Margaret Thatcher romped home with a massive majority of 142. Although the Conservatives secured just under 43 per cent of the popular vote, less than in 1979, the British system worked for them in terms of the 397 seats won. Conservative strength lay in the South and Midlands. In a sense, Britain was being polarised geographically as never before. On the other hand, there was less traditional class identification with particular political parties. The Conservatives won 31 per cent of the trade union vote. Only

40 per cent voted Labour. In large numbers, the working class or the ex-working class were voting Conservative, at least in the South and Midlands. On the other hand, the Conservatives were losing their hold on the professional middle classes, many of whom identified with the Alliance. This was a significant part of the Thatcher revolution.

Unit summary

What have you learned in this unit?

This unit has covered a considerable amount of information even though it is focused on only four years of the Thatcher premiership. You have learned what it was that Thatcher and her close colleagues, such as Geoffrey Howe, wished to achieve and why. You have learned about the tough changes introduced in successive Budgets and their economic consequences and the criticisms made. You have learned about the challenge posed by the SDP and the damaging developments within the Labour Party. Finally, the unlooked for war in the South Atlantic has been addressed and its political consequences in Britain considered.

What skills have you used in this unit?

You have encountered a large number of secondary sources relating to this period and these can pose rather special problems for few periods have excited so much controversy and debate amongst contemporaries and historians. In a sense this reflects the fact that it was in these years that 'consensus politics' broke down.

Exam style question

This is the type of question that you will find on the examination paper as a (b) question. You will use the sources provided, with your own knowledge.

Study Sources P, U and V.

How far do you agree that it was the 'Falklands factor' that was the decisive factor in the Conservative victory in the election of June 1983?

Explain your answer using the evidence of Sources P, U and V, and your own knowledge.

Exam tips

Do use the sources to structure your answer, carefully identifying in which direction each source points. Clearly Source P points out the Falkland factor but Source V draws attention to the deficiencies of the Labour Party. Source U nicely sits between the two, both literally and in its views.

Make sure that you understand this latter point. Each viewpoint needs unpacking and developing using your own knowledge. Feel free to throw in important points not dealt with in the sources, such as the economic recovery underway in 1983 and the regional split in the voting reflecting the differences in the economic experience of 1979–83.

RESEARCH TOPIC

The Margaret Thatcher Foundation offers a massive resource for research. It has put on-line all of her public statements. It also contains material from other associated politicians such as Keith Joseph and gives access to a number of other archival sources. To access this website go to www.pearsonschoolsandfecolleges.co.uk/hotlinks, enter the express code 5056P and select the appropriate chapter.

9 The high tide and ebb tide of Thatcherism, 1983–90

What is this unit about?

This unit examines the period of Margaret Thatcher's last six and a half years as prime minister. A major conflict with the miners developed at home and, after a bitter struggle, it was felt by many Conservatives that revenge had been gained for the humiliations of 1972 and 1974. Privatisation accelerated and it appeared that the growing boom and prosperity was creating a new consensus around a free-market state. Despite the stresses and strains induced by Conservative reforms, the Labour Party still seemed in no shape to mount an effective challenge and a third large electoral Tory victory resulted in June 1987. Despite this, there were strains within the Cabinet and within the Tory party, where Mrs Thatcher's autocratic approach was resented by an increasing number of her followers. There were particular difficulties over the relationship with Europe, which widened fissures in the party. The attempt to reform the financing of local government produced a serious popular backlash and a growing sense that, without a change of leadership, the Tories would lose the next election.

Key questions

- What were the characteristics of Thatcher's style of government in these years?
- Why did conflict develop with the miners and with what result?
- In what ways was Britain altered in these years?
- Why did the Labour Party do so badly in the 1987 election?
- Why was Thatcher forced to resign in 1990?

Timeline

1983	June	Election victory for the Conservatives
1984	March	Miners' strike begins
1985	March	Miners' strike ends in defeat
	October	Kinnock attacks the Militant Tendency at the Labour Party conference
1986	January	Michael Heseltine resigns
	October	Big Bang in the City
1987	June	General election: Conservatives 376, Labour 229, Liberal-SDP 22
	October	Stock market crash
1988	September	Thatcher makes 'Bruges' speech opposing further European integration

1989	October	Resignation of Nigel Lawson
1990	November	Resignation of Geoffrey Howe
	December	Fall of Thatcher

Second term: the high tide of Thatcherism

Not surprisingly, the new Cabinet was even drier than before. Francis Pym was sacked as Foreign Secretary and replaced by the quiet but loyal Geoffrey Howe. The dry but flamboyant Nigel Lawson took over the Exchequer. Leon Brittan became Home Secretary in place of Willie Whitelaw, who went to the Lords as deputy prime minister. He was still capable of exercising some restraint and guidance on his increasingly confident chief. Mrs Thatcher accepted that every prime minister needed a Willie (not strong on humour, the inadvertent joke had to be explained to her). A few leading wets survived. Peter Walker was sent to energy to prepare for battle with the miners. Thatcher appreciated his abilities. Jim Prior hung on for a further 12 months as Secretary for Northern Ireland, but then resigned in 1984. Perhaps the most dangerous and unconventional of the 'wets' was Michael Heseltine. He was the darling of Conservative Party conferences with his flowing blond hair and colourful speeches. He was popularly nicknamed 'Tarzan'. He desperately wanted Thatcher's job and she knew it. He became Secretary for Defence.

The enemy within

The central drama of the second term was the great miners' strike of 1984–85. Once again, Thatcher was lucky in her enemies. The canny and moderate miners' leader, Joe Gormley, had retired and in his place the NUM overwhelmingly elected the Yorkshire miners' leader, Arthur Scargill in 1981. Scargill was an avowed Marxist, but he had left the Communist Party and joined the Labour Party. He still had some revolutionary aspirations. Since the ballot box had proved unsatisfactory in removing the Conservatives in 1983, then direct action could possibly be tried. Andrew Marr has a colourful and illuminating section on Scargill in his section on the miners' strike.

Source A

Many found Scargill inspiring, many others found him frankly scary. He had been a Communist and retained strong Marxist views and a penchant for denouncing anyone who disagreed with him as a traitor. Some found a megalomaniac atmosphere at his Barnsley headquarters, already known as Arthur's Castle. Kim Howells, then a Communist and later a New Labour minister, visited him there and was taken aback to find him sitting at 'this Mussolini desk with a great space in front of it' and behind him a huge painting of himself on the back of a lorry, posed like Lenin, urging picketing workers in London to overthrow the ruling class. Howells thought anyone who could put up a painting like that was nuts and returned to express his fears to the Welsh miners. 'And of course the South Wales Executive almost to a man agreed with me. But then said "He's the only one we've got, see boy." The Left has decided.'

From Andrew Marr, *A History of Modern Britain*, published in 2007

The central issue between the miners and the government was the closure of uneconomic pits. This was all part of the government's drive to reduce government subsidies to inefficient nationalised industries. The union, which in the 1950s and 1960s had accepted this, now dug their heels in and virtually refused to contemplate the closure of any pit no matter how uneconomic. No government could ultimately tolerate this and a show-down was inevitable. Many Tories, including the prime minister, looked forward to revenge for past humiliations and Peter Walker, as the new Secretary for Energy, made preparations for conflict. To Margaret Thatcher, Scargill was 'the enemy within' to be defeated as roundly as General Galtieri had been. In many ways, it was a battle between a new southern England and an older northern England, in some ways reminiscent of the Northern Rebellion of 1569, when northern feudal earls took on the majesty of Elizabeth Tudor. Margaret Thatcher now played the part of Elizabeth I with relish and with a certainty that she was right and had to win if her vision of a new revived Britain was to become reality.

There was considerable resistance within the mining communities to striking. In the run up to the outbreak of the strike, 50,000 out of 70,000 balloted on a local basis opposed striking. In view of this, Scargill committed a double blunder. He began the strike in the spring, not early winter and decided not to hold a national ballot, which he feared he might lose, but begin with a series of local strikes in areas where militancy was high and strike action would be approved in local votes. The idea was to escalate the action using militants from one area to pressurise others. This tactic initially worked and by April, four out of five miners were on strike. However, in the crucial area of Nottinghamshire, large numbers chose to keep working and the government was determined to use the police to allow those who wished to work to do so and to prevent secondary picketing. The result was repeated scenes of confrontation and violence. Tony Benn describes the conflict at one of the most notorious centres of confrontation in his diary entry for 31 May 1984.

Source B

Over the last few days there have been terrible scenes outside the Orgreave Coke Depot, where 7000 pickets have been attacked by mounted and foot police with riot shields and helmets. It looks like a civil war. You see the police charging with big staves and police dogs chasing miners across fields, then miners respond by throwing stones and trying to drag a telegraph pole across a road; there are burning buildings and roadblocks.

From Tony Benn, *The Benn Diaries*, published in 1995

To Conservatives and many non-Conservatives, it was a struggle about parliamentary democracy and the rule of law on one side and an ideologically motivated egotist, who wished to be the British Lenin, on the other. Such a view is expressed in the following cartoon:

Source C

9.1 Cartoon by 'Trog' Wally Fawkes, *Observer*, 18 November 1984

To Tony Benn and many others on the more extreme left of the political spectrum, it was a class struggle. Benn's diary entry for 5 May 1984 is detailed in Source D.

The strike dragged on throughout 1984, the mining communities showing intense loyalty in a strike that many had never wanted but could not stand aside from once the battle was joined. The government were equally determined to win and police were used from all over the country. Flying pickets were answered with flying police, some it has been alleged were, in fact troops, in police uniforms. By early 1985, more and more miners were seeking to go back to work and the government was determined to protect their rights to do so. Heart-breaking divisions were created in communities, which have never healed. By the end of February more than half the NUM's members were back in the pits. The dispute ended in early March. Arthur Scargill's scalp had joined that of General Galtieri on Margaret Thatcher's belt.

The defeat of the miners was symbolic and probably necessary to the modernisation of the economy. This was clearly illustrated shortly afterwards, as the following extract from the *Penguin History of Britain* makes clear.

Source D

The miners won't budge, and it is a very long strike, already longer than the 1926 strike. The TUC has got to back them, because, to put it bluntly, if the miners are beaten, the Government will ride all over everybody and workers couldn't stand up to it again, so the miners must not be beaten.

From Tony Benn, *The Benn Diaries*, published in 1995

Source E

The humbling of the miners, with their reputation as the shock troops of the Labour movement, was shortly to be complemented by the equally forthright defeat of the newspaper printers, whose tight hold over Fleet Street had made them a byword for restrictive practices. When Murdoch, intent on asserting his right to manage, installed new computerised technology for Times Newspapers at a vast, fortified new plant at Wapping, in the old docklands, he was able to invoke the cover of the law in a final confrontation with the old print unions. Neither of these bitter industrial disputes were over pay. The coal strike had the greater political resonance but the Wapping dispute had the wider economic significance, by overcoming union resistance to changes in working practices.

From Peter Clarke, *Hope and Glory*, published in 1996

More radical reform: rolling back the state

The second term was marked by a concerted effort to reduce the roll of the state in the economy by privatising state-owned and local government-owned property. Here was a determined attempt to overthrow the post-war settlement, which had left 20 per cent of the country's industry in the state's hands. Some privatisation had begun in the first term. Cable and Wireless was sold in 1981 for £240 million. In 1983, the prime minister justified the strategy to the House of Commons, see Source F.

There were other advantages to the government. It raised revenue. It weakened trade unions, which tended to be very strong in the public sector. It also, it was hoped, created more Tory voters by creating more share-owning citizens. Popular capitalism and efficiency could go hand in hand. After 1983, every year saw more sales and in every year the government raised more than £1 billion from the sale of companies. This reached a climax in 1988–89 when £7.1 billion was raised. The sale of Jaguar Cars in 1984 seemed to illustrate the case by the prime minister in Source F. As part of nationalised British Leyland, it was making a loss of £32 million on a turn over of £224 million. By 1985, as a private company, it was making a profit of £121 million on a turnover of £747 million. In November 1984, came the far bigger sale of British Telecom. Kenneth Harris, the biographer of Thatcher, points out its remarkable success.

Source F

Privatisation, through exposing former state owned companies more fully to the disciplines and opportunities of the market, improves the efficiency of business' that are crucial to our overall economic performance. As such it forms an important part of the Government's overall strategy for long term economic growth, further reinforcing the enterprise culture that is essential for economic success.

From a speech by Margaret Thatcher in the House of Commons, February 1983

Source G

To the amazement of the City, and even to some members of the government, the public response was overwhelming, the offer was four times oversubscribed with the private investor putting up more than £6 billion for shares worth £1.5 billion in a partly paid form. The response had exceeded all expectations, and the government's undue caution was demonstrated in the first day of trading of the new BT shares when the excessively low price doubled in value. Over two million people became shareholders, half of them as direct investors for the first time. Mrs. Thatcher's popular capitalism had hit the big time.

From Kenneth Harris, *Thatcher*, published in 1988

A roll call of companies followed, British Gas privatised for £5.5 billion, Trustees Savings Bank, British Airways, Rolls Royce and BP. The number of shareholders rose from three million in 1979 to nine million by the end of the decade. The percentage of the electorate in trade unions declined from 30 per cent in 1979 to 22 per cent in 1987. These changes amounted to almost a social and economic revolution. By 1990, a greater proportion of the population owned shares than in France or Germany. Nigel Lawson's introduction of Personal Equity Plans (PEPs) also encouraged savers to buy shares and shelter them in their PEPs, free from taxation. In his 1988 Budget, income tax was, in fact, reduced to 25 per cent at the standard rate and 40 per cent at the top rate. This was a far cry from the 1970s when some unearned income had been taxed at 98 per cent.

Another aspect of this same revolution was the sale of houses owned by local councils. In 1979, a third of all housing was so owned. In 1980, the government introduced 'right to buy' legislation for all tenants who had lived in a property for a minimum of three years. This was lowered to two years in 1984. It appeared enormously popular and over a million council houses were sold in the 1980s. This helped to cement Britain as a property owning democracy.

If the restrictive practices of trade unions were attacked, so were the restrictive practices of the City of London. The gentlemanly world of the stock exchange with its leisurely class-ridden culture of brokers and jobbers was suddenly exposed to the full blast of the free market. Foreign banks and foreign dealers poured into London following the **'Big Bang'** of October 1986. American and Japanese Banks took over smallish British investment banks and brokers. Computerised trading was introduced and the city began a crazed expansion, massively enriching some but also hugely contributing to the increase in national wealth. From being a poor third behind Tokyo and New York, by the 21st century London had recaptured its place as the world's leading financial centre, a position not held since 1914. As Andrew Marr asserts, 'The truth is that without the Big Bang, Britain's books would be in much worse condition.'

> **Definition**
>
> **'Big Bang'**
> The nickname given to the reform of the stock exchange introduced on 27 October 1986. It basically opened up trading to more people and freed up the market by de-regulation.

The problem of Northern Ireland

Running through the whole decade was the bloody, unsolved problem of Northern Ireland. The violence that had exploded in the early 1970s continued and from time to time erupted in some dramatic fashion on the mainland. Just as the election campaign of 1979 was gathering pace, Airey Neave, the Tory MP who had done so much to get Margaret Thatcher elected leader, was murdered when a bomb blew up in the Palace of Westminster. Ian Gow, probably the MP closest to Thatcher, was murdered on his drive in Sussex in 1990, just before the prime minister left office. Most shocking of all was the attempt to kill the prime minister herself by exploding a massive bomb in the middle of the night at the Grand Hotel Brighton where most of the Cabinet were staying for the 1984 Tory Party conference. Five were killed and Norman Tebbit's wife crippled for life. Thatcher appeared immaculate as ever in the conference chamber at 9.30 sharp the next morning and later faultlessly delivered her speech. No one could ever deny her courage.

In Northern Ireland, the violence continued but at a reduced level compared to the crisis years of 1971–73. Perhaps two dozen or so police and members of the armed services and around 50 civilians were killed each year. The cost in terms of subsidies to the economic infrastructure and the deployment of around 12,000 troops was a considerable drain on the Exchequer. Thatcher was basically a devout Unionist and could see no reason for altering her position while the majority of Northern Ireland's population wished to remain part of the UK, as undoubtedly they did. The challenges to her were enormous and the pressure from both Dublin and the USA for a compromise settlement considerable. One of the IRA's most effective tactics was the campaign of hunger strikes by prisoners in the Maze Prison, beginning in 1980. The demand was for status as political prisoners not ordinary criminals. This was totally unacceptable to the British government, who in view of their acts saw them simply as criminals. The Maze was in every respect a model prison, conforming to all aspects of the charter of human rights, yet the IRA denounced it as a 'British death camp'. This was total nonsense, but the power of propaganda convinced many of the Catholic community in both the Irish Republic and within the Irish community in the USA that this was the scene of a modern atrocity. When Bobby Sands starved himself to death in May 1981, there was outrage, yet Thatcher was rightly unmoved. It was self-inflicted and totally unjustified by any objective criteria, but it took political courage to say so and accept other deaths. Once again this was a display of moral courage and determination on the prime minister's part but one that was not popular in liberal circles.

In 1984, Jim Prior decided to resign as Northern Ireland Secretary and was replaced by Douglas Hurd. His memoirs give some of the flavour of what it was like to have to live with the ever-present danger. In October, he was due to open a new bridge over the river Foyle at Londonderry:

Source H

We drove into Londonderry past the statue of Queen Victoria, her hands amputated by a bomb. The young Mayor was shaking with nervousness. I was not allowed to drive across the bridge but snipped the tape at one end, resolving to come back on a less tense occasion.

I never myself felt physical fear in Northern Ireland. Those who protected me did not conceal the fact that they were unlikely to be able to save my life in an ambush, but could probably kill or catch my assailants afterwards.

From Douglas Hurd, *Memoirs*, published in 2003

Clearly the answer was a political deal but this proved impossible. The Irish Republic demanded a commitment to some modification of British sovereignty and this, Thatcher would never agree to. Had she done so, then the ire of the Ulster Protestants would have made such a deal unworkable. The nearest she came to a deal, which some see as a forerunner of the Good Friday Agreement of 1997, which seems to have ended the 'Troubles' was the Anglo-Irish Agreement of November 1985. It was a modest concession to Irish Nationalism, merely agreeing to regular consultations with Dublin about Northern Ireland. Even so, it produced outrage among Unionists and Thatcher herself felt guilty that she may have betrayed them. Basically, the problem remained unsolved, but it was contained.

Neil Kinnock and the Labour Party's long road back to sanity

The Election of 1983 was a disaster for the Labour Party and many began to wonder what had gone wrong. It was clear that the party had lost touch with its own supporters. Michael Foot immediately resigned and a young left-wing activist, who like Foot was a keen supporter of CND, was elected in his place. Neil Kinnock was personable and young, and, in a rather long-winded fashion, an able speaker. He was immediately embarrassed by the miners' strike. He came to detest Scargill, but found himself having to support the strike, even though he felt the tactics were idiotic. It was an unfortunate beginning to his leadership. He found himself equally embarrassed by the antics of the far left Militant Tendency, which was pushing the party further into unelectability. Derek Hatton, a leading militant and effective leader of Liverpool City Council, successfully got the 1984 Labour conference to pass a resolution supporting councils that broke the law by resisting the government's attempts to set limits to rate increases. Kinnock got his chance to counter-attack the next year when he delivered a stinging attack on Hatton and his fellow militants in Liverpool. Their resistance to the government's policy had ended in a fiasco.

Source I

I'll tell you what happens with impossible promises. You start with far-fetched resolutions. They are pickled into a rigid dogma, a code, and you go through the years sticking to that, out-dated, misplaced, irrelevant to the real needs, and you end in the grotesque chaos of a Labour council – a Labour council – hiring taxis to scuttle round the city handing out redundancy notices to its own workers. I am telling you no matter how entertaining, how fulfilling to short-term egos – I'm telling you and you'll listen – you can't play politics with people's jobs and with people's services or with their homes.

From a speech by Neil Kinnock to the Labour Party conference in Bournemouth, October 1985

He was booed and heckled, and Eric Heffer, a left-wing Labour MP from Liverpool stormed off the platform; but it was the beginning of Labour's fight back for electability. Not surprisingly, Tony Benn gives a very different impression of the days' events in his diary entry for 1 October 1985.

Source J

Kinnock spoke as if the Liverpool councillors wanted to fire people, when actually they are themselves victims of government policy. It was all part of his strategy to kill off any left wing challenge by appealing for unity and on that basis to get a right wing NEC and accuse the left of being divisive. Kinnock has released the hatred of the Tory press against his own people in the middle of a struggle.

From Tony Benn, *The Benn Diaries*, published in 1995

SKILLS BUILDER

How do Sources I and J differ in their attitudes towards the militants in the Labour Party?

After the conference, an internal Labour investigation was launched into activities of the militants in Liverpool, and Hatton and many of his colleagues were expelled from the Party. Slowly Kinnock, with the support of such figures from the 'soft left' as David Blunkett of Sheffield, recaptured the NEC. By the time of the 1987 election, some of Labour's more extreme policies, such as withdrawal from Europe and opposition to the sale of council houses, had been dropped. There was still a commitment to unilateral nuclear disarmament and the repeal of Tory trade union legislation. No one in the party expected to win, but it was hoped that there would be an improvement on the disastrous result of 1983. There was an improvement (see page 175) and the attempt by the hard left campaign group to stop the return to moderation and 'consensus politics' was decisively beaten off in 1988 when Tony Benn and Eric Heffer chose to stand against Kinnock and Roy Hattersley for the leadership and deputy leadership positions.

Source K

'This may take some time — the horse has died laughing'

9.2 Cartoon by 'Mac' Stan McMurty, *Daily Mail*, 25 March 1988

SKILLS BUILDER

How far does Source L support the view expressed in Source K?

Source L

When the result came it was appalling. My total of the electoral vote came to 11 per cent. I did my best to look impassive and cheerful on the platform. I just touched Neil Kinnock on the shoulder and smiled.

From Tony Benn, *The Benn Diaries*, published in 1995

General election, 1987

The election of 1987 was in many ways unexciting. Everyone expected a Tory victory. The economy appeared to be booming, the Liberals and Social Democrats appeared less than happy in their alliance and for all the improvements in the Labour Party, it still seemed too extreme and riven with faction. The notable Conservative wet, Julian Critchley, remembers little of the election in his memoir but gives this simple explanation of the result.

The result was a convincing Conservative victory. They won 376 seats with 42.3 per cent of the vote. Labour increased their share slightly and gained 229. The Alliance lost votes and finished with 22 seats. Once again the Conservatives swept the South and Midlands but faced near extinction in Scotland.

Reform of Health and Education

Many had come to question the quality of state education provision, particularly when compared with other leading industrial states. Callaghan, in a speech in 1976, had asked serious questions about why so many pupils leaving British secondary schools lacked basic literacy and numeracy skills. It was particularly worrying that large numbers of middle-class families chose to by-pass the state system altogether, particularly in London, and send their children to private schools. Private education had flourished as never before as the drive for comprehensives had removed the grammar schools.

The Thatcher governments did not prioritise education but an Act in 1981, which came into effect in 1983, extended education provision for those with special needs. This certainly helped some of the most challenged

Source M

The bubble of the Lawson boom had not yet burst, Neil Kinnock was almost as unsatisfactory a party leader as Michael Foot had been and the Liberals cheerfully split the anti-Conservative vote.

From Julian Critchley, *A Bag of Boiled Sweets: An Autobiography*, published in 1994

Source N

A poll published today gives the Tories an 18 per cent lead. Mrs Thatcher was so confident on the television news, and Kinnock was so boastful and wordy and weak. His popularity is falling rapidly.

From Tony Benn's Diary, Friday 15 May 1987

Source O

9.3 Cartoon by Michael Cummings, *Daily Express*, 21 June 1987

SKILLS BUILDER

How far do Sources M, N and O agree on the reasons for the Conservative victory in 1987?

pupils. A more wide-ranging Act was passed in 1988 with the intention of freeing schools from tight local authority control. Increased powers were given to school governors and parents' representatives were to dominate these bodies rather than the nominees of the local authorities. Schools were to enjoy greater control over their budgets and colleges became freed altogether from local authority control. The strategy reflected a faith in greater freedom and a belief that some element of competition could be introduced to raise standards. The other prong of the attack involved the exact opposite approach, namely greater central government control through the imposition of the national curriculum on all state schools. How far this twin approach worked to the benefit of children is difficult to judge.

With regard to that other great drain on the public purse, the National Health Service, there was a similar mixed approach which tried to raise standards of efficiency through introducing the principles of competition and the market place but also imposed greater bureaucratic accountability and the extra costs of more management. Health costs had continued to spiral as more and more treatments became available and people lived longer. In 1981 twice as many people were over 80 compared to 1951. Various reforms were considered but it was not until 1989 that the principles of reform were unveiled in the government White Paper *Working for Patients*. This attempted to introduce the so-called 'internal market'. GPs would control their budgets and choose where to refer their patients for further treatment which meant they could 'shop around'. Hospital Trusts would run large hospitals and health authorities would buy their services. The theory was that, as with education, delegation of budgets and choice would improve efficiency. One thing it did do was increase the numbers of managers and their cost. The implementation of the reforms came largely after the fall of Thatcher.

Decline and fall

There was always something unusual in Margaret Thatcher's relationship with her Cabinet. She was not a team player and inclined to be bossy. This latter quality became worse with time. Trivial incidents illustrate this. Paddy Ashdown, the new Liberal leader in succession to David Steel, gives an illuminating insight into the prime minister at a Remembrance Day ceremony in 1988, in Source P.

She had already clashed in dramatic fashion with one of her most talented ministers before the 1987 election. Michael Heseltine, nicknamed 'Tarzan' for his flowing locks and macho behaviour, entered a lengthy confrontation with the prime minister over a bid for a British helicopter company, Westland. Thatcher and her protégé Leon Brittan, as Minister for Trade and Industry, preferred an American bid; Heseltine as Minister of Defence argued for a European consortium. It ended in a theatrical walk out from the Cabinet by Heseltine in January 1986. There had been clear leaks to the press in breach of regulations and these, it eventually transpired, had come from Number 10, although Brittan resigned and took the blame instead. Thatcher was let off the hook, partially because Neil Kinnock failed to ask the right questions in the Commons. She had, however, lost

Source P

Maggie fussed around, bullied us into two lines . . . then she proceeded to go down the lined up Cabinet like a sergeant major, inspecting new recruits, straightening the Foreign Secretary's tie, flicking specks of dust off the Chancellor's coat etc.

From Paddy Ashdown, *The Ashdown Diaries vol I*, published in 2000 two more ministers. In the prime ministerial league table of ministerial resignations, she heads the list.

Source Q

"No, Michael, YOU'VE got it wrong—YOU Michael, ME Tarzan!"

9.4 Cartoon by 'Jak' Raymond Jackson, *Evening Standard*, 23 December 1985

Source R

After her third general election victory in 1987, she developed an arrogant sense that she was politically immortal. In truth the cracks appeared almost at once. They were later to develop into connected chasms in which her leadership perished; the poll tax, the economy and Europe.

From John Cole, *As it Seemed to Me: Political Memoirs*, published in 1995

The election victory of 1987 added to Thatcher's sense of certainty and self-belief, and this prepared the way for her downfall.

In the course of 1987–88, it appeared that the economic miracle was spurious. A stock market crash in October 1987 was followed by a whole series of undesirable developments. The pound fell dramatically and inflation took off again. Lawson's answer was to raise interest rates, which hurt mortgage holders, and to try to tie the pound more closely to European currencies, in particular the German mark. Both Lawson and the Foreign Secretary, Geoffrey Howe, seemed in favour of joining the European Exchange Rate Mechanism, a precursor of the Euro and single European currency. The prime minister would have none of this and bitter arguments ensued. Lawson, the Chancellor of the Exchequer, was not an easy-going colleague and had an arrogance to match the prime minister. Her insistence on retaining the services of Professor Alan Walters, as an independent financial adviser, led to Lawson's resignation in October 1989.

Thatcher herself stirred up widespread discontent with her government by enthusiastically backing the reform of the financing of local government. The roots of this were varied. The existing system of rates based on antique valuations of houses was unfair and unpopular with many. A single old-age pensioner, who consumed little in the way of local services, could be paying considerably more than all five adult occupants of a smaller house. Thatcher wished to make local councils more responsible to their

Source S

Cummings

THE
ECONOMY

"As you're such a good back-seat driver, I've resigned as
chauffeur — so you can change the wheel, yourself!"

9.5 Cartoon by Michael Cummings, *Daily Express*, 29 October 1989

electors by ensuring that rate-payers experience the pain of free-spending local authorities and thus control them. If local electors chose left-wing councils, who in her judgement frittered away public money, they should have to suffer the cost of their choice. The answer seemed obvious – a poll tax. All adults should pay the same amount since all gained from it. This would mean a considerable increase in local taxes for those living in smaller properties. The last poll tax had produced the Peasant's Revolt in 1381 and this was rather similar. There were riots and the loss of by-elections by the government. Large numbers of Tory MPs feared for their seats. The mood grew that 'the Lady' must at long last go.

9.6 The poll tax riots

The final trigger that brought about her fall was the resignation of Geoffrey Howe. He had been demoted in 1989 and repeatedly humiliated by the prime minister in Cabinet. He finally chose to resign over the issue of Europe in November 1990. This most mild-mannered of men (Denis Healey had likened an attack by him to being savaged by a dead sheep) now delivered one of the most effective parliamentary attacks in history. The Tory MP Alan Clark describes the scene in his diary entry for 13 November 1990.

Howe finished with what seemed like a call for a challenge to Thatcher's leadership. Heseltine responded and, in the resulting ballot, Thatcher, although the winner, was short of the necessary majority called for by the rules. After consultation with her Cabinet colleagues, she resigned.

The fall of one of the most powerful post-war prime ministers was sudden and dramatic. It was proof, as a French commentator at the time remarked that Britain really was a 'parliamentary' democracy. Margaret Thatcher had alienated her cabinet colleagues with her increasing bossiness and they took their revenge. She had also lost touch with the Tory back-benchers and in the past had relied on the services of such loyal acolytes as Ian Gow and the robust common sense of Willie Whitelaw to keep her in touch. But both Gow and Whitelaw had gone by 1990. She was increasingly isolated, frozen inside her own certainties. The economic downturn, the disputes over Europe and the deep unpopularity of the poll tax all seem to point to a politician whose time had passed. Tory back-benchers feared that unless they jettisoned her, their seats would be lost. She was removed and her successor, John Major, won a further term in office. Her only consolation was that it was not the hated Heseltine who replaced her. He had been denied the crown he so desperately wanted.

Assessment of Margaret Thatcher's government

Margaret Thatcher must rank as the most controversial of post-war politicians. For long adored and toasted in the golf clubs of southern England, she was reviled in the working men's clubs of much of the North. She was despised by the chattering classes as a crude philistine and Oxford, her old university, refused to grant her an honorary degree much less

Source T

From the moment he rose to his feet Geoffrey got into it. He was personally wounding – to a far greater extent than mere policy differences would justify. Elspeth's [his wife's] hand in every line.

The Labour benches loved it. Grinning from ear to ear they 'Oooh'd' and 'Aaah'd' dead on cue. At one point he illustrated his sense of betrayal with some cricketing analogy, being sent into bat for Britain . . . only to find that before the game the bats had been broken by the team captain. Everyone gasped.

From Alan Clark, *Diaries*, published in 2001

Source U

The university teachers on masse – if so petty a swarm could be described as a masse – voted against her being allowed an honorary degree by 738 votes to 319. All sorts of bogus justifications were produced for this exhibition of Lilliputian malice – Thatcher's supposed philistinism, or cuts in expenditure on libraries, the arts and so forth. As a matter of fact, Thatcher was no more philistine than many politicians and she was considerably more intelligent. Whatever view might be taken of her politics, it was surely quite an achievement to have risen from modest origins to become the first woman prime minister and it might have been thought that the university would have been big enough to see that her journey was unimaginable without Oxford, that she was Oxford's daughter and as such deserved an honour.

From A.N. Wilson, *Our Times: The Age of Elizabeth II*, published in 2008 accept her in the prestigious post of Chancellor. They preferred Roy Jenkins of the SDP. A.N. Wilson, in his very personal survey of modern Britain, vents his spleen over the decision (see Source U).

Perhaps some of the hostility shown in Oxford can be explained by the following extract from Professor Eric Evans.

Source V

True, Thatcherism believed in the beneficence of market forces, using these 'to turn Britain around' and re-establish an era of national greatness. But not in much else. The list of those things Thatcherism attacked or demeaned is far longer: welfare, the power of the state to improve people's lives, the professional ethic of service, local government, trade unions, the notion of community, Europe. Margaret Thatcher's conviction politics led her more readily to destroy than to create and her abiding narrowness of vision prevented her from seeing the likely medium- and long-term consequences of her policies.

From Eric J. Evans, *Thatcher and Thatcherism*, second edition published in 2004

In contrast Geoffrey Howe, who as we have seen had no reason to make very positive claims for his leader, makes a very positive case.

Source W

And so came the years of triumph that ended in tragedy. Margaret Thatcher's eleven years as Prime Minister still stand as a period of remarkable achievement, albeit marred by decisive and fatal errors in her final term of office. It is all too easy to allow conflict of later years to eclipse the scale of earlier successes. Most difficult and most lasting has been the dismantling of the malign, if unspoken, compact between state ownership and monopoly trade unionism in Britain's bloated public sector. The culmination came with the divisive but essential victory over Arthur Scargill.

Margaret Thatcher is entitled to much of the credit for the renewed economic vitality with which we entered (and won) the 1987 election, still more so for the broader revival of self confidence which sprang from the Falklands victory.

From Geoffrey Howe, *Conflict of Loyalty*, published in 1994

Clearly the assessment of a major political figure will be very much influenced by the political prejudices of the historian and it can be useful to know something of their beliefs in valuing their opinions. It is interesting to finish with two eminent historians of very different political persuasions. First, the concluding judgement of the Labour peer, Kenneth O. Morgan, see Source X.

By comparison, John Charmley is more sympathetic to the Conservative position, see Source Y.

Any final judgement on Margaret Thatcher is impossible as yet, other than that she was an important political phenomena. As Zhou Enlai, the Chinese prime minister of the 1950s and 1960s, famously replied to the question: What was the impact of the French Revolution? – 'It was too soon to tell.' She set herself to reverse a long-term decline in the British

Source X

The logic of Mrs Thatcher's programme since 1979 had been to reverse the main lines of her country's history as it had evolved since the Second World War – the conventional wisdom, the corporatism, the 'debilitating consensus'. Through ceaseless activity and a triumph of will-power, she had by 1987 come as near to success as was possible for one self-sufficient human being. The nation had formally rejected neither her nor her policies by the end of 1990. But below the surface, it had defeated her, just the same.

From Kenneth O. Morgan, *Britain since 1945: The People's Peace*, third edition published in 2001

Source Y

She probably overestimated the capacity of the British people to cope with the downside of 'Freedom' after so many years of having the State take responsibility when things went wrong, but it was inevitable that she would do so. She certainly overestimated the capacity of the Conservative Party to cope with the negative consequences of freeing up the economy. But the depth of emotions stirred in local Conservative associations by her departure was testimony to how well she had kept the faith in which she had been brought up. She had won an unprecedented three elections, she was a figure with a world reputation, and yet in the end the sheer funk of her party and Cabinet meant that she had to go; it was, as she told her colleagues, 'a funny old world'. But it was, both for the British people and for her own party, a world which had been changed by her actions.

From John Charmley, *A History of Conservative Politics 1900–1906*, published in 1996

> ## SKILLS BUILDER
>
> In what ways do Sources X and Y agree with one another and in what ways do they disagree?

economy. Up to 2007, it appeared that she really had succeeded, as British wealth per head once more overtook Italy, then France and even Germany. The pattern of relative decline appeared to have at long last been reversed. Britain became no longer the sick man of Europe but a free-market model to be emulated. France, with its statist rigidities, now seemed to be the social and economic basket case. Some commentators explained Britain's transformation by the fact that Britain had stopped doing what she was poor at, heavy manufacturing, and become focused on what she was good at: financial services, entertainment, education and all the many aspects of a sophisticated service economy. The collapse of manufacturing in the early 1980s has to be acknowledged, but most would agree that this was probably inevitable. Margaret Thatcher merely turned off the life-support system on a near corpse. However, the banking collapse and dramatic economic downturn of 2008–09 brought this whole interpretation into question. Time alone will tell whether long-term economic decline was really reversed in 1979–90, but the decade witnessed the most sustained and single-minded attempt to bring this about.

Unit summary

What have you learned in this unit?

This unit has covered a considerable amount of information. You have learned about how the bitter miners' dispute came about, was conducted and what the implications of this were. You have considered the growing drive to roll back the economic powers of the state by privatising many state-owned enterprises and the impact this had. You have learned about developments within the Labour Party and its attempt to broaden its appeal by marginalising its left-wing radicals. Despite this it went down to defeat again in 1987. Finally you have studied the events leading up to the resignation of Margaret Thatcher in December 1990.

What skills have you used in this unit?

You have encountered a large number of secondary sources relating to this period as well as some primary ones and as with the previous section on the Thatcher premiership, you have encountered the obvious partisan approach of so much of the material. This should have enabled you to realise that bias and prejudice does not invalidate sources but must be considered when judging such sources as evidence.

Exam style question

This is the type of question that you will find on the examination paper as a (b) question. You will use the sources provided, with your own knowledge.

Study Sources E, V and W.

How far do you agree that the Thatcher governments were marked primarily by their positive impact on Britain?

Explain your answer using the evidence of Sources E, V and W, and your own knowledge.

Exam tips

Once again the sources set out the debate for you with Source W being essentially positive and Source V disagreeing with the proposition under consideration. Do contextualise the sources with your own knowledge where appropriate. In this case, Howe as a Thatcher Cabinet minister might be expected to take this line but as you are aware he had reasons not to like Mrs Thatcher. Source E can be cross-referenced with the claims made by Geoffrey Howe. Your own knowledge can be used to bring in areas not directly addressed such as privatisation and taxation policies and to unpack the general charges levelled in Source V.

RESEARCH TOPIC

An obvious area for further research is the reputation of Margaret Thatcher in the 21st century. She still tends to elicit violently opposed reactions. Try to find two people with such views and interview them, asking them to explain what it is that either causes them to detest or admire the 'Iron Lady'.

10 Conclusion

What is this unit about?

This seeks to reflect briefly on the whole 45 years covered by this book and the salient themes addressed.

Key questions

• How was Britain's international position different in 1990 compared to 1945?
• How had British society changed?
• In what ways had the political system changed?
• Political success or failure?

Timeline

1945	End of World War II – first majority Labour Government under Attlee
1948	National Health Service inaugurated
1951	Labour loses power to Conservatives under Churchill
1955	Churchill finally retires to be replaced by Eden
1956	Suez operation – symbolises Britain's decline as a world power
1957	Macmillan becomes prime minister – 'You've never had it so good'
1964	Harold Wilson becomes prime minister with small majority
1966	Labour win large majority
1969	*In Place of Strife* – Labour fail to reform the Unions
1970	Heath unexpectedly beats Wilson to become prime minister
1973	Britain finally joins the European Economic Community
1974	Heath beaten in 'who governs Britain election'
1976	Wilson retires to be replaced by Callaghan. IMF crisis marks beginning of change in policy
1979	Margaret Thatcher becomes the first woman prime minister – Keynesian economic policies openly abandoned
1982	Victorious Falklands' War
1983	Big Conservative victory in general election
1984–85	Miners' strike
1987	Third Conservative election victory
1990	Thatcher fails to defeat challenge to her leadership and resigns

How had Britain changed?

In 1940, during the War, John Betjeman wrote a satirical poem imagining an upper class lady praying in Westminster Abbey, see Source A.

By 1990 many of the assumptions in this poem were no longer applicable. The transformation in the relationship with Germany is perhaps the most obvious. No longer enemies, Britain and Germany were close trading partners in the EEC. In 1990, one of Margaret Thatcher's cabinet colleagues, a notable 'dry,' Nicholas Ridley was forced to resign as Secretary for Trade and Industry, for making disparaging comments about the Germans in an interview with the editor of the Spectator. It was a far cry from *'Gracious Lord, oh bomb the Germans'*. 1990, in some ways marked the final ending of the most direct and obvious consequences of the war, which had for so-longed shaped Britain's position in the world. Germany was finally re-united, not without some trepidation on Margaret Thatcher's part, but it was something she could not resist. The Cold War and the confrontation with the Soviet Union ended in the same year with the collapse of the Soviet Union and the whole of Communism in Eastern Europe. This confrontation had begun in 1945 and both Britain's major political parties had accepted it and the consequent need for a close alliance with the USA. In many ways it was one of the key planks in consensus politics and a determinant of how Britain saw herself in the world. This was now removed, as the Communist bogey man disintegrated.

God had preserved the Empire 'undismembered' throughout the war but he had not extended his protection thereafter and the fifth of the globe that had been ruled from London rapidly became independent, leaving the Commonwealth as a ghost sitting upon the Empire's grave. No longer a world power, isolated islands and territories remained as faded flowers from the imperial garland, reminders of former glories. From time to time these could cause problems and attract attention. The Falklands War can perhaps be seen as a last imperial hurrah. Quite a few of *'the gallant blacks from far Jamaica'* had decided to risk the British climate and settle in the United Kingdom, beginning a process whereby various peoples from former imperial possessions became British citizens and began to transform an almost wholly 'white' Britain into a more ethnically-diverse society. This must rank as one of the most important development in these 45 years but the process still left Britain essentially of the same ethnicity in 1990, as the journalist Andrew Marr observes in Source B.

Boots no longer lent books but as a high street chain had flourished nonetheless. In fact the unrestrained consumerism of Britain in the 1990s is one of the starkest contrasts with the rationed world of the 1940s. Some of the country lanes survived but most resounded with the throb of motor vehicles, massively greater in numbers than in 1945. Few would now draw attention to the quality of British drains, once regarded as a mark of superiority over

Source B

The British [in 1990] were fewer than they are today. The population was smaller by at least three million souls. Also the ethnic mix of the country was simpler. Of roughly three million non-white British, the largest group were Indian (840,000), black Caribbean (500,000) and Pakistani (476,000), pretty much what an extrapolation from the seventies would have predicted. No serious concern was expressed politically about whether Muslims could fully integrate. In the interests of keeping an eye on troublemakers, and maintaining Britain's traditions of tolerance, a number of the most radical Islamic militants, on the run from their own countries, had been given safe haven in London. The largest white migrant group was from Ireland, which was still relatively poor. Any Poles or Russians in Britain were diplomats or refugees from communism. The term 'bogus asylum seeker' would have met with a puzzled frown. Looking to east or west, Britain was less penetrated by overseas culture and people than she would soon become.

Extract from Andrew Marr's *A History of Modern Britain*, published 2007

Britain's French neighbours. Nevertheless, affluence marked the Britain of the 1990s when compared with the starting point of this book. The historian Kenneth Morgan lists many aspects of this in Source C.

Source C

Overall, the wealth of most families had steadily risen. Average incomes rose through the 1980s; one factor that enhanced family incomes was the greater range of employment for women, which increased their financial independence, even if much of it was part-time. One curious outcome was that domestic service, long thought of as a relic of Victorian times, showed an increase, with growing demand for nannies and child-minders to act as substitute mothers in double-income households, along with cleaners and gardeners. Small savers had windfall gains from free shares or bonuses as building societies floated as limited companies; tax-free nest eggs were easily accumulated in saving schemes like PEPs or TESSAs; supermarkets offered financial services like cheap loans or instant credit. Earlier retirement commonly meant more leisure and comfort for the elderly. For them and others, foreign holidays became the norm. . . . Almost every family had a car, frequently two or more, with hazardous consequences for a polluted environment. In England in 1933 there were 369 cars per 1,000 people. The average home invariably featured leisure facilities like a video (77 per cent), kitchen conveniences like a microwave (67 per cent), comforts like central heating, and increasingly such working aids as a home computer. In 1997 there were 8 million mobile phones. Surveys of regional trends showed that these were distributed comparatively equally throughout the different parts of the country.

Kenneth Morgan, *Britain since 1945: The People's Peace*, third edition, published 2001

In most ways 'freedom' had increased for all classes. Most important was probably freedom from want and freedom from the fear of the poverty ill health could bring. The welfare state massively extended by the post war Labour Government was not essentially challenged by any subsequent governments. Claims could be made about under-funding as the costs of providing more and more sophisticated treatments to an ever aging population drove up the costs of the NHS but the fundamental principle laid down by Bevan, of healthcare, free at the point of delivery, remained. Freedom was also extended by the relaxation of censorship and moral codes. Homosexuals were no longer persecuted by the police and the dreaded backstreet abortion faded into nightmare memory with the legalisation of abortion in the 1960s.

Class distinction, a salient aspect of Britain in the first half of the 20th century had softened, if not quite disappeared. Alec Douglas-Home, in 1963, had been the last prime minister to be drawn from the traditional ruling British elite. Wilson and Heath were lower-middle class grammar school boys and Callaghan genuinely working class. Thatcher as both a woman and lower-middle class in origin was doubly different from the traditional governors of the country. Her cabinet was notable both for ministers of humble background and of Jewish extraction. In Macmillan's words, *'Out went the Etonians. In came the Estonians.'* Britain's social structure in 1990 was much more solidly based on merit than birth and background, as it had been in 1945. Both political parties had changed in their social composition as the extract in Source D makes clear.

Source D

The Governing elite of the country has clearly changed. Etonians are still represented out of all proportion to their numbers but from forming 25 per cent of all Conservative MPs in 1957, they were down to 12 per cent in 1987. The Labour Party has similarly reduced its proportion of the proletarian equivalents to Etonians. Miners formed 15 per cent of Labour MPs in 1951. By 1987 they were 6 per cent. 56 per cent of Labour MPs were graduates in 1987. Both parties were therefore in essence middle class. 40 per cent of Labour MPs were professionals compared to 42 per cent of Conservatives, but they were more likely to be of working-class origins and from state schools. Class differences clearly distinguish the two parliamentary parties but not as obviously as in the inter-war years. Women continued to be massively under-represented in both parties with only 20 Conservative MPs and only 38 Labour MPs in 1992. Perhaps in this way more than any other the parliamentary elite remained unrepresentative of late twentieth century Britain.

Extract from Malcom Pearce and Geoffrey Stewart, *British Political History 1867–2001*, third edition published in 2002

SKILLS BUILDER

How far do Sources B, C and D support the view that Britain experienced sweeping political and social changes between 1945 and 1990?

Democracy is a difficult concept to define precisely. If it means government elected by the people and responsive to the people, then Britain remained a democracy throughout these years yet no government was elected by more than 50% of the electorate and many, as a result of the 'first past the post' voting system, enjoyed large parliamentary majorities with considerably less than 50% of the votes cast. The Liberal Party consistently gained a share of the popular vote out of all proportion to the number of Liberal MPs elected, hence their support for a change in the voting system to proportional representation. Such a change would theoretically have enhanced fairness but as with all systems it would have thrown up different problems, by ensuring that all governments were coalitions. A 'fairer system' would not necessarily have produced a better

Source E

Margaret Thatcher's favourite minister had another disadvantage. He had a total contempt for presentational skills. Ridley once quizzically asked me whether I realised that his predecessor as Industry Secretary forty years before would have expended 75 per cent of his time and energy taking policy decisions, and 25 per cent explaining them to parliament and the public (including, he derisively implied, the media). Now the percentages were the other way about. On that day, he had already been to Brighton to make a speech, he had to open an exhibition at Battersea, and he was devoting lunchtime to me! This was clearly not his preferred set of priorities.

From John Cole's *As it Seemed to Me*, published 1995

Source F

Thoroughly delighted with myself I held court in the Lobby. Around me I had John Cole, Colin Browne (the *Independent*), a swarthy little fellow from the *FT* and a very short cheeky chappie from one of the comics (tabloids).

I said Nick's performance was a welcome return to the old doings of the nineteenth century, when a major figure in the Govt. could digress giftedly and constructively on the issues of the day without constantly being hauled over the coals by some wanker from the Foreign Office Press Office.

Extract from Alan Clark's *Diaries*, Friday 13th July 1990

SKILLS BUILDER

How far do Sources E and F support the claim that the presentation of policy and manipulation of the media was an increasingly important aspect of British politics in these years.

system of government and might very likely have produced a worse one. Weimar Germany enjoyed a system of proportional representation and ended up with Hitler.

If governments in this period were not elected by a majority of the votes cast, all governments showed an increasing obsession with relating to the public and winning their favour through the media. The press office became a vital department in every ministry particularly at number 10. John Cole, the BBC correspondent and a notable beneficiary of this tendency records the complaints of Nicholas Ridley, the resigning minister referred to in Source E, about these developments.

Ridley's lack of sensitivity to the media and the importance of presentational skills was to cost him his political career. The Tory MP and diarist, Alan Clark, clearly sympathised with Ridley as can be seen in Source F.

Politicians were increasingly becoming media stars and increasing exposure robbed them of both the privacy and some of the respect that they could command automatically in the 1940s. Sleaze and scandal dogged many in the 1980s and 1990s, who would have escaped in a previous age with a less intrusive press. On the whole, the intellectual calibre and moral integrity of MPs and particularly ministers remained high and governments of both parties handled the range of problems the country faced with skill. The loss of great power status and Empire was managed without too much national humiliation. The decline of old industries was similarly handled with only the occasional twinge of painful stress as in the miners' strike of 1984–85. Despite the dire predictions of Enoch Powell in 1968, immigration did not produce 'rivers of blood' and an essentially cohesive society was maintained.

Reform of Trade Union power was eventually accomplished. Standards of living and life expectancy continued to rise even if for much of the period Britain grew more slowly than her continental neighbours. In certain areas Britain's performance was outstanding, in the arts, scientific discovery, and latterly in the financial sector, the country appeared second to none.

In the years 1939–45, Britain had played a leading part in saving Europe from the horrors of Nazi Germany at great cost to herself. Between 1945 and 1990, she played a leading role in confronting with ultimate success that other totalitarian state of the 20th century, Soviet Russia. On balance the years from 1945 to 1990 were years of achievement. As Churchill had predicted in 1940, victory would enable the world to move into 'broad sunlit uplands'. It had, and so had Britain.

Thematic review: source-based debate and evaluation

It is important, especially when dealing with a topic that addresses change over time, to stand back and review the period you have been studying. You need to ask yourself not only what happened, but why it happened and why it happened then and not, say, 100 years earlier or 20 years later. What had driven change? Which factors were significant and which were not? Were there any events that were critical turning points? Thematic review questions, spanning the whole time period, will help to focus your thinking.

Here are the thematic review questions that relate to British Political History: Consensus and Conflict 1945–1990. You can probably think of more, but for the moment these are the ones with which you will be working.

- How far was there 'consensus' between the two main parties during these years?

- To what extent did the power of trade unions create problems for different governments?

- How far and in what ways were the housing needs of the country met throughout these years?

- To what extent was education provision changed?

- How successful were governments in dealing with Britain's economic problems in these years?

Choose one of these thematic review questions that you plan to answer. Working through this section will make much more sense if you have an actual question in mind.

Answering a thematic review question

There are two key approaches to answering a thematic review question: *select* and *deploy*.

Select   You need to select appropriate source material. You need to select appropriate knowledge.

Deploy   You need to deploy what you have selected so that you answer the question in as direct a way as possible.

Unpacking 'select'

You will see that all the thematic review questions are asking for an evaluation. They ask 'How far . . .', 'To what extent . . .', 'How successful . . .', which means that you will have to weigh up the evidence given by the sources you have selected. You will, therefore, have to select sources that will give you a range of evidence. Six diary entries, for example, will not give you the range you want. You will also need to select sources that seem to provide evidence that pulls in different directions. Eight sources saying more or less the same thing but in different ways will not help you weigh up the significance of different sorts of evidence and reach a reasoned, supported conclusion.

So now go ahead.

1 Look back through this book and select the sources, primary and secondary, that you think will give you the appropriate range, balance and evidence.

2 Make notes of the knowledge you will need to use to contextualise the sources and create an argument.

You can't, of course, simply put some sources into an answer and hope that whoever is reading what you have written can sort things out for themselves. You need to evaluate the sources you have selected and use that evaluation to create the argument you will be making when you answer the question. You have already had practice doing this, but here is a reminder of some of the questions you will need to ask of a source before you can turn it into evidence.

- Is the *content* appropriate for the question I am answering?

- Can I supply the appropriate *context* for the source?

- How *reliable* is the source as evidence? Was the author or artist *in a position to know* what he or she was talking about or drawing?

- What was the intended *audience* of the source? What was the *purpose* of the source?

- If the source is a photograph or cartoon, did the photographer or cartoonist *pose* the people in the picture/cartoon? Was the photographer or cartoonist *selective* in what he or she chose to photograph or draw?

- How *useful* is this source in developing an answer to the question? Remember that a source that is unreliable can still be useful.

Now you have your selection of source material, you need to think about it as a package. Does it do the job you want it to do? Does it supply you with enough evidence to argue your case, while at the same time providing you with enough evidence of different points of view so that you can show you have considered what weight the evidence will bear in reaching a reasoned, supported conclusion? In other words, can you effectively *cross-reference* between the sources, showing where they support and where they challenge each other?

Unpacking 'deploy'

The key to successful deployment of evidence and knowledge in answering a question like the one you have selected, is always to keep the question in the forefront of your mind. Keep focused! Don't be tempted to go off into interesting byways. Make every paragraph count as you build your argument.

You have already had a lot of practice in essay planning and writing, so this is just a reminder of the main things you need to bear in mind.

Plan

Plan carefully how you are going to construct your answer and make out your case.

Structure

You should structure your answer. (You can use this framework as a guide.)

Introduction

'Set out your stall', briefly outlining your argument and approach.

Paragraphs

The main body of your answer should develop your argument, using the evidence you have gathered by questioning the sources. As you outline your case, remember to cross-reference between the sources that you are using and to show on which source you place the most weight.

Conclusion

This should demonstrate that you have weighed up the evidence in order to reach your conclusion. It will pull your case together, giving a supported summary of your arguments and show how you reached a reasoned judgement.

In other words: say what you are going to do, do it, and show that you have done it.

You do not, of course, have to respond to these thematic review questions by writing an essay all by yourself. You could work collaboratively in a small group or you could use one or more of the questions to prepare for a class debate. In whatever way you are going to use these thematic review questions, the approach will be the same: select, deploy and keep to the point.

Good luck!

Exam zone

Relax and prepare

Hot tips: What other students have said

From GCSE to AS level

- I really enjoyed studying modern world history at GCSE, but I am glad that I had the chance to look at some 19th and 20th century English history at AS level. It has been challenging but enjoyable to study a different period.

- Many of the skills that I learned at GCSE were built upon at AS level, especially in Unit 2 where the skills of source evaluation and analysis are very important.

- AS-level history seems like a big step up at first with more demands made on independent reading and more complex source passages to cope with. However, by the end of the first term, I felt as if my written work had improved considerably.

- The more practice source-based questions I attempted, the more confident I became and quite quickly I picked up the necessary style and technique required for success.

- I found it really helpful to look at mark schemes in the textbook. It was reassuring to see what the examiners were looking for and how I could gain top marks.

What I wish I had known at the start of the year

- I used the textbook a lot during the revision period to learn the key facts and to practise key skills. I really wished that I had used it from the beginning of the course in order to consolidate my class notes.

- I wished that I had done more reading and taken more notes from other material such as the photocopied handouts issued by my teacher. Reading around the subject and undertaking independent research would have made my understanding more complete and made the whole topic more interesting.

- AS history is not just about learning the relevant material but also developing the skills to use the material effectively. I wish that I had spent more time throughout the year practising source questions to improve my style and technique.

- I wish I had paid more attention to the advice and comments made by my teacher on the written work I had done. This would have helped me to improve my scores throughout the year.

How to revise

- I started my revision by buying a new folder and some dividers. I put all my revision work into the folder and used the dividers to separate the different topics. I really took pride in my revision notes and made them as thorough and effective as I could.

- Before I started the revision process, I found it helpful to plan out my history revision. I used the Edexcel specification given to me by my teacher as a guideline for which topics to revise and I ticked off each one as I covered it.

- I found it useful to revise in short, sharp bursts. I would set myself a target of revising one particular topic in an hour and a half. I would spend one hour taking revision notes and then half an hour testing myself with a short practice question or a facts test.

- I found it useful to always include some practice work in my revision. If I could get that work to my teacher to mark, then all the better, but just attempting questions to time helped me improve my technique.

- Sometimes I found it helpful to revise with a friend. We might spend 45 minutes revising by ourselves and then half an hour testing each other. Often we were able to sort out any problems between us and it was reassuring to see that someone else had the same worries and pressures at that time.

Refresh your memory

Revision checklist

The following checklists provide the key points from each unit that you need to revise for your exam.

Unit 1: Introduction: Britain in 1945

- How was Britain socially and economically different from today?
- How did the British political system work?
- What had been the impact of war on society, the economy and politics?

Unit 2: Labour in power, 1945–48

- Why did Labour win so convincingly in the 1945 election?
- Building the New Jerusalem – reforms – the National Health Service
- Wrestling with economic problems

Unit 3: Labour in power, 1948–51

- Cripps and austerity
- Changing Conservative Party
- The elections of 1950 and 1951
- Legacy of the Attlee government

Unit 4: The return of the Conservatives, 1951–56

- Butler and economic policies
- Harold Macmillan as Minister of Housing

- Eden and the election of 1955
- Impact of the Suez crisis

Unit 5: Conservative rule, 1957–64

- Macmillan as prime minister – never had it so good
- General election of 1959
- Continuing economic problems – the attempt to join the EEC
- Decline and fall

Unit 6: Labour in power, 1964–70

- Wilson as prime minister – style and beliefs
- Economic policies and problems
- Civilised society
- Trying to deal with the unions – 'In Place of Strife'

Unit 7: Ted, Harold and Jim, 1970–79

- In what ways did Edward Heath seek to solve the economic problems facing Britain?
- Why did Heath go down in defeat in 1974?
- How successfully had Wilson and Callaghan dealt with the economic problems they faced?
- Why did Labour lose the election of 1979?

Unit 8: The breaking of consensus politics (the Thatcher revolution), 1979–83

- Economic and financial policies – impact and response
- Developments in the Labour Party and the formation of the SDP
- The Falklands War and its impact
- The election of 1983

Unit 9: The high tide and ebb tide of Thatcherism, 1983–90

- Conflict with the miners
- Privatisation
- The Labour Party in opposition
- The fall of Margaret Thatcher – her legacy?

This revision checklist looks very knowledge-based. The examination, however, will test your source-based skills as well. So remember that when dealing with sources you must be able to: comprehend a source and break it down into key points, interpret a source and draw inferences and deductions from it rather than treat it as a source of information. This may involve considering the language and tone used as well.

- Cross-reference points of evidence between sources to reinforce and challenge.

- Evaluate the evidence by assessing its quality and its reliability in terms of how much weight it will bear and how secure are the conclusions that can be drawn from it. This may include considering the provenance of the source.

- Deal with the sources as a set to build a body of evidence.

Result

You have spent a lot of time working on plans and constructing answers to the (a) and (b) questions. In Units 1, 3, 6 and 7 you worked with (a) questions; in Units 2, 4, 5, 8 and 9 you worked with (b) questions. So you now have a pretty good idea about how to plan an answer and write a response to the questions of the exam paper. But what are the examiners looking for? And what marks will you get?

What will the exam paper look like?

There will be three questions on the paper.

(a) Compulsory: everyone has to do this.

(b) (i) and (b) (ii) You will have a choice here and will only have to answer one (b) question.

There will be nine sources on the examination paper. But don't worry: you won't have to deal with them all! You'll only need to deal with six sources – three for each of the questions you will be answering. And here is the good news. So far, you have worked with very long sources, some of which were complicated. In the exam, because you will only have one hour and 20 minutes to answer the two questions, the sources will be much

shorter. You'll probably be dealing with no more than around 550 words altogether.

Question (a)

What will you have to do and what marks will you get for doing it?

You will have to focus on reaching a judgement by analysis, cross-referencing and evaluation of source material. The maximum number of marks you can get is 20. You will be working at any one of four levels. Try to get as high up in the levels as you can.

Remember that the only knowledge, outside of that which you can find in the sources, is what examiners call 'contextual' knowledge. This means you can write enough to enable you to interpret the source, but no more. For example, if one of the three sources is by Margaret Thatcher, you should show the examiners that you know she was the leader of the Conservative Party, but you should not describe other features of her leadership unless this information helps the understanding of a particular source.

Level 1
1–5 marks

- Have you shown that you understand the surface features of the sources?

- Have you shown that you have selected material relevant to the question?

- Does your response consist mainly of direct quotations from the sources?

Level 2
6–10 marks

- Have you identified points of similarity and difference in the sources in relation to the question asked?

- Have you made at least one developed comparison or a range of undeveloped ones?

- Have you summarised the information you have found in the sources?

- Have you noted the provenance of at least one of the sources?

Level 3
11–15 marks

- Have you cross-referenced between the sources, making detailed comparisons supported by evidence from the sources?

- Have you shown that you understand you have to weigh the evidence by looking at the nature, origins, purpose and audience of the sources?

- Have you shown that you have thought about considering 'how far' by trying to use the sources as a set?

Level 4
16–20 marks

- Have you reached a judgement in relation to the issue posed by the question?

- Is this judgement supported by careful examination of the evidence of the sources?

- Have you cross-referenced between the sources and analysed the points of similarity and disagreement?

- Have you taken account of the different qualities of the sources in order to establish what weight the evidence will bear?

- Have you used the sources as a set when addressing 'how far' in the question?

Now try this (a) question:

- Study Sources A, B and C. How far do Sources A, B and C agree on the characteristics that marked Margaret Thatcher's political leadership?

Source A

You had only to talk to her in the couple of years before the election, when the Labour Government's popularity had gone, to savour her self-confidence. In part this was ideological: all over the world, she told me, the long night of collectivism was receding. 'Impoverishment' and 'socialism' went together in her conversation, with the hammer-beat of a doctrinaire non-doubter. With Margaret Thatcher, Keynesian orthodoxy had been abandoned. She came nearer to *laissez-faire* liberalism than any Tory leader in this century.

From John Cole, *As It Seemed To Me*, published in 1995

Source B

One of her remarkable characteristics, which stamps her as a superb politician, is her ability to put up with things and go along with them, even though she doesn't agree with them, until the time comes when they can be dealt with. Now, not possessing that quality myself – having the loquacity which always impels me to say: 'I don't agree' – I admire this.

From Enoch Powell, speaking in 1989

Source C

She was different. It was partly that she carried with her into No. 10 a greater baggage of ideology than her predecessors. It was partly that she was a scientist by training, not for once a product of the humanities. It was partly that she was a woman. She was also intensely serious. The camaraderie, the relaxed jokey, allusive style, the affectation of doing things well without trying, the view of politics, and most other things as a game, these expressions of the ruling male culture, which with Harold Macmillan had been carried to extreme lengths, all these were alien to her.

From Percy Craddock, *In Pursuit of British Interests*, published in 1979

Now use the marking criteria to assess your response.

How did you do?

What could you have done to have achieved a better mark?

Question (b)

What will you have to do and what marks will you get for doing it?

You will have to analyse and evaluate a historical view or claim using two or three sources and your own knowledge. There are 40 marks for this question. You will get 24 marks for your own knowledge and 16 marks for your source evaluation. You can be working at any one of four levels. Try to get as high up in the levels as you can.

The examiners will be marking your answer twice: once for knowledge and a second time for source evaluation. This is what the examiners will be looking for as they mark the ways in which you have selected and used your knowledge to answer the question.

Level 1
1–6 marks

- Have you written in simple sentences without making any links between them?

- Have you provided only limited support for the points you are making?

- Have you written what you know separately from the sources?

- Is what you have written mostly generalised and not really directed at the focus of the question?

- Have you made a lot of spelling mistakes and is your answer disorganised?

Level 2
7–12 marks

- Have you produced a series of statements that are supported by mostly accurate and relevant factual material?

- Have you made some limited links between the statements you have written?

- Is your answer mainly 'telling the story' and not really analysing what happened?

- Have you kept your own knowledge and the sources separate?

- Have you made a judgement that isn't supported by facts?

- Is your answer a bit disorganised with some spelling and grammatical mistakes?

Level 3
13–18 marks

- Is your answer focused on the question?

- Have you shown that you understand the key issues involved?

- Have you included a lot of descriptive material along with your analysis of the issues?

- Is your material factually accurate but a bit lacking in depth and/or relevance?

- Have you begun to integrate your own knowledge with the source material?

- Have you made a few spelling and grammatical mistakes?

- Is your work mostly well organised?

Level 4
19–24 marks

- Does your answer relate well to the focus of the question?

- Have you shown that you understand the issues involved?

- Have you analysed the key issues?

- Is the material you have used relevant to the question and factually accurate?

- Have you begun to integrate what you know with the evidence you have gleaned from the source material?

- Is the material you have selected balanced?

- Is the way you have expressed your answer clear and coherent? Is your spelling and grammar mostly accurate?

This is what the examiners are looking for as they mark your source evaluation skills.

Level 1
1–4 marks

- Have you shown that you understand the sources?

- Is the material you have selected from them relevant to the question?

- Is your answer mostly direct quotations from the sources or rewrites of them in your own words?

Level 2
5–8 marks

- Have you shown that you understand the sources?

- Have you selected from them in order to support or challenge the view given in the question?

- Have you used the sources mainly as sources of information?

Level 3
9–12 marks

- Have you analysed the sources, drawing from them points of challenge and/or support for the view contained in the question?
- Have you developed these points, using the source material?
- Have you shown that you realise you are dealing with just one viewpoint and that the sources point to other, perhaps equally valid, ones?
- Have you reached a judgement?
- Have you supported that judgement with evidence from the sources?

Level 4
13–16 marks

- Have you analysed the sources, raising issues from them?
- Have you discussed the viewpoint in the question by relating it to the issues raised by your analysis of the source material?
- Have you weighed the evidence in order to reach a judgement?
- Is your judgement fully explained and supported by carefully selected evidence?

Now try this (b) question:

- Read Sources D, E and F and use your own knowledge. Do you agree with the view that the 1950s and 1960s were marked by steady and substantial progress in the provision of education?

Source D

School building to house the post-war baby boom came to a halt and pupil–teacher ratios in primary schools declined in 1953–54. At the other end of the process the total of university students fell from 85,000 in 1950 to 82,000 in 1954. Not until a strong-minded minister, David Eccles, succeeded Horsbrough in October 1954 and remade the case for education as a national investment rather than as a taxpayer's burden did matters improve.

From P. Hennessy, *Having it So Good: Britain in the Fifties*, published in 2006

Source E

As busily as the new government built new places of higher learning – thirty polytechnics were commissioned by the Education and Science Department in 1967 – it worked diligently to destroy the solid groundwork of traditional schooling, which would have made these new colleges into intellectual powerhouses. The man who commissioned the polytechnics, Antony Crosland, is known to history for one sentence – his ambition to destroy 'every ****ing grammar school in England'. This is not to say that the development of comprehensive schools (about 60 per cent of British pupils were educated in them by 1970, and about 90 per cent by 1980) was not introduced with the kindliest of motives. Whether standards of numeracy, literacy, scientific knowledge or technological skill arose across the nation, and whether there was more chance for the clever children of the economically disadvantaged than in the old system, will remain a matter of debate. It is hard to imagine Roy Jenkins, Roy Hattersley, Margaret Thatcher, Denis Healey, Edward Heath or Harold Wilson himself having been quite as successful as they were had they not been educated in the despised grammar school tradition.

From A.N. Wilson, *Our Times*, published in 2008

Source F

Now in 1969 came the inauguration of a brain-child of mine, worked out by me privately in the early sixties, announced by me as Leader of the opposition, and now coming to fruition through the efforts of my ministerial colleagues – the Open University.

From Harold Wilson, *The Labour Government 1964–1970*, published in 1971

Now use the marking criteria to assess your response.

How did you do?

What could you have done to have achieved higher marks?

The examiners will not be nit-picking their way through your answer, ticking things off as they go.

Rather, they will be looking to see which levels best fit the response you have written to the question, and you should do the same when assessing your own responses.

How will I time my responses?

You have 1 hour 20 minutes to answer two questions.

- The (a) question is compulsory and you will have a choice of one from two.

- You must choose one (b) question. Take time, say 5 minutes, to read through the paper before making your choice.

The (a) question is worth half the marks of the (b) question, so you should aim to spend twice the time on the (b) question. This means that, including planning time, you should spend about 25 minutes on the (a) question and about 50 minutes (again including planning) on the (b) question.

Practising questions

Each unit finishes with an exam style question – either an (a) style (sources only) or a (b) style (sources and own knowledge). Use these to get plenty of practice.

You have now had a lot of practice in planning, writing and assessing your responses to the sort of questions you can expect to find on the exam paper. You are well prepared and you should be able to tackle the examination with confidence.

Good luck!

References

Alanbrooke, Field Marshall Lord (2002) *War Diaries 1939–1945*

Barnett, C. (1986) *The Audit of War: The Illusion and Reality of Britain as a Great Nation*

Benn, T. (1995) *The Benn Diaries*

Blake, R. (1970) *The Conservative Party From Peel to Churchill*

Brittan, S. (1966) *The Treasury under the Tories 1951–1964*

Butler, D. *et al.*, (1951–88) *British General Elections from 1950 to 1987 (Nuffield Studies)*

Butler, R.A. (1971) *The Art of the Possible: The Memoirs of Lord Butler*

Callaghan, J. (1987) *Time and Chance*

Campbell, J. (2009) *Margaret Thatcher*, revised edition

Castle, B. (1984) *The Castle Diaries 1964–1976*

Channon C. edit. James, R.R. (1996) *'Chips': The Diaries of Sir Henry Channon*

Charmley, J. (1996) *A History of Conservative Politics 1900–1996*

Clark, A. (2001) *Diaries*

Clarke, P. (1996) *Hope and Glory: Britain 1900–2000*

Cockerell, M. (1988) *Live from Number 10: The Inside Story of Prime Ministers and Television*

Cole, J. (1995) *As It Seemed to Me: Political Memoirs*

Colville, J.R. (2005) *The Fringes of Power: Downing Street Diaries 1939–1955*

Cooper, S. (1963) *'Snoek Piquante'* in *The Age of Austerity 1945–51*, edited by Michael Sissons and Philip French

Craddock, P. (1997) *In Pursuit of British Interests*

Critchley, J. (1994) *A Bag of Boiled Sweets: An Autobiography*

Crosland, S. (1982) *Tony Crosland*

Crossman, R. (1979) *The Crossman Diaries*

Dalton, H. (1987) *The Political Diary, 1918–40, 1945–60*

Dell, E. (1993) *A Hard Pounding: Politics and Economic Crisis, 1974–76*

Evans, E.J. (2004) *Thatcher and Thatcherism*, second edition

Fisher, N. (1973) *Iain Macleod*

Foot, M. (1986) *Loyalists and Loners*

Fyfe, D.P.M (1962) *Political Adventures: The Memoirs of the Earl of Kilmuir*

Gardiner, J. (2004) *Wartime: Britain 1939–1945*

Harris, K. (1982) *Attlee*

Harris, K. (1988) *Thatcher*

Harrison, B. (2009) *Seeking a Role, The United Kingdom 1951–1970*

Healey, D. (1989) *The Time of My Life*

Hennessy, P. (1992) *Never Again: Britain 1945–51*

Hennessy, P. (1999) *Whitehall*

Hennessy, P. (2000) *The Prime Minister: The Office and Its Holders since 1945*

Hennessy, P. (2006) *Having it So Good; Britain in the Fifties*

Horne, A. (1988) *Macmillan Volume I 1894–1956*

Howard, A. (1987) *RAB: Life of R.A. Butler*

Howe, Sir G. (1994) *Conflict of Loyalty*

Hughes, D. (1964) *'The Spivs'* in *The Age of Austerity*, edited by Michael Sissons and Philip French

Hurd, D. (2003) *Memoirs*

James, R.R. (1986) *Anthony Eden*

Jenkins, R. (1991) *A Life at the Centre*

Marr, A. (2007) *A History of Modern Britain*

Maudling, R. (1978) *Memoirs*

Moran, Lord C. (1966) *Churchill: The Struggle for Survival 1945–60* *You should get more recognition, Kenneth. – R. 13*

Morgan, K.O. (2001) *The People's Peace*, third edition

Morgan, K.O. (2007) *Michael Foot: A Life*

Perkins, A. (2003) *Red Queen: The Authorised Biography of Barbara Castle*

Pierce, M. and Stewart, G. (1996) *British Political History 1867–1995*, second edition

Pimlott, B. (1985) *Hugh Dalton: A Life*

Pym, F. (1985) *The Politics of Consent*

Sandbrook, D. (2005) *Never Had it So Good: A History of Britain from Suez to the Beatles*

Sked, A. and Chris Cook, C. (1979) *Post-War Britain: A Political History, 1945–92*

Taylor, A.J.P. (1965) *English History 1914–1945*

Vinen, R. (2009) *Thatcher's Britain: The Politics and Social Upheaval of the Thatcher Era*

Wilson, A.N. (2008) *Our Times: The Age of Elizabeth II*

Wilson, Sir H. (1971) *The Labour Government 1964–70: A Personal Record*

Young, H. (1989) *One of Us: Life of Margaret Thatcher*

Ziegler, P. (1993) *Wilson: The Authorised Life*

Glossary

1922 Committee   This was a committee of Conservative back-benchers named after the famous revolt by Tory MPs against continuing support for the Lloyd George coalition. Here the bulk of ordinary Conservative MPs had voted against the wishes of the Tory leadership who wished to continue the coalition. The post of chairman of the 1922 Committee was a very prestigious one for a back-bencher (ie non-minister) and the committee had considerable influence and acted as a barometer for the feelings of the back-bench MPs.

Balance of payments   This refers to the relationship between payments made by the country for imports and the earnings gained from exports. If the cost of imports exceeds that of earnings from exports then there is a negative balance and the country is effectively spending more money than it is earning. Ultimately if this persists over a long time then an economic crisis can ensue as the country gets into high levels of debt.

Bank rate   This is the rate at which the Bank of England lends money to other banks and therefore controls the cost of borrowing throughout the economy.

Berlin airlift   On 24 June 1948, the Soviet Union closed all land routes to Berlin in breach of post-war agreements. The Western powers were faced with either using force against the vastly superior Red Army or accepting defeat and the abandonment of their occupation of Berlin. They hit on the idea of using their superior air power to fly food and supplies to the two million West Berliners. In all, 272,000 sorties were flown and, in May 1949, Russia lifted the blockade.

'Big Bang'   The nickname given to the reform of the stock exchange introduced on 27 October 1986. It basically opened up trading to more people and freed up the market by de-regulation.

Block vote   Unions voted at Labour Party conferences with as many votes as they had members, not on the basis of one vote per union.

Thus the Transport and General Workers Union had enormous voting power. All the votes from each union would also vote the same way.

Cabinet   The Cabinet was at the heart of government in Britain. It was a committee of the senior members of the government, meeting regularly under the chairmanship of the prime minister to discuss and approve the general line of government policy. Senior ministers like the Foreign and Home Secretaries and the Chancellor of the Exchequer would always be members. Sub-committees of the Cabinet were often established for more detailed work and these reported back. Government ministers not in the Cabinet are normally referred to as junior ministers.

CBI   The Confederation of British Industry (CBI) is a pressure group representing the interests of the boards of directors of companies in Britain.

Chief Whip   The Cabinet member responsible for party discipline. They ensure that the government has a majority in any votes by making sure their party's MPs attend and vote as the government wishes.

Clause 4   A clause of the 1918 Labour Party constitution committing the party to the 'common ownership of the means of production, distribution and exchange'. In practice this would mean widespread nationalisation. It was dear to the left of the party but not taken very seriously by most senior Labour politicians.

Closed shop   As with picketing this was a key issue with regard to trade unions and the law. A closed shop was a business or company where a worker had to belong to a particular union or group of unions in order to be employed. It could be said to violate the freedom of the individual to choose whether to belong to a union or not.

Cold War   The expression was coined to describe the confrontation between the USA and Britain on one side and the Soviet Union on the other. It developed almost immediately after the 'hot war' with Nazi Germany. Although it never led to a direct military conflict, there were many close shaves and indirect confrontations such as in Korea. It finally ended in 1990 with the collapse of Communism in Eastern Europe and the disintegration of the Soviet Union. It is an essential part of the background of the time period covered by this book.

Commodity prices These are the costs of various raw materials needed for industry to produce finished goods, and are a vital ingredient in the balance of payments. Britain needed to import large amounts of raw materials, notably oil. If the commodity prices fell on the world market then Britain benefited.

Consensus politics This refers to the broad agreement between the two main political parties on most important issues e.g. foreign policy, acceptance of the welfare state, the desire to avoid 1930s style unemployment.

Conservative Party The name 'conservative' dated back to the 1830s and was devised by Sir Robert Peel as a way of repackaging the old 'Tory' Party and making it more acceptable to the increasingly influential middle classes. It was traditionally the party of the landed gentry and the Church of England. It gradually became more and more middle class itself, with business men replacing landed gentlemen and aristocrats as its leading members. All the leaders from 1911 to 1940 had business backgrounds, including Neville Chamberlain whom Churchill replaced.

Devaluation – holding the pound at $2.80 This phrase refers to the attempts of the government to maintain a fixed rate of exchange for the pound sterling against the dollar and other currencies. If large numbers of banks around the world decided that the pound was likely to fall, they would sell their holding of pounds, forcing the value down and fulfilling their fears. Some might speculate against the pound in the hope of making money, i.e. selling pounds to force the value down so that they could then buy them back more cheaply. The government's weapon to prevent this was to get the Bank of England to buy pounds, using its reserves of dollars and other currencies. If it could keep buying for longer than the speculators could keep selling, they would force the speculators into a loss instead of a profit, hopefully teaching them a lesson.

Direct taxes These are taxes on income that include the basic income tax and 'surtax', a higher

rate charged on higher incomes. Such taxes are said to be 'progressive' because they hit the rich harder.

Dollar gap A shortage of dollars earned from exports which were necessary to pay for imports – see balance of payments definition on previous page.

Embourgeoisification This is the name given to the process of more and more people becoming 'middle class' in their lifestyle and attitudes.

First-past-the-post system This is the traditional British voting system in which MPs are elected for a particular geographical area and the winner is the candidate with the most votes regardless of whether this is a majority of over 50% or not.

Fellow travellers This is a phrase used to describe secret Communist sympathisers, who had chosen to stand as Labour MPs knowing that they stood little chance of being elected if their true colours as Communists were known by the electorate.

Flying pickets and picketing Picketing is the placing of striking workers outside their place of employment with the object of persuading other workers not to go in to work but to support the strike. The law since 1875 allowed 'peaceful picketing' such as persuasion, but this often became blatant intimidation and the forcible prevention of working, which was illegal. Flying pickets are small bands of strikers that can quickly move to any workplace associated with the strike. They would often intimidate rather than 'peacefully persuade' other workers.

Gang of four This was a reference to four leading Labour politicians: Shirley Williams, Bill Rodgers, David Owen and, most prestigious and famous of all, Roy Jenkins, newly returned from being president of the European Commission. Jenkins was often satirically referred to as the 'prince from over the water' or in view of his pronounced lisp, 'the pwince'. The phrase 'gang of four' had become famous in the 1970s from Chinese politics.

GNP A measure of the total value of the goods and services produced in a country and its overseas earnings from trade and investments. Divided by the number of people, GNP will give an approximate indication of standard of living. It is a useful way of comparing the relative economic importance of countries.

Greasy pole This phrase likens political life to the fairground amusement of trying to climb a greased pole and was attributed to Disraeli, who on first being appointed prime minister in February 1868 is reputed to have said, 'Well, I've climbed to the top of the greasy pole.'

Hire purchase   Known traditionally in Britain as the 'never-never', this was buying goods and services on credit. It was a system of purchase widely developed in the United States before the Second World War but only really began developing in Britain during the 1950s.

Hung parliament   This is a parliament in which no party has an overall majority.

Indirect taxes   These are taxes on the buying and selling of goods such as excise duty on alcoholic drinks.

Incomes policy   An attempt by governments to control the rise in incomes and salaries. This could be informal such as under Labour in 1974–79 or statutory (backed up by law), as under Heath in 1970–74.

KGB   These initials stand for the feared post-war secret police of the USSR. Before the war, they had been called the NKVD and between 1936 and 1938 had arrested, tortured and shot hundreds of thousands of Soviet citizens. In 1938, Lavrentiy Beria had taken over management of the organisation and he was still the dreaded chief after the war.

King's/queen's speech   The speech given at the beginning of a parliament or a session of parliament that sets out the government's agenda or programme. It is usually delivered by the monarch but is written by the prime minister and his colleagues. Private Eye had a famous front cover in October 1964 with the Queen delivering the Wilson government's programme with a speech bubble coming from her mouth with the words, 'and I hope you realise I didn't write this crap'.

Kitchen cabinet   This term is used to describe the group of close advisers that a prime minister might choose to serve him or her in Number 10. They are likely to be outside the formal Cabinet and might not even be MPs.

Labour Party   This was the new party of the 20th century, being originally established in 1900 as 'The Labour Representation Committee', an alliance between three small political groups and the trade unions. It won 29 seats in 1906 and changed its name to the Labour Party. After the First World War it expanded rapidly at the expense of the Liberals and formed a government for the first time in 1924. In 1918 the Party adopted a new constitution which committed it to 'socialism'. The Labour Party drew its support from the big cities and the mining areas. The parliamentary party tended to be a mixture of trade unionists and middle-class intellectuals.

Liberal Party   The Liberals had been the dominant party in Britain between 1832 and 1886. It was essentially the party of reform and drew its support from the middle classes and non-conformist churches. It enjoyed one last spectacular burst of power between 1905 and 1915 when Liberal governments introduced a spate of reforms which laid the basis for the welfare state. The party split in 1916 which gave the new Labour Party a chance to take its place as the main challenger to the Conservative Party.

Marshall aid   This was the programme of economic aid to Europe proposed by George Marshall, the US foreign secretary in 1947. The suggestion was enthusiastically encouraged and helped by Bevin. Congress agreed in 1948 and set up the European Recovery Programme. Eventually $13 billion was spent. Britain and France were the two chief beneficiaries. The aim was to reduce the influence and attraction of Communism, very strong in France, and to enable Western Europe to buy US products. It was enlightened self-interest by the USA, but it was generous and did much to help Europe develop as a prosperous, free and essentially capitalist corner of the globe.

Mixed economy   This refers to the presence of both state run and privately run economic ventures. Extreme socialists wanted most economic ventures to be state owned and run.

Monetarism   This is a belief in controlling the money supply as a means of controlling inflation and it is often seen as the most important element in the economic policy of the Thatcher government from 1979 to 1982. It is often used as shorthand for a belief in free-market economics and a rejection of Keynesian demand management, as practised by all governments from 1945 to the 1970s.

In theory, monetarism looks easy and uncontroversial, but the real problem is measuring the money supply in a modern economy. Is it simply cash in circulation – M0? Is it cash plus money in bank accounts M1 or M3, depending on whether it includes all bank accounts? Does it include building society accounts? The chief weapon of monetarists was interest rates making money dearer to borrow by raising them.

New Jerusalem   This is a phrase often used in this period and comes from the language of religious visionaries like William Blake, whose famous poem talks of Jerusalem being built in 'England's green and pleasant land'. It refers to the creation of a near perfect environment for human beings.

Pairing   Usually allowed by the party whips, pairing is a parliamentary convention by which an MP of one party can be allowed to miss a vote in the Commons if his 'pair' in the rival party agrees not to vote, thereby preserving the balance.

Polytechnic   These were advanced technical colleges offering a more practical approach to higher education than the traditional universities. Most eventually were re-designated universities and enjoy that status today.

Private members' bills   Draft law introduced into the Commons by a back-bench MP, not by government sponsored legislation which is the norm. Without government support there is little chance of a bill becoming law.

Purchase tax   An indirect tax on sales and a fore-runner of VAT.

Quango   Quasi-autonomous Non-governmental Organisation, or quangos for short, were bodies that, whilst funded by government and controlled by government appointees, were meant to act with some degree of independence from the government.

Selsdon Park conference   This conference was a meeting in January 1970 of Heath and his shadow Cabinet. The communiqué issued afterwards gave the impression of a shift to the right in Conservative thinking, i.e. a smaller role for the state and an emphasis on law and order. Wilson seized on it with the image of 'Selsdon Man', a wild right-wing extremist tearing up consensus politics. In reality, the communiqué was a last-minute improvisation. Heath had forgotten that he was holding a press conference to catch the Sunday papers and, when reminded one was about to happen, in desperation cried to his colleagues, 'What on earth am I going to say to them? We haven't decided anything.' Iain Macleod, a liberal in the Macmillan mould, responded, 'It's quite easy, Ted, you just tell them we believe in law and order.' The newspaper reports then carried a story of a shift to the right.

Wets and drys   These became terms used to describe the two wings of the Conservative Party in the 1980s. Wets were traditional consensus Tories anxious to avoid confrontation with the unions and supportive of a large economic management role for the state. Drys were suspicious of Keynesian economic policies which they feared had led the country to disaster. They believed the role of the state should be slimmed down and union power disciplined by both legislation and the impact of higher unemployment.

Whitehall   Originally the site of Cardinal Wolsey's London palace it was seized by Henry VIII and became a great royal palace but was largely burnt down in 1698. The site became occupied over the next two centuries by government departments such as the Admiralty, the Treasury and the Foreign Office. The word became a synonym for government and the civil servants who worked there.

Index

Page references in italic indicate sources.